Hugh Tennant.

Xmas. 1959.

HENRY COTTON

My

Golfing Album

THE INCOMPARABLE THRILL OF DRIVING DOWN HILL: TEMPLE GOLF CLUB

HENRY COTTON

My Golfing Album

COUNTRY LIFE LIMITED LONDON

Published in 1959
by Country Life Limited
Tavistock Street London W C 2
Printed in Great Britain by
Balding & Mansell Ltd
London and Wisbech

TO DEAR TOOTS

We have climbed many a hill together, hand in hand, and you know, better than anyone else, what it means to be at the top of the golf game, but despite all the ups and downs of life, your helping hand has always been there!

Thanks a million!

LIST OF CONTENTS

HOW QUICKLY THE YEARS FLY!

How quickly the years fly! I look forward annually to the warmth of spring and summer and that clean smell of mown fairways, and then before I can say I have enjoyed them to the full, here I am looking forward to the next spring and summer, and in my excitement I forget I am steadily running out of time. Things are so arranged in this world by our Creator that whatever happens we all run out of time finally.

I have now gone fifty, which I suppose one day will be a sort of half-way mark in human life, but to-day it means that more than the best half has already gone; one can say that 'the future is behind one'. Anyway, I feel like doing some summing-up. When one is young, one seeks all the honours one can get, and there always seems to be time to obtain them, and then all of a sudden how grateful one becomes for what one has got — never mind what one missed.

My generation of golfers had the long years of World War II cut into their lives, but those of us who were spared, while, may be, having a regret at having missed chances to add to our laurels, can be thankful anyway.

I decided at one moment to stop playing in major golf tournaments, to rest on my laurels, but then I suddenly became aware that, while my well-wishing friends were giving me good advice, which I thought seemed sound common sense, about retiring from competitive golf, I did after all love golf very much. I love the competition, and the personal challenge a well-prepared course made to me, and I felt that if I could still play decently enough to be considered a competitor, not a passenger merely crowding the field, I would go on enjoying this sort of tough golf. While it is to me a sort of torture, it is that sweet sort of suffering which gives much satisfaction to the sufferer. Although past fifty, I realized that I could play within a stroke or two as well as I did twenty years previously if I felt really fit, and even if I did notice that my recuperative powers had diminished, provided that my heart was sound, I could still get a big kick out of playing against the young golfers.

At the same time I could test out some theories I had worked on since I was very young — namely, that my action was one which would not only last me all my life, but would produce satisfactory results when one-time rivals had dropped back on the golfing ladder.

I decided years ago that easy golf was a game of hands and arms, and that no trouble should be spared to build up the hands and arms, so that the club could be swung fast and truly. I felt then, as I still feel to-day, that many of the great champions are apt to overlook the fact that they have excessively strong hands, a grip like a vice in fact, and so they unconsciously mislead others when giving advice. They put the accent on other parts of the body, simply because their hands have never been a problem to them.

All I can say is that if you give Mr Jim Snooks Sam Snead's or my own hands, he will be almost scratch the next day, even using his own special sort of swing. In fact, I will go even further and say that his special sort of swing, which he and his teachers claim lets him down, is only so condemned because he tries somehow to cover up the weakness of his hands and fingers and make do with the muscles he has, which are non-golfing ones.

So in the following pages are comments on various points which I found interesting to golfers during discussions both on and off the course. Fifty years is not perhaps considered a great age, but I think that I have accumulated in that time some information which I can pass on to interest and entertain golfers everywhere. I have not tried to cover all the golf game nor the styles of all the great golfers I have seen in my lifetime — others better qualified than myself set about this task regularly — but I have tried to hit the various nails right on the head as they have come before me. I have not tried to set out any ordered sequence of chapters, such as driver to putter, which I have previously done in other books, but to flit about among my photographs and memories for ideas, and so I present:

My Golfing Album!

THE BEST THINGS IN LIFE

I SIMPLY have to put these lines in my album. They are not exactly words of golfing advice, which I set out to give, but all the same I feel I need not apologise for them, for they just about sum up life to me, as I am sure they will to many others who read them.

After all we are all three people in one: 'The person we think we are, the person others think we are, and the person we really are.'

'Youth is not a time of life — it is a state of mind. It is not a matter of ripe cheeks, red lips, and *supple knees*, it is a temper of the will, a quality of the imagination, a vigour of the emotions, a predominance of courage over timidity, of the appetite for adventure over love of ease. This often exists in a man of fifty more than in a boy of twenty.

Nobody grows old by merely living a number of years, people grow old only by deserting their ideals. Years wrinkle the skin, but to give up enthusiasm wrinkles the soul. Worry, doubt, self-distrust, fear and despair — these are the long, long years that bow the head and turn the growing spirit back to dust.

Whether 70 or 16, there is in every being's heart the love of wonder, the sweet amazement at the stars and the star-like things and thoughts, the undaunted challenge of events, the unfailing appetite for what next, and the joy and the game of life.

You are as young as your faith, as old as your doubt, as young as your self-confidence, as old as your fear, as young as your hope, as old as your despair.

So long as your heart receives messages of beauty, cheer, courage, grandeur and power from the earth, from man and from the *infinite*, so long you are young.

When the wires are all down and all the central place of your heart is covered with the snows of pessimism, than you are grown old indeed and *may God have mercy on your soul*.'

— AUTHOR UNKNOWN: quoted from *The Best Things in Life*, by Harry Hepner (B. C. Forbes Publishing Co.)

LET'S START

The beginning of the round of golf — even this takes a beginner time to learn. The simple act of teeing up the ball does not need two hands, after all, he finds.

The way I do it. Some golfers put the back of their hand on the ground so that they press the tee peg between their fingers and so get the same height of tee each time — the thickness of the hand is the measure. Not a bad idea!

BUILDING UP THE HEART OF THE GOLF SWING

FROM what I have seen of handicap golfers, very few ever experience that solid impact of the ball being struck in the centre of the club face, where the shaft vibrates in their hands. So many seem to brush away the ball, and it must feel dead, as if the clubhead cover had not been removed.

Players learn to go from A to B (top of the swing to end of follow-through) without ever building up the heart of the swing — i.e., the hitting area. Some exercises I have found which help are:

Hit the ball and swish the clubhead straight back immediately after impact — this teaches the player to hang on, as it puts a double strain on the wrists and forearms and keeps the head down.

Hit and stop, using the left arm and wrist as a buffer for the right hand's hit. I usually put over the feel of the hand action in these strokes by placing my right hand on the shaft, taking the place of the pupil's right hand, and then we swing the club together.

Remember that your hands cannot be too strong. I have never yet met a golfer whose hands were too strong. You see it is not the amount of practice which counts in golf — *it is how you practise*. If you want to succeed, exercise your hands and fingers with spring grips, heavy clubs, by doing press ups, hanging from a bar, squeezing a rubber ball, rolling up sheets of newspaper one-handed into tiny balls, beginning at one corner,

Here is a pupil doing his 'hit and stop' drill. All 'Cotton School' pupils will have worked on this drill, I trust with advantage, because it does put the maximum strain on the hands and arms.

I can hit the ball within 20 yards of my best possible efforts with my driver, using this action. The clubhead does not follow-through more than this. It is an exercise to fit into every practice session.

rolling up a weight on a stick, playing rapidly seven or more golf balls to get them into the air at one time; this is very good drill, and so on. They will all help your impact.

THE LATEST SECRET

THE word 'secret', when mentioned in connection with the golf game, makes all golfers prick their ears, and everyone, from the very beginner who thinks the professional is 'holding one back' from him, to the near-champion, who still turns and twists in the hope of unearthing that something new, which will make him outshine the rest — all think this idea of a secret fascinating.

Following on Ben Hogan's 10,000 dollars-worth of 'secret', I read an amusing couple of paragraphs by Jimmy Hines, who followed Ben as professional at the Thunderbird Club in Palm Springs. Jimmy is quite a wit; I like this: 'There is only one theory on golf, but I have one, too, and that is that if fewer theories were tried, sounder golf would result. But why should I give the usual wrinkles the golf professional strings his pupils along with, when I have just decided to reveal the real secrets of the game? A sure-fire method is to take lessons from at least half-a-dozen professionals, then sort it out yourself. If two heads are better than one, why not six? Besides, there is a variety and spice to all this which makes the game a real challenge. Instead of having the simple fundamentals grooved into an easy swing, that permits you to give full concentration to a particular type of shot you wish to play, you can reconstruct the picture a half-dozen times. If it does not quite come off, try "What's-his-name's" suggestion next time. You're sure to get it. In fact, you'll get it any number of times for years to come.

'Don't stay with one thought too long. It gets you in a rut. Have a little new theory ready once a month, week, or each hole if you prefer. You might try this one on the first tee to-morrow. Without thinking of anything else, "just stare at the back of the ball where you plan to hit it". Or you might give this one a whirl. "Clench your

Golf magazines in the 1920–30 period claimed these two swings as classical: Bobby Jones (LEFT), Tommy Armour (RIGHT). In my eyes they are still right to-day. The left wrist under the shaft at the top is right for the vast majority of golfers — no danger of disc trouble in this method.

teeth and literally hit with your chin, ankles, elbows or knees — never the hands, as that is too obvious — and we know it is the catch-phrase that really gets us on to our game."

'Now this is good, sound thinking which, in closing, I would like to say is the key to the whole game. When you continue to think soundly it develops the ability to concentrate for sustained periods.'

There really is no *one* secret, unless Ben Hogan's infinite capacity for taking pains can be called a secret. The alterations players make from time to time to sections of their swings — a movement of the thumb or the foot, however small — will never work permanently: they are nothing more than temporary adjustments, almost fault-correctors. You see, it could be that, in the case of that great player Ben Hogan, his newly-found left-wrist position, where the back of the left hand, instead of being held flat in line with the left forearm, was now angled to an 8° position — the wrist was brought under the shaft — was nothing more than his insurance against a tendency to hook when under pressure.

Every player has a weakness under pressure —

it can be a tendency to drift to one side of the fairway or the other. Dai Rees was telling me that Sam Snead quick-hooked seven drives in 36 holes they once played together, which means (with eight short holes) one drive in every four. Some players tend to cut, others to hit the ball 'thin'. So, if a player all of a sudden cuts down his percentage of poor shots by doing some new-for-him action, then he might claim it as a 'secret', if it produced him a big success. But, as Jimmy Hines said: 'Don't stay with one thought too long: it gets you in a rut.' And this is what most amateurs' secrets become: they become ruts which are hard to get out of.

When I was asked during a lecture in the St Andrew's Hall, Glasgow, 'Did I believe in the forward press?', I answered: 'Yes, if you need it, but like everything else in golf, it can be exaggerated.' When Ben Hogan says he put his left wrist under the shaft to make an angle of 8° between the forearm and the back of the hand, he means that he found that at the time he achieved a great triumph (or triumphs), this was just the amount which worked. It may or may not be right to-day — more than

Ben Hogan's newly-found left-wrist position.

14

likely he would want to alter this in some way slightly.

Once a golfer has the basic principles right and holds the club correctly, and does a smooth swing with his club, the fine adjustments have to be learned as much in competitive play as on the practice tee. There is a correct peg to hang your hat on for each day. *For a period it may be the same peg, but it is never — I repeat, never — the same peg all the time.* If a golfer plays occasional golf, such as the week-end player does, he may make a 'secret' last longer, but the hard practiser soon needs another peg for his hat.

I am certain that the inside-out theory is the soundest for the majority of golfers; to drift into a power-fade or controlled slice, as is now talked of, is a waste of time for most golfers; it means an all-round loss of length.

Golf for the big majority is an exercise and fun, and in our country there are no facilities for hitting a hundred or so balls to 'warm up', and tune-up one's swing, without the greatest inconvenience, so any method which puts the accent on the hands, and which is natural, must be right. It seems the wheel has turned and, taking a line from a popular song of the 'thirties, the latest secret is 'the oldest yet the latest thing'!

ABOVE: *Cary Middlecoff's left hand position is very sound indeed — club-face fully open.*

LEFT: *Willie Macfarlane, a U.S. Open Champion of 1925 and a great stylist. This position at the top of the back-swing taken in his heyday shows this famous player in a classical position with the club held firmly in the fingers, the left wrist well under the shaft, and the club-face fully open. This action is still worth the attention of every student and while it could be claimed that there are other positions of the wrists at this moment in the swing just as good, there are none better, and as I pen these words I cannot see the possibilities (very remote, they are) of a better one coming along.*

If any golfer can get into this position at the top of his back-swing, I cannot see how he can fail to hit good golf shots.

15

The first Golf Buggy ever was called a 'Linksmobile' — around 1929 it appeared, being motor-driven. Now they are mostly electric, but there are a few petrol-engine driven buggies coming in, to get rid of the battery-charging problems. This scene was in California — ideal country for such riding round, and golf is played there all the year round, too.

The first commercial sand wedge — a concave-faced job, which sold in thousands, but which was declared illegal later. This photograph is from an advertisement in a golfing magazine in 1930. It was a great club, so easy to play. I suppose it was too easy, that is why it was banned. Horton Smith brought it to Britain in 1930.

WHAT IS NEW IN GOLF AFTER ALL?

I HAVE watched the cycles of golf instruction change during the past thirty years. I have studied all the available information on golfing methods since the earliest days and I have concluded there is nothing very much new coming.

After all, what can be new? We are hitting a little white ball with a stick as far and as straight as we can, and then trying to regulate the distance and direction once the hole is within reach. There's nothing new in this.

I have watched the back-swings vary from the most upright swing to the flattest round-the-corner action possible. Yet in the hitting area *all* successful golfers arrive in a comparable position.

My picture shows the swing of James (Jimmy) Bruen from Cork, Eire, the former Amateur Champion and Walker Cup player who, as a boy prodigy in the immediate pre-war years, amazed everyone by the way he hit the ball from this super-upright back-swing. This swing is not for every golfer. Jimmy must have almost double-jointed shoulders, if such a thing is possible.

From this position he whipped the ball with an impact like the crack of a big whip and sent it enormous distances. He came on to the ball just from inside-to-out, giving it a slight hook. A ball can be hit from inside-to-out, not only from a flat back-swing but also from an upright one.

The end of the Bruen swing was classical, with the hands high.

James Bruen at the top of his back-swing (LEFT) *and at the end of his swing* (RIGHT).

16

ON BEING ORIGINAL

WHEN the courses run fast and the greens are not soaked to the extent of being puddings, then a great variety of golf shots is called for, because the ordinary pitch shot, a wedge shot if you like to push it, landing from any angle on to the putting surface, does not sit down like an egg dropped on to the pavement.

It is perhaps rather futile to tell a beginner to be original in his shots to the pin, when he is trying as hard as he can to remember what he had learned in order to hit the ball at all, but this advice to be original can be borne in mind by any golfers who consider themselves outside the beginner stage.

I know that the idea in learning golf is to groove the swing, and to simplify the game by striking every shot as nearly as possible with one swing in the same way, but the good player is always prepared to play his shot according to the occasion. It is possible, of course, to be too clever, and one sometimes meets good players who are not better ones, because they wish to complicate every shot and turn it almost into a trick one.

The beginner will ask his caddie (if he has one, that is!) how long the shot is, and then take the appropriate club and hit the shot, missing through lack of experience a few details concerning the lie, the wind or the nature of the ground and the putting surface to which he is playing — things that a more experienced player would notice.

I wonder if many of you realize what passes through the mind of a first-class player when he is playing, say, a pitch to the green. Before he plays the shot he has decided many points. For example, he has decided that for the lie in question and the certain type of green being approached, it is better to play a full No. 8 than a half No. 7, as he can get more grip on the ball.

He has noticed the wind; if he is not quite sure of the direction he has found out with a handkerchief held high or by throwing up some little bits of grass. He has observed, too, which side of the green the pin is placed, so if there is any serious trouble near the pin, he can play safe, if the occasion demands, and a risk must not be taken.

Serious trouble such as a bad bunker, a clump of gorse, a pond or some long grass or even an out of bounds fence, are all looked for. So, before he plays his shot, he has weighed up all these points, for it is one of the conditions of being a first-class player to think first and not afterwards.

It might be interesting for some of you who travel around and play on different courses to ask yourselves after your first round what you remember of the course, apart from the approximate length of the holes and the scratch score. I am certain many golfers have a job to remember where the serious trouble lies on every hole, unless they have visited it and been punished.

As an old competition player, I found myself looking for all the two-stroke penalties automatically — the out of bounds boundaries and the places where a ball could be lost. One-stroke penalties, although severe, seem to impress one less, but long grass near the green or deep straight-sided bunkers must be avoided at all costs.

Let us return to the question of being original with those little shots around the green. One of the

An interesting study of the 'Old Maestro' James Braid playing a pitch and run shot. This famous old champion, living most of his life on fast-running Walton Heath, where there are few built-up greens — most of the greens run straight off the fairway and so are on the same level — used this shot as one of the main features of his armoury.

In this stroke he has made the ball run. The whole angle of the body and weight situation show that he has been ahead of the ball all the time, so as to play it down, but has used his hands to push the clubhead to the hole, allowing the club-face to turn over very slightly. This is really playing the shot naturally.

Note the white linen jacket — a relic of the days when pullovers had not yet come into fashion.

ABOVE: *English Amateur Golf Championship at the Royal Cinque Ports Golf Club, Deal, Kent. H. G. Bentley is approaching the 13th green. He has gone right down the grip and has used his club-face as the extension of his right hand. He was an ace at making-up shots. Anthony Spalding, who wrote the golf articles in the London* Star *for many years, is the hatless spectator.*

RIGHT: *These shots are not stunts — but actual efficient, legal golf strokes, and the only real way to get a good result from such lies. In the drawing (page 19) taken from an actual photograph, the golfer broke his club (1) but he could have got the same result standing in the position seen in drawing (2).*

I am seen demonstrating a shot backwards and through the legs, made necessary because of the lie by the tree. The other shot was necessary, because the bunker, just through the gap at St Andrews on the 13th hole, is so deep that even if I had stood in it I still could not play the ball. I could hardly see it from the sand. I had no room to stand if I stood normally to the ball, but this way I knocked it forward a few yards. A left-hander, of course, could have played this shot readily, but I could not guarantee a successful shot at all with a right-handed club held nose downwards, especially from a poor lie. To-day few people carry a left-handed club; luckily such situations are rare, but this is a way to meet one.

hardest is the shot played against the grain of the grass, from the walk to the next tee for example. Here the club buries itself on the down-and-through action and the ball never seems to get into the air properly. There is no doubt that a tight grip of the club is essential, and that an action whereby the follow-through is 'lifted', the opposite of the chop type of stroke, is best. These shots are a guess anyway. I have tried them with straighter-faced clubs, too, but that is not the answer, though

it might work for some shots, where loft is not needed on the ball, because there is less tendency to dig for the ball.

Pitch and run shots are the shots which seem to have gone out of fashion since the wedge came into modern golf, yet they are the real safety ones for the handicap golfer. I have one golfing friend who still uses one of those special short-shafted, square-handled run-up clubs which were popular not long ago; now they are rarely to be seen. This

18

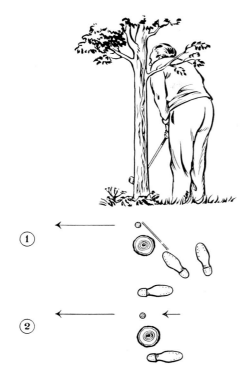

Playing from behind a tree (see page 18).

day, has been Harry Bradshaw, and he overlaps two or three fingers.

James Braid, living so long on fast-running Walton Heath, with scarcely any built-up greens, was a great player of original strokes, and these were very wristy affairs, often accompanied by a kick through with the right knee and a pronounced rolling over of the club-face as if to make sure the ball was to roll. He made a run-up shot look like one in the way he played it.

In the category of original shots would come the chop shot when a ball lying poorly cannot safely be 'got at' with the standard stroke. I often feel that this shot is justified if there is a danger of 'hitting one thin' or of being timid about forcing the ball up a slope as on a double plateau green, because this stroke, which of necessity has a definite attack on the ball, gives less time for a change of mind, as often happens during the normal stroke, if the player has any doubts about the power required. Naturally only when the ground is firm can this sort of shot be a great success. I know some middle handicap range players who rely on the chop to win their half-crowns! To stab at the ball, as often occurs in this sort of shot,

was the only club in his bag he really knew. He scuffled the ball along with the minimum of pitch on it, and through experience often gauged the fairway and semi-rough a treat. There used to be a club called a 'scuffler', which like other clubs such as the jigger and lofting iron has also had its day.

Since top golfers began to use their body action in a pronounced way on the shorter shots, original shots have fallen out of the repertoire of many good golfers. They do not seek to play them, they 'play round' them.

Few handicap golfers notice when sand bunkers have no lips on them, and so often miss a chance to roll the ball out of trouble; and if the ball has to be rolled, then always use a putter — a straight-faced iron does not give the same result.

If you are in front of a big green and need to produce a shot which you could do best if you could lob it by hand, underarm, do not overlook the fact that if you overlap two fingers of the right hand on the left, the right shoulder comes up a fraction and it becomes easier to flip the ball forward cleanly. A divot is not required for such shots, and remember that possibly the best pitch and runner in the business, since Bobby Jones's

ABOVE: *Single-figure handicap, experienced American golfer, Mr Paul Summers, from Lewisburg, W. Virginia, plays a difficult shot from the top of this bunker. The feature of this successful shot, which incidentally went to the hole side, is the body balance and the long back swing. There is a tendency from such positions to swing too quickly and snatch at the shot. There is no doubt that Mr Summers trusted his swing here and 'waited for it'.*

is by no means a classical stroke, but it should not be overlooked by those who are inclined to come up too readily on the shorter shots to the pin, even if it is only used to learn to strike the ball definitely.

With the old-fashioned thin-soled niblick, with a sharpish cutting edge, the modern skid through blast from the sand was 'never on', and so the leading golfers learned to shock the ball from the sand, by actually burying the head behind the ball, varying distances, and shocking the ball on the green by the force of the explosion. This explosion shot to-day is almost out of date, but if the ball lies badly in soft sand, it *is* often easiest to lay open the face of the narrow-soled No. 9 iron and explode the ball, following the old-fashioned method. The broad-soled wedge or sand iron with the lower back edge to the sole, made for skidding, is more difficult to handle if the lie of the ball is bad and, being heavy, is more difficult to swing fast at the ball. The sand iron is made for skidding slowly, not for exploding.

So many golfers would benefit from playing rounds with only five clubs — and I do not mean only club golfers; I include the top players, too — because it is the only way to learn to play golf. It is possible, and fable has it that it did happen, for a golfer to go straight from a driving range complete with sand bunker and putting green, where he had trained, to win an open competition. He would be playing on soft watered greens and on a course with no rough, but just set him off for the first time on a real seaside links, or the Walton

This is one of the hardest shots to judge in the whole game — playing the ball from a ditch. The only way to succeed in such a stroke, if you must take the risk of playing it, is to keep very still with the body and rely on your hands to lead the clubhead to the ball — doing the minimum of arm swing. Marcel Chassagny of Paris in action.

Heath courses, where originality pays off, and he could never have acquired enough experience to handle the problems which arise in every round. I did not hear how he got a handicap, if he had one worse than scratch!

ANALYSING YOUR OWN MISTAKES

THE average golfer, who can be counted upon to mishit the ball more times in a round than not, never tries even to analyse his faults. He never stops to work out, from the unsatisfactory flight of the ball he has produced, why it happened.

Its direction and trajectory should be studied — there is always an explanation. Take, as an example for study, a ball that starts off flying low to the left and then rises quickly, curves to the right, and on landing breaks to the right and stops — a sort of pulled slice. Or consider the ball which starts off to the right, then curves to the left, ducks downward, and then scuttles along the ground as if it would never stop — the quick hook.

The first thing to do is to study the mechanics of the golf swing, to figure out which fundamental or fundamentals must have been violated, then find a trick or a tip which will serve to prevent a repeti-

tion of the violation. In the first example, the clubhead is obviously coming across the ball from outside to inside, and the hit is made particularly late with the club-face striking a glancing blow as well, accompanied by a determined effort with the hands to hold the club-face down. This outside-in attack, plus the glancing blow, produces a very fast spinning ball which, once the initial pull flight, due to the swing being out of line, is beaten by the power of the spin, curves away to the right.

The cause of this type of error? Insufficient body pivot in the back-swing fails to bring the club-shaft pointing parallel to the line from the ball to the hole (some players, Locke and O'Connor, for example, point not just to the hole, but far to the right of it, as viewed from behind), so from this position the club descends all too easily on the inside of the line of play and then has to travel on

20

the inside-to-out path to strike the ball at all.

It can also happen that the player, even if getting into the correct position at the top of the swing, begins to unwind his shoulders too early; that is, before the arms have had a chance to drag the hands and the club into the correct groove.

Also, if too much right shoulder is applied, the wrists will not have enough time to get the club-head through to strike the ball a square blow; it will be from outside-in again, with the club-face generally open at impact. To cure this fault, the player must learn to attack the ball on an inside-to-out path, and so it is a good idea to set up a simple sort of control for acquiring this movement, such as I have set out.

Draw a line on a bare piece of ground with a peg tee, using a club-shaft as a guide, and tee up low or place on the ground a golf ball in the centre of the line. Place long peg tees in the ground as indicated in the sketch. It should be possible to strike the ball without touching the tees; and if the hands are bringing the clubhead through correctly and in time, there should be a good result. Make sure that the left arm is in charge and that the clubhead is being swung straight on. The shoulders must move under the head and not around it, so that the clubhead can get on the inside-to-out path. If the peg tees, which must be tall ones, are touched during the swing, then the player can see for himself where his error lies. It is important in this action that the hands do not get too far ahead of the ball as impact approaches.

In the second example the line of attack of the clubhead is on an excessive inside-to-out path,

It is difficult to slice the ball from here. Christy O'Connor points the clubhead to the right of the hole. Note how he relaxes the left hand. This is not suitable for everyone, but it relieves tension and if the club-shaft does not turn all can be well.

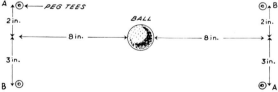

with the toe of the face of the club making contact with the ball first and with the hit being early as well. This is just about as much the opposite of the first example as is possible, for slices and hooks are in pairs, so the very points which are down to be cured in the first example can be accentuated in the second. By this I mean that a swing at the ball from inside-to-out, as in the drawing from A to A, can send the ball out to the right, as a push, if the face is square to the line hit, or if the face is square 'line to hole', then the ball will have a hook on it. Thus a push and a hook are a pair; they come from the same angle of attack on the ball.

Conversely the slice and pull are a pair for the same reason that the clubhead travels on line B to B. It is important to know all this.

To cure a quick hook

An effort must be made to take the clubhead forward (towards the tee box, that is); a shoulder turn can be used, the right side can be rolled round to throw the club towards an outside-to-in path, and the left arm drag-down can be accentuated to produce a later hit, which will tend to hold the club-face more open as impact approaches, to stop the toe of the club-face from leading up to the ball first.

Part of the cause of this second error can come from the grip itself. The placing of the hands on the shaft has a very big bearing on the angle of the swing and on the wrist action itself, and one slight alteration may often call for other adjustments which must be done to get any benefit.

To help to develop a hook, see that the left hand does not show *more* than two knuckles and that the backs of the hands are parallel.

To help to cure a hook, see that the thumb of the right hand is on top of the shaft and that the right hand is being used to guide the club-face.

These tips are my own, but I have found, despite their apparent contradiction to the accepted doctrines, they are 100% right.

21

THE NATURAL GOLFER

Is there such a person? It has always been admitted by players who have never taken a lesson, and who play well, that they have copied from other players, stealing something here and there as they develop their own style. This means that, honestly speaking, they have a sort of composite style which masquerades under the name of 'The Natural Golfer'. Yet, all the same, I did come across a golfer who had never taken a lesson, and who had not copied anyone.

A strong young fellow he was, rather stocky and with thick short-fingered hands, who had gone round a golf course more or less regularly for ten years, slogging at his game on the course and never practising. After reaching some sort of peak to his game — in which a pitch shot always meant a try to scoop the ball in the air and where 'one off the sole' which skidded along the ground caused him to comment naturally, 'I didn't get under that one' — his whole game had fallen to pieces. There

was nothing one could do to help.

Even the standard expressions 'look at the ball', 'swing slower', 'take your time', etc., had no helping effect; in fact, at one moment I felt that any suggestion I made was making the worst quite horrible. The picture of the 'Natural Golfer' — I regret I did not photograph him — was like this: a narrow stance, hands somewhat apart, with right hand well underneath, ball well outside the left toe, and the general aim to mid-on, anticipating a slice; but it was 'even money' that the catching hold of the club again on the way down, as the shaft turned during the back swing, brought the face of the club often very closed to the ball, and this meant a smother or a pulled ball as often as a slice, which of course happened when the face of the club arrived square at impact.

'I have done jolly well my own way until recently', said the 'Natural Golfer', 'but now it has all gone. I am afraid to take any lessons in case I go worse.' 'Sir', I had to reply, 'there is no way to go worse except to miss the ball altogether.'

The swing, I forgot to mention, consisted of a short, waist-high action with a lot of 'ballet' footwork accompanied by a shoulder roll, as it were, just to make it more difficult.

We managed to fit in four lessons, in which some of the mysteries were unfolded, but during the round where we met I managed to get the 'Natural Golfer' stabbing successfully at his wedge shots, and so hitting the ball downwards, to make it rise, and not expecting it to come upwards with a scooping action. This was the best I could get while playing on the course. To learn to swing inside-to-out, to use the hands correctly, to pivot sufficiently, to swing back to the horizontal, to hold on to the club, to follow through towards the hole, to keep the head steady — these made a fine collection of things to do, or to attempt to do.

Progress was made, and I thought that the swing finally achieved did look like a golf swing, but it could not be claimed as precise. What was gained definitely was that when I asked the 'Natural Golfer' to show me what his old swing looked like, he had already forgotten it enough to be against trying to reproduce it.

I suppose what really is meant by a natural golfer is 'one who makes the game look easy' in a natural sort of way. Just two extremes flash to mind — a natural player making the game look easy — Percy Alliss (senior); and one making it look difficult — Max Faulkner, when he has no need to do so.

Harry Bradshaw, who overlaps two or three fingers of his right hand on his left, is a natural player all right. Not for him any thoughts of straight left arm, unwinding of the hips first, etc. This sturdy Irishman has as his programme 'A ball is there! I must hit it straight and hard.' He thinks of nothing else.

The Duke of Norfolk is a natural golfer and is an above-average player, for the time he can give the game. LEFT: *A good left-hand grip, but a palm grip with the right hand.* CENTRE: *The club slips into the fingers quite naturally coming through.* RIGHT: *A classical putting stroke with an old-time wooden putter.*

Monsignor Hugh O'Flaherty and Father John Murray, S.J., at the Rome Golf Club.

LEFT: *Monsignor Hugh O'Flaherty of Rome, the 'Scarlet Pimpernel of the Vatican', who helped so many allied prisoners to safety during the last war, loves his game of golf. He plays to a 5 handicap with this 'natural' grip of the club. A natural golfer if ever there was one!* CENTRE: *Horace G. Hutchinson, Amateur Champion in 1886–7. This is how a golfer played at the turn of the century. Note bent left arm, bent right leg action, Norfolk Jacket and palm grip and open right hand.* RIGHT: *This was the back-swing of a legendary hero, Lt. F. G. Tait, killed in the Boer War as a young man. Note here the left hand position and the grip of the right hand. This is certainly a natural action!*

23

CURING THE TWITCH

'TWITCHING' on the short shots, from the little holing-out putts up to the 30-yard pitch or pitch and run, is not perhaps the most common fault of the average golfer, but once I was a bit shaken to come across two such 'sufferers' in one week. One 19 handicap and the other 9, both 'crazy' golfers being driven almost crazy by this appalling disease. Even from the front of an open green, with just a well-cut apron before them and a No. 6 iron in their hands, the clubhead could not be brought to the ball except in a jerk — a jerk in which the club either hit the ball very cleanly or caught the ground behind the ball suddenly!

One of these golfers told me the tale, very sadly, of how he was given up by his pro., whom he had taken out one evening in the summer to get him to help him. After trying out many ideas, the pro. had taken a club to show him how to play the stroke, and after finding himself twitching on three successive shots, had decided to leave him before he, too, became permanently affected. Rather cowardly, I thought! This may or may not be exactly true, but there are many golfers who believe that such twitching is entirely mental and a job for the psychiatrist.

I believe that it can develop from a doubt about

Charles Ward tries the reverse hands style for putting, to get rid of the 'over 40 twitch'. He uses this as a temporary cure, then goes back to his old style.

being able to play such a shot smoothly in the first place, and that successive failures can bring this twitch about; but there is also a fundamental error in technique.

In the case of the player who nearly gave it to his pro., on closer observation, when I asked him to grip a near-by umbrella, I could see he was always going to have trouble from holding the club in the way he did — his right hand was not well placed; it was in a curious bunched-up position and so much under the shaft that a real wrist cock with this hand seemed unlikely.

I said I would look at his action on the first occasion and, following a 'phone call, he came round to show me 'the real thing' in my garden, where it is possible to pitch into a net from ten to twelve yards.

Yes! there it was, alive, a real twitch. It was repeated consistently, accompanied by a change in complexion, for as the terror grew his face became more red, not entirely from shame, for we were alone, but from the effort of concentrating and the job of trying to make the clubhead swing. It did not swing, it was taken back from the ball a short distance and then suddenly it tried to fly at the ball, like a dog at a rat. In a dozen attempts, a 'mixed bag' was offered, including 'one off the pipe' which hit some stone steps on the right, whence the ball popped back into the garden pond.

What should one do? I am always sure a cure can be effected, because there is a physical reason for such mistakes. 'Chop down on it. Do not follow through, get the hands ahead of the shaft and then squeeze the ball into the mat! Pinch it!'

No! this did not help much, for there was not enough golfing ability in the player to get this idea quickly enough, and I did not intend, therefore, to plug this suggestion.

'Now get your hands lower at the address', I suggested. Yes, this was a bit better, a series of quite satisfying shots pitched down the paving-stones of the yard correctly and bounced into the net. But after another dozen shots or so, the old twitch showed up again. That was not it!

A change of stance was helpful, but with the right foot wanting all the time to point outwards like paraded feet, toes out 45°, it was not easy to move the right hip and knee with the stroke.

Here it was — not in the grip or hand-work really, but as much in the feet as the hips. The right side locked, and the shoulders did not move freely, as there was no rhythm in the action — there never could be.

'Oh, I keep my head still. I never look up', the golfer said, and that was true; he had added a 'head-frozen-into-position' section to this already paralysed motion.

How did he ever get on to the green at all? For I could see it would sometimes need a chain of these strokes to advance twenty yards? Well, he finally took a putter and with this 22-ounce club he could record every time a success, for he always made a contact with the ball and so got on to the putting surface. It was just that one shot, from in front of the green, which 'killed him'. I could not get him to stay put with his feet parallel — his right foot always wanted to turn out — but by not getting the weight on the heels, and by using the inside edges of the shoes, the body began to come 'into' the swing of the clubhead.

What sort of an eye had he got? Yes, he had played all the games at school, and decently, too! Let me check on that. 'Here are five balls on the mat! Just knock them into the net without addressing the ball and without a pause of any sort.' BANG, BANG, BANG, BANG and BANG — the whole lot flew immediately to the centre of the net.

Joe Davis, the billiards and snooker ace, tries out his hand for steadiness at the 'News of the World' Garden Party in the Chairman's garden. The idea is to pass the wire loop he is holding along the electrified line without touching it. A bell rings if contact is made and the distance covered is measured, a prize being given if you get to the end. This is not difficult to do if you have good sight, I found. As the years pass, it is difficult for the eyes to hold the focus on the loop in the wire, to judge exactly 'where it is'. Joe, a keen golfer, is just a sound putter, not a master on the greens as one might expect. His handicap at his pet game, snooker, to-day is just 'scratch' in golf terms, he reckons. Anno domini and eyesight problems have put up his handicap, for he was plus 10 for years. Unbeatable that means — and he was for twenty years.

Sam Snead practising putting at Boca Raton — beyond, his golf buggy waits for him to begin a round. He is trying out my old putter and his left hand action holding the blade down is interesting, but on short putts this closed face action can provoke pushing out the ball to the right.

As I thought, he could produce a result if he could get the club back from the ball.

'Now play me some shots with no wrist work. Swing from the shoulders, point the left shoulder towards the ball and without help from the wrists swing the clubhead under your head, allowing the knees and hips to work — a sort of wooden doll action!' This was it — it worked like magic, shot after shot went sweetly into the centre of the net. But the ball was perched up nicely on the bristles of the mat, quite teed up in fact.

25

Sam Snead, one of the greatest golfers ever, snapped without his straw hat on this occasion, suffered for a while from a twitch in his short putts. On a long putt, as shown here, he is perhaps the equal of anybody in the game. This photograph shows the follow-through on a 30-foot putt at Boca Raton, Florida, where he goes in the winter.

the flag in the centre of the fairway. They anticipated another easy win. He never came back, so I trust it *is* all over. A doctor friend of mine claims to have satisfied himself that 'jitters' and 'putting paralysis' come from concentrating on the clubhead instead of the hands only. He claims that the hands form the most sensitive part of the golfer's body, for in them are placed highly sensitive sensory organs which can give the golfer the most vital information.

No golfer twitches when he moves his hands backwards and forwards as when making a golf stroke, if he has no club in his hands. I have checked this point with various golfers. To ask a not very skilful golfer to watch his hands move and not to have his eye on the ball might prove to be a mixed blessing, but there is something in it.

Charles Ward, as can be seen in the photograph on page 24, is using a reverse hands grip of the club to get rid of a twitch. I have seen low handicap golfers and professionals, too, even putt left-handed to get the missing rhythm back and to cut out that jerk.

If I were setting out to cure all twitches, I would not consult a psychiatrist but a physician, and get my metabolism fixed up. I think the nerves need feeding; just my humble opinion!

Would it work off the fairway? Yes, if the lie was good. Winter rules, anyway, I told him, would see him through for the present. I do not guarantee that this suggestion will prove to be the permanent cure, but it did seem as if it would break the spell.

This player was afraid to move away from the ball because he felt that to take the clubhead back more than nine or ten inches was risking an inaccurate blow, yet he was soon satisfied that he could 'find the ball' easily, even 'on the run'.

I did not mention the right-hand position again after I moved the right thumb from a sort of floating position so that it was right down the top of the shaft.

I do not know if there is to be a 'happy ever after ending', but my golfer was going to test it out the very next week-end on his regular 'clients'. He hoped to stop them rubbing their hands together with glee when they saw his good second shots finish just that right number of yards from

Another get-rid-of-twitch method. This is perhaps the most popular of all. Charles Mills in action. Several well-known amateurs, including Leonard Crawley and John Beck, are putting croquet-fashion.

26

GOOD GOLF WITHOUT PRACTICE?

To the European golf fan, unless he has visited America, it is difficult to imagine what goes on in the golf world there, for there is an enthusiasm for the game which cannot be described — it must be seen. Down in Florida, where golf courses are being built by the dozen, as this all-the-year-round holiday State grows in popularity annually, golf course construction design incorporates facilities for practice which I have never yet seen in Europe, except in the American military courses in Germany. Even at a long-established club like the elegant Gulf Stream Golf Club, where Bobby Cruikshank has been pro. for some twenty years, one finds two huge putting greens, a small pitching green and practice bunker, and a driving range where a pail of one hundred balls costs two dollars. The interest in reading about the game was never greater, and short golf articles by Tommy Armour, Cary Middlecoff and Sam Snead appear in many daily papers, often illustrated by drawings, year after year.

Ben Hogan had a similar series running for some time. He wrote also a long article for *Life*, in which he gave *the secret* of his success — for just ten thousand dollars — built around the permitting of his left wrist to go a little more under the shaft at the top of the back swing, and for the forearm and back of the hand not to be in line, as he had recommended at one time.

In the elaborate series (about 8,000 words in each article), which was beautifully illustrated with coloured drawings (now published in book form), Ben wrote of his own action in the greatest detail, developing all his ideas most carefully. No golfer can fail to be interested in how this golfing wizard plays, for even nearing fifty years of age he is still one of the world's top players. He practises with a determination few youngsters show. I enjoyed following this series because they set out so clearly all the points Hogan studies when he plays and practises, but, of course, they must be read with the understanding that the writer is very strong and wiry, and has *exceptionally* strong hands.

If you would give me a would-be golfer with hands as strong as any top professional's, then three-quarters of the problems of learning to play golf are solved. Most golfers fail because they have *no hands*, not because they do a bad swing. All the efforts they make to swing the club at the ball are finally transmitted by the hands, and if the hands are weak, then the back-swing, however good, all too frequently leads to nothing, because there is no control of the club in the hitting area.

Gulf Stream Golf Club. One of the putting greens in front of the clubhouse. Florida, 1957.

Peter Mills, one of our best professionals, is not considered a good practiser by his colleagues here — he prefers to play. My camera has caught him practising in Spain at the Barcelona Golf Club, 1957. His action is classical. I like the firm left hand and the club-face position.

While studying the Hogan series for the first time it struck me that the author had accepted too readily that those he had set out to guide have strong hands and muscular bodies, because he

The veteran Earl of Rosebery is a natural ball-games player and has rarely practised golf, despite having a private 9 holes course on his estate at Dalmeny, near Edinburgh. After a few holes he gets loosened up, and is always a hard man to beat on handicap. He is annoyed that he tends to fall away from his shots, but it is only his flat-footed action which causes this. Barnton, 1953.

inferred that breaking 80 should be within every golfer's scope. All golf champions, without exception, have built up their game by practising ; this practice breeds confidence and strengthens the hands and the body, but average golfers, as we readily call the mass of people who do play golf, have not time and probably no inclination to practise hard, so they would be more interested in learning how to play *without* practising.

Hogan's explanations of why he uses certain actions in his own game are very clearly reasoned, but to me it seems as if he is always setting out to harness immense power, to subjugate his wrist flick rather than use 'the lot'. In my own case, while I have developed my hands and arms, they do not compare with the strength available to Hogan and Snead, and I feel that I have always needed to use 'the lot' to whip the ball, not cut down on my freedom of action — to push the ball, as it were.

The stance is not just a position taken for aiming the ball, but for striking it properly. While every credit must be given to the strong men for the skill and ball control they exhibit, I am always very

interested in studying how the less physically-gifted golfers get by and manage to give competition to the real tigers. That there is an ideal combination of strength and flexibility to succeed in golf is, I think, generally accepted, but such natural talent is rare; what is almost rarer is for someone to built up a strong golf game from a 'below average' physical start. I think that the latest Ben Hogan series, which marks many changes from his first book, *Power Golf,* published over ten years ago, is a fine contribution to golf instruction, but if all golfers go copying the elbows together, wristless action, tight grip of the club, they will meet with new problems.

There is in this series the idea that a flat swing is a main key to a successful attack on the ball, but such an action cannot be everybody's 'meat'. Hogan is one of the many golfers of the new American school who admits that his game deteriorates fast if he does not practise; his swing is a built-up one, but admittedly this does not diminish in any way his great talent, because he has such a knowledge of his own play that he can work on the weak links and steadily build up a great chain of mechanical movements, in just a few weeks, following a beneficial rest. As results alone count, the man who can play a good game, say around scratch, playing only once a week, receives little credit except to hear that he has a natural swing. I think the next successful series must be 'How to play golf well without hard practice.' Surely this will create a rush on the bookstalls!

Ben Hogan, a glutton for practice — just look at the power in these arms. Note rigid start back.

28

VARIETY

HERCULES AS A GOLFER

Hercules, a statue by Bertoldo di Giovanni, 1420–91, doing a golf swing. I added the club, but his swing is not bad — only he forgot to keep his head down.

LOST BALL ON THE TEE

Stanley Holloway, of 'My Fair Lady', put his ball in the ball washer, having pulled out the wooden handle completely, and of course the ball went to the bottom and was lost, making him holder of a world's record — 'The first man to lose his ball on the tee.'

TOM THUMB GOLF

Few of my golfing followers will have seen me struggling round a Tom Thumb course. I was taken to one by a young friend, William Carr, when staying at Deauville, and went round the local 'track'. Said the owner to his wife, not knowing who we were and not for our hearing, as we started off: 'Funny how all these Englishmen hold the club so much better than Frenchmen.'

BELIEVE IT OR NOT!

Sam Snead with his favourite driver, which has had five new shafts in its life. The neck is cracked, the metal plate is worn paper-thin. I sent him a copy of my own driver, which he liked and which he has in reserve. Look how far the wrapping on the neck goes down — it helps the head to stay on the shaft.

29

THE GOLF SECRET

Tʜɪs is the title of a golf book by a West Country doctor, Dr H. A. Murray.

Golf books and articles are poured out by the thousand, it seems, for there is no other sport in the world which is submitted to such an annual barrage of words the year round, the world over.

Dr Murray has done what so many other instructional writers on golf do: he has selected one section of the golf swing and developed his theme to the point of 'proving it a secret'. There is a lot of sound sense in this book, and it is a great credit to the writer. Winding up his work, the Doctor says: 'Apart from maintaining a firm grip, there are only four anatomical parts with which we are consciously concerned in executing the golf swing. They are the upper part of the spine, the left shoulder and the left and right upper arms. The first is used in preparation for the swing, the third and fourth can be left to themselves; the second is indispensable. Therefore, the LEFT SHOULDER is our sheet-anchor.'

I still have to be convinced that golf, for the world in general, means using more body than I teach, for I give the body only 15% of the effort to get speed, the arms, hands and wrists 85%. (Seymour Dunn, a great teacher and student, gave the same percentages).

When one teaches golf to dozens of different people of all ages, shapes and sizes, it becomes increasingly clear that each one is an individual case. There are fundamentals, maybe, that one can follow, but it is always a question of using one's experience of trial and error methods to save the pupil from wasting his or her time, attempting to do the impossible. And yet at the outset every pupil imagines he or she will develop that perfect 'pro. swing'.

Just as further evidence of the need to be original when teaching — a very broad-shouldered person, who cannot get his elbows anywhere near touching when his arms are extended before him, cannot possibly hit the ball with that ideal sort of flapping action of the right hand, because his right hand will lie too much under the shaft at the address, so he will need to use a pushing action, or even a 'hand slide' by the club shaft to get his best results.

I am often amused by golfers who are afraid to go to a certain professional because they feel they cannot 'do' his method. They might as well say: 'We have not your power or flexibility, therefore we could not adopt your method.'

This would imply that the pro. only gets pupils to teach who can or do use his method. How wrong! I do think that a *stiff-armed, body emphasized swing* is no good for the average golfer, who is a person past the dashing activity of youth; it is, in fact, a spine-twisting menace. A pivot is essential — it goes along with the swing — but I hesitate to make my pupils do a pivot forcibly or to insist on the body winding and unwinding any more than will happen with the steady to-and-fro swinging of a heavy club.

The instructor who has long experience usually tries out his stock phrases and methods on every beginner, and is then prepared to adjust, because every person requires a different approach. To perhaps three people in six, a simple sort of accepted explanation fails to ring the bell; another phrase, maybe, has to be tried to put over the idea — perhaps several attempts are needed. Because of this, I always view with suspicion a method which says 'this is it'. Do you remember the much vaunted 'scissor' action — the crossing over of the wrists? The secret of the game, it was said to be. It is forgotten to-day, considered almost as out-of-date as the hickory shaft, *yet* it could be the right medicine for some players to-day who are afraid to let the wrists go free.

Treat your left shoulder as a key pivot of the swing. It points to the ball 'going up', and then it revolves around and under the head till it is pulled behind the head as the swing proceeds, the right shoulder taking its place momentarily; but would it count for you as '*the* secret'?

It could possibly be the very thing you need to accentuate, but, like other tips, it can be overdone and so exceed its real rôle. There are several types of golf swing and, I am sure, they will one day be set out in the form of a chart. Swing one — this will be a certain grip, and certain body and foot actions to go with it; variations for certain builds and degrees of flexibility. So a player could find his swing and then add all the bits that fit together for him as parts for his own jigsaw puzzle. That will be the day! Swing two — this will be a different grip and its accompanying variations of body and foot action, but it will then be understood that parts of swing one and swing two are not interchangeable. So many mistakes are made by keen golfers in copying swings or bits of swings and adding them to their own actions, which they just won't fit.

WHAT SHAPE ARE YOU?

EVERYONE is built differently physically. And from this simple statement comes the great truth, that it is no use trying to imitate another player in every detail — it does not work out.

It was interesting to read some words of Bill Campbell's, captain of the 1955 U.S. Walker Cup team which butchered our players at St Andrews, in which he was acknowledging his deep admiration for golfer Sam Snead and at the same time pointing out that Sam's powerful double-jointed, much broken and repaired bones in his hands give him a unique grip of the club.

His long arms and loose shoulders enable him to develop as wide an arc at impact as can be found in the whole game. Most golfers would love to have, as one golfer imaginatively said in a New Year's wish, a swing like Slamming Sam's, 'just for a couple of days, then I'd show the boys!'

I have watched over the years the champions of yester-year having to alter their actions to fit their changing bodies, as with the fleeting years their legs have got weaker and bodies thicker. Ben Hogan decided to free himself gradually from the dreadful strain of big golf and its preparation; he put on 20 lb. and went to around 12 stone in weight. This alone made him alter his body action and made his hands and arms play an ever bigger rôle.

The tall thin players have completely different problems from thick-set, short types, and I have seen that the thick-set players, when they have put

What's my line? Don't kid yourself! It really does make a difference, if you want to copy someone, just to see where your line runs.

on weight, rely very much on an opening and closing of the hands during the swing in order to play a decent game at all — and then their play would only be a patch on their best, younger days.

When one knows this, and when one sees a fifty-year-old beginner struggling to do a swing which a pro. with almost forty years of contact with the game could not reproduce, one realises that the golf game must always be approached with a very open mind. To be prepared to try everything and anything should be every golfer's plan, because every golfer can improve up to the limit of his own capabilities. Few senior golfers, even the very keenest ones, are disposed to try and develop muscles or loosen up tight ones with exercises and massage. They rightly regard golf as a game, but this does not get them away from the fact that golf muscles are needed to do a golfing swing. Ask your own professional (or several professionals) what he thinks your peak would be in golf, according to the amount of practice and play you can manage, and this will give you a goal. If you get there, then obviously you will raise your sights.

I have always stuck to my theories about the right physique for golf, because golf is more difficult for extremes; very tall or very short people have entirely different problems to handle. Gene Sazaren, one of the best little (in size) golfers of the past three decades, had to use a considerable body sway going up to get his back-swing arc wide enough, because with his shorter radius, left shoulder-joint to clubhead, he naturally had too narrow or steep an arc for wooden shots, if he stayed still on the back-swing.

Fred Daly uses his most personal shoulder roll-away from the ball to get width in his back-swing

Marcel Dallemagne of Paris, tall and slim.

Archie Compston   *Byron Nelson*   *Eric Brown*

because he too is a short man. The very tall players (Archie Compston, David Thomas, 'Long Jim' Barnes, Bernard Hunt, Peter Alliss, come to mind) have the opposite problem; their radius, left shoulder to clubhead, is large, and so has to be narrowed for most fairway shots, and Compston uses a very delayed hit and as narrow an arc as possible, with a body sway into the ball on the way down.

Tall (Open Champions) Jim Barnes and Cary Middlecoff sway noticeably into the ball. They have to, because a small golf ball when lying on the ground can only be attacked within a limited range of arcs. An arc can be too wide and hit the ground behind the ball, or too steep and squeeze the ball too much. The larger-sized ball does ease matters slightly, as the centre of the back of the ball is 0·84 inches off bare ground level as against 0·81 inches with the small ball; and this little bit makes a mighty difference, because allowing for spongy turf the larger balls sit up higher off bare ground-level, and it is, therefore, possible to hit the ball more 'coming up'.

The players of ideal average physique (Snead, Hogan, Locke, Nelson and myself — I immodestly include myself for being of similar height) have fewer problems of the arc to solve — our natural wide arc is just right to hit the ball in the back off the tee and through the green.

The smaller players usually become expert short-game players, for their natural steepish arcs are very convenient for the shorter-shafted pitch-ing clubs, with which the ball has always to be hit a descending blow. Peter Thomson is a slightly stiffer edition of the immortal Bobby Jones. Jones was not considered a great pitcher, but that was just because he played his shots to the pin with the same lazy rhythm which he used for his long shots. I am not positive, but I feel I am correct in blaming his training with hickory shafts as being responsible

Peter Thomson, a stockier Bobby Jones. Note sitting action for this No. 3 iron shot.

32

Bobby Locke (1959), *a heavy-weight to-day, still manages to hit from inside to out. Note how his left hand is closing the club-face as he rolls his right shoulder but keeps his right arm bent. All Champions do this. Note the very closed stance — this suits some heavy-weights.* (RIGHT): *Locke in 1938 — still the same action.*

Ed. ('Porky') Oliver weighs 220 pounds, but despite his bulk is one of the great golfers in America, capable of winning at any time.

    Here he is practising at White Sulphur Springs in 1956. His action is classical in every way. Note the way he holds the club-face square at impact with the side of his left hand; this is unusual but there, as always, is the bent right arm.

The late Aga Khan, a delightful person, and a keen golfer with little sartorial enthusiasm, found that with the left thumb outside, on this double-handed grip, he could get more rhythm in his shots. With extra weight, a privilege of age, his body action and footwork became slow, but that did not stop him from getting the maximum pleasure out of his regular game.

In his heydey a scratch golfer, Henry Longhurst, brilliant scribe and broadcaster, whom the fleeting years have made thicker-and-thicker-set, always wanted a little more freedom to make golf easy.

    His compact build has been a good base for his excellent short game and from being a regular slicer he has at last a gentle hook on his tee shots. I hope it lasts!!

There must be a difference in the swings of these two golfers. Mario Gonzales from Brazil, 'the Walking Pencil' as he was called in 1948, had a hip action which could be called snake-like. He used it to get power and to hold the club-face open, as his grip was part of the beginning of a shut-faced club action.

Harry Lipman, of the sturdy figure, has the opposite problems — the problems of the short golfer with the extra weight on; his objective is to move more, not less, and to try to get some hip action into his swing to stop the shoulders doing too much. He should never stand still at the address, his feet should be 'alive', he should begin his swing back from a 'little dance'.

LEFT: *Double-jointed James Adams, pro. at Royal Mid-Surrey Golf Club, can do the most rhythmic full swing even with both feet flat on the ground. Although now a veteran he can still swing as fully and as smoothly as he ever did.*

CENTRE: *Thick-set, short, sturdy Lionel Hebert, U.S. Ryder Cup player, a successful player on the Tournament Circuit, stands very near to the ball for his short shots. He is really 'crowding the ball'. I find this is a personal position — it looks cramped to me. Many would shank the ball from here.*

RIGHT: *The shoulders here work horizontally instead of under the head — the head has moved far to the right, throwing the whole swing off balance, and the bent right leg stops the swing from ever being firm. This closed club-face position and crumpled-up backswing make it difficult to stay on the 'inside of the ball'. This golfer does not use his height, and the ball is generally cut miserably. The real golf muscles are missing — that is why this happens.*

LEFT: *A thick-set veteran lady golfer, Mrs J. Hagander, gets well away from the ball at the address and uses a wide stance to get a solid whack at the ball. She remembers, too, to look at the ball with her left eye, which helps the backswing and the 'looking at the ball.'*

RIGHT: *Heavyweight W. J. ('Bill') Cox blasts his ball from powdery sand, cutting across the ball as he crashes into the sand behind the ball.*

for this, just as much as his rubber-jointed body. Peter Thomson, like most players who have grown up with steel shafts, punches the ball more — his swing is commercially efficient as opposed to Jones's wonderfully elegant action — but Thomson is of a more stocky build. Of our pros., Eric Brown has an ideal build — Peter Alliss, Bernard Hunt and David Thomas have the problems of the tall golfers to solve. Peter Alliss finds the mystery of the short game still his biggest problem — his natural arc is too wide. His father, Percy, a beautiful player at his best, was the ideal build, I thought, and few players have ever been more machine-like through the green. Little Australian Norman Von Nida had a fine free action, with his fingers being very active during his swing. He had much success over here just after the war.

These few examples at random should give golfers reason to think about their own physique relative to what they are trying to do. There are particular actions which suit each player best. Have you found yours?

BALL IN THE CENTRE

This is how I like to begin my backswing for any full shot. Here I am playing a No. 3 iron shot — wide stance, ball off the centre. There is no doubt here that the left side is playing its part in pushing the club away from the ball, as the left knee is working inwards towards the ball.

OH, MY ACHING BACK!

CONTORTIONISTS . . . SLIPPED DISCS . . . AND 'JUST DANGLING'

| *Cary Middlecoff* | *Sam Snead* | *Harry Weetman* | *Henry Cotton* |

THERE is a lot of strain in the golf game. The need for the highest degree of mental concentration over an extended period of time 'kills off' the giants even more quickly than the physical strain of wielding a club at a great speed, with the body twisted because the right hand fits below the left.

If the hands completely overlapped one over the other, the game would be easier, because the shoulders would then be level. But while this is possible physically, from a point of applying maximum power and control it would be useless.

Just look at the photograph of Cary Middlecoff finishing his swing. Everything is twisted from the ankles to the neck, and it needs an extra strong, supple body to stand this strain, not only when playing a round but also in the continual practising. In an actual round a player of Middlecoff's power would play only very few full shots with any chosen club, but it is the hours on the practice-tee which will take their toll unless contra- or corrective exercises of some sort are done.

The fact that Sam Snead's game is so smooth and yet so strong is due to his magnificent physique. He does regular exercises night and morning. The man from the mountains of Virginia has long realised that physical fitness pays off.

Just look at those arms! Slamming Sam has 'arms like legs' and two hundred exercises a day (with a spring-grip, with each arm) keep them like this.

It is all very well to say 'sweep the ball away'. But no golf ball was ever sent a long way without some sort of resistance creeping into the swing — without hitting past the body and allowing the

clubhead to overtake the hands. If the towing or tugging down from the top continued without some resistance somewhere, the clubhead would never catch up with the hands and the body. It would trail all the time.

Now what sort of resistance can be found? I have played with the maximum amount of hands and arms in my swing all my life, limiting the body action to the minimum so far as helping the clubhead through is concerned. I have been content to let my arms take the body through.

I worked this out for myself in a way, because, although slipped discs were not talked of in my early days — possibly they were rarer, anyway — I think golfers had a different angle on the swing and practised less and rode less in cars, and maybe they were tougher specimens, too!

Middlecoff has had back trouble for some time now, and it is not surprising when one realises the twist he gives his body. Harry Weetman, one of the game's really long hitters, possessing an exquisite touch around the greens, has had odd back pains. But I suspect these are more muscular than from spinal strain, because, as this photograph shows, he has a normal sort of position coming through the ball. Photograph No. 3 shows him playing from 'open to shut'.

It can be claimed also that years ago, when I 'came in', players did not practise as they do now. I often wonder how a glutton for practice like Ben Hogan would have handled the hickory shaft situation. He would never have hit as many balls, I feel, because the shafts, however good, would never have stood up to the 'bashing'. Even with the power I had in my early days, when there were

36

not enough hours of daylight in the day for me, I found I had to have a practice set and a 'best' set — a bit like the everyday suit and the Sunday suit.

This alone may have saved the backs of many players, but I am now of the opinion that if contra-exercises are done all along while practising — stretching exercises particularly — the human body is flexible enough to take the toughest punishment.

I have landed on daily stretching in the easy way, by using a telescopic expanding gym. bar which I fit in a door frame and take everywhere I go. After any spell in a slumped-up position, such as happens when reading, writing or golfing, just a few seconds of hanging seem to get my muscles all rested and relaxed again and strengthen my back.

After fifty years of age, it is not a question of looking for much improvement in one's physical condition. One is grateful if one can hold one's own, as it were. Golf is a great game, an ideal relaxation for all, but played incorrectly it can become tiring and can at odd times put a big strain on certain sectors of the body. The lower part of the spine and the left elbow are the two vulnerable points in the golfer, I have found from my experience as player and teacher.

Teaching, as I do, that golf is a game of the hands and arms where the club is swung and the body is almost encouraged to follow, I feel that I am guiding my pupils as far away as possible from physical damage. But when the player wants to hit full out, and so bring some resistance into the shot, then trained muscles are needed, not only to get good results, but to minimize the danger of strains.

You see, it is as easy as this. If the hands are under too much strain, the club just slips round in the fingers. This happens, for example, when a ball is hit outside the centre section of the club-face. If there is too much strain coming on the ankles, knees and spine, then the foot should slew round and save the day. That is where the shorter shoe-spikes have great value. I have used all lengths of spike in my golf shoes from ordinary hobnails to actual running spikes. But I am sure that long spikes are dangerous for many elderly golfers, for they are inclined to lock the feet in the turf.

If you are experiencing back trouble, I suggest that you begin hanging daily, and then check on your method and think of golf as a hand and arm game — cut down the body work. It is safest to consult your doctor, but orthopaedic surgeons and professors of anatomy have all spoken to me of the advantages of this regular stretching. We do not stretch enough. Most animals set us an example on how to keep fit by stretching. But few of us ever stop to copy. I am sure that my own golf has improved lately as a result of my 'hanging'. Do not try to pull up if you are over forty; leave that to youth. 'Just dangle to feel worth a million!'

VERY OPEN TO SHUT

Norman Drew, a promising North of Ireland professional, is here seen using the 'maximum shut-face method'. This particular action originates in the grip (photograph 1). In photograph 2 his action is caught by the camera at its 'shuttest'. In the third photograph he has manoeuvred his body well in advance of the clubhead to make sure the face will be square at impact. In the last photograph is seen the exceptional strain put on the spine. This is why I contend that this is only a young man's method.

'Doing the bridge' in 1946, aged 39 — just checked up to see if I could do these exercises today and found I still could, but as it is a bit of a strain, I desist — I think wisely. There are other exercises less strenuous, such as swinging a heavy club, skipping and hanging, but I can still do this for a bet.

TAKE MY TIP AND KEEP FIT - EVEN AT 50!

MUCH as I dislike reminding myself that I am past 50, the grey hairs and the wrinkles are there. I cannot miss them. But I am beginning to realize that while a lot is past, there may still be much to come. And I am satisfied that the period from 30 to 50 is the most important of one's life in forming good health and exercise patterns. For most of us they are the busy years. And they pass all too quickly. But they are also the years during which a sane physical fitness programme must be followed if later life is to be enjoyed usefully.

After 30 most people are interested in economic or social success. And, not having the excess energy of the 20's, they rapidly deteriorate physically unless an intelligent balance is arrived at between work, feeding, resting and exercise. In other words, a great many people find it a lot easier to make a living than to *live*.

Most business men neglect exercise except at the week-end, when it is often too exhausting to do any good, while the womenfolk get thoroughly fatigued by the daily care of the house and children. In fact many men arrive at the office or works on Monday tired out after a week-end on the links or the tennis court, in the garden, or driving the car on crowded roads.

All this week-end 'living-it-up' can be mentally diverting, but from a health standpoint it's just dissipation. That's why I think the 30's to 50's are the years in which we must learn to *regulate* our

I spent ten weeks that winter doing P.T. I can still do all this!

38

I have a portable gym bar.   *I won the Dunlop five rounds event by five strokes.*

energy. If one has been physically very active during the 20's, it is important to maintain most of this capacity as the 30's are reached.

Athletes who keep up their exercises have a longer life expectancy than non-athletes. Even those who neglect training for a spell can gradually work to a peak of physical fitness that gives the maximum functioning of the body for daily living. If you take my tip and decide to get yourself into the best possible shape for your age, you must have a medical check-up first. When did you last have one? Or are you one of those people who say 'Never had a doctor in my life'? Such people often go the quickest, remember. I've learned a lot from bitter experience. I wouldn't make the same mistakes again, but we get no second chances. There is just time, sometimes, to correct part of the errors.

When I decided to retire from big-time golf in 1948 and just play the rôle of spectator (almost business man-golfer you might call it) I found not only that my game deteriorated, the competitive edge being absent, but also that my design for living was missing. That is, there was no incentive to keep me in peak condition.

I stuck it out till 1952, making only a few mediocre shows in tournaments. But after Christmas,

1952 (I was rising 46), I thought I would have another big try just to see how much skill I had lost and how good the others who had taken my place were.

I spent ten weeks of that winter doing physical training exercises with an instructor who got me out of bed at 8 a.m. no matter how tired I was — and I *was* tired — playing and practising golf daily and carrying on with my usual social and business life.

By the end of April I had really toughened up.

The first event I played in I won easily, and I felt that my efforts and sacrifices had been worth while. But I had forgotten my age, in the excitement, and played in another big tournament two weeks later.

I did well, but not as well as in the first one. Then I tried a third. And when the ground began to heave like an ocean swell I guessed something was wrong. So it was that in June, 1953, I was pushed off to rest in France, for my heart was tired. I had done too much.

'No more big golf this year, my boy, and thereafter just a few events a year is your quota', said the doctor. I got a wigging from the Press for not playing in the Ryder Cup match at Wentworth (that October) which we nearly won, but was

39

forbidden by Lord Evans, the famous physician, to put myself under great strain so soon.

All got well again. The heart rested up and the latest news (1959) is that it is better than at any time for years, but I must not overdo things.

I think I am best when I stick to my old pattern of keeping as fit as possible for coming tournaments. Though I play only a few now, they keep me trying, and this incentive is sufficient to make me keep in good general shape.

But it is no use expecting most middle-aged men and women to take time off each day to get down on the mat and do their daily dozen.

They all know they should. They all know they feel better for it. But it requires an abnormal amount of will-power, and too many drift along thinking they are fit.

What is the answer?

I have found that a few seconds at a time of s-t-r-e-t-c-h-i-n-g is just enough to keep one in shape.

I find it corrects the usually slumping postures we settle into during most of our day, and the natural extending of the spine acts as a relief as well as toughening up the all-important back muscles, and golfing muscles in particular, for those engaging in the sport.

Most people slump and slouch. And this poor posture contributes to all forms of ill health.

I have been hanging on the tops of door frames all my life — but you need very strong fingers for this, and besides the tops of door frames are always dirty. That is why the simple gym. bar is the thing. I have one in my luggage everywhere I go. I use one at home, on a ship, in hotel rooms.

Take my tip. Learn from my experience.

You must be fit to enjoy life. Just look around you. How many of your friends are really fit, how many try to keep in shape by diet and exercises? The answer, I'll bet, is a handful only.

The rest just let themselves go in the years from 30 to 50 in what I call the constructive years, too. Then they live (if they live on) to regret it.

So start stretching to-day. You'll never be sorry.

A TYPE OF PITCH

Tony Holguin, a pro. on the circuit in America, is seen here practising pitch shots (watched by Frank Stranahan and 'Toots', right. He is using a stiff-wristed action with lots of body as can be seen by the way he has finished this short stroke.

The wrists, the right especially, are locked at the top of the back swing and never move throughout the stroke; the knees and hips supply any flexibility in this action, passing through the ball.

TALKING ON THE COURSE

Some players keep relaxed through chatting as they go round, but I have found that I do play better if I concentrate to the maximum, and that means talking little and getting on with the job.

We all know the breezy type who tries to talk you out of it, and often does. He could be reminded of the saying of the old Scotsman who said: 'Golf is a game to be enjoyed or endured in silence.'

PRACTISING

WHETHER one practises a little or much depends on individual taste, but to practise regularly and frequently is a 'must' for everyone who wants to be good. Few golfers have remained great without regular practice, and none has arrived at being great without much practice.

Some players are gluttons for practice. One who comes to mind is Ben Hogan — he felt that $2\frac{1}{2}$ hours was a sort of daily warming-up drill. I wonder what some of the giants of the past would think of this for a spell of hard labour. I have felt, as I have grown older, that it is only necessary to play 'like mad' when one is learning to play, but once a swing 'that works' has been acquired, then it is enough to keep the muscles toned up and to check on direction by hitting a certain number of balls.

Another American who is a slaving practiser is Frank Stranahan. I have studied him while practising, and after reaching a peak when he hit very many perfect shots in succession, he often continued to play on enthusiastically and then gradually passed this peak, and became tired. He then spent the rest of his time on the practice-ground correcting faults caused by the fatigue, which produced faults which were never really his normal errors. This sort of practice, except that it passes the time, is not really as beneficial as it should be. The time to stop is when you have the feeling that all is going well.

Every player has his own formula for practice. Some work hard on the short game, others only enjoy hitting full shots. Francis Ouimet once wrote that the best way to improve was to practise your best shots the most, and there are many golfers who support this theory. If perfection in putting was achieved in direct proportion to the hours practised, it would be only necessary to 'clock' a lot of time to be superlative, but, alas, the best putters often practise the least.

I have putting 'secrets' sent to me regularly; tapes on the ground, tape on the clubhead — one travels along the other — mirrors or reflectors or guides for the pendulum stroke, but these 'stunts' rarely make a bad putter into a Locke.

I do not say they do not work at all, because this is not true. Someone has usually benefited from the invention, but the really good putter is born, I am satisfied. Practising on the putting green for sixpence a putt — that means trying on every single putt — is by far the best method of improving. Laying dozens of balls down and putting them one after the other is a way of getting the touch of the green, but the stroke, while it can be claimed it becomes mechanical, does not tax the co-ordination, for it becomes too automatic from a distance-judging point of view, and ball after ball is sent to the hole side from habit, not from the direct orders of the delicate distance-controlling mechanism of the body.

I still love practising, and while I always have a sort of regret at cutting-up lovely close-knit turf, it is, of course, the only way to expect to play iron shots consistently. I recall a single-figure handicap golfing friend of mine ruining his short game, through playing up and down his perfect tennis lawn without taking a divot. He developed a frightened sort of half-topped stroke which was very difficult to cure. 'Cut up your lawn', I said, 'You never play tennis, and besides, the gardener can always re-turf it.' It never happened, and he went on half-topping.

If you set out to hit a lot of balls and you are not used to this training, put on a left-hand glove, which fits tightly, *before* your hand gets sore. Once you have the slightest sign of a blister, stop!

I think it is a good idea to hit the full shots while you are fresh, as at the beginning of a practice session, and finish on the shorter ones.

Fit in some practice using each hand separately, but once the hand and arm tire, change over and give it a rest. Do not hesitate to try out extremes in stances and grips — it is the only way to learn about golf.

Dai Rees practising putting with a long row of balls lined up ready for striking.

THEY ALL PRACTISE

LEFT: *A scene by the score-board at the Seminole Club, Florida, U.S.A., during a lunch-time break at a tournament. Dozens of bags of practice balls belonging to the professionals lie around unguarded, which makes one think the Americans must be very honest people, leaving such treasures about!*

RIGHT: *A few minutes later, after the players have had a light lunch, the practice-ground is crowded again. Walter Burkemo and Billy Maxwell are in the foreground.*

LEFT: *1958 U.S. Open Champion, Tommy Bolt, practising. Note the way his left hand and arm are working. While there is a 'climb over' right over left, there is no sign of collapse by the left; it is still guiding the club, elbow down.*

CENTRE: *Dick Mayer practising in May, 1957. Mayer became U.S. Open Champion a month later, and then won the 50,000 dollar prize in Chicago that August. Note left hand and open club-face.*

RIGHT: *Sam Snead playing 30-yard pitches to a green. Note how firmly these shots are played — no slackening of the grip or arm muscles, and what arms! Sam does not flick the ball; he has no need to do so, anyhow, and, secondly, he prefers to go slowly 'through the ball'. Note also the practice balls are opposite the right toe.*

LEARN TO MOVE

Holding the shoulders steady by placing the hands on the top of the club and then working the hips quickly from left to right is a good exercise. This can be done anywhere, but a little daily drill in the door-frame of the bathroom is perhaps the best place to give the muscles of the back, midriff and legs a beneficial work-out. The knees are pushed in towards the ball (left-right, left-right) repeatedly.

CHECK YOUR LEFT ARM AND GRIP

LEFT: *This is the only way to find out exactly how good your left arm really is and if it could respond to any demand to play a bigger part in the swing if called upon. Most handicap golfers find this very difficult to do. Good golfers can hit balls quite readily, even if they have never done it before. Here Spanish Amateur Champion, Mr A. Maura, is trying one-armed shots for the first time. The young caddie seems to be unconsciously expressing doubts about his master's ability to do it, judging by his pose.*

RIGHT: *In this swing the left arm has not played its best rôle in the swing, for the elbow has bent. This action can be used to ensure that the club-face is held open, as in 'cutting the ball', but it is a weak action and here the ball was definitely pushed, not whipped. Compare this left arm action with that of Tommy Bolt on the opposite page, where the elbow points down.*

ANOTHER PAIL OF BALLS GONE

Myself practising at the Piping Rock Club, Long Island, U.S.A. Note size of practice-ground — actually two full-size adjoining polo fields — which must form the biggest practice-ground in the world. I am overlapping two fingers of the right hand on the left at this moment.

CHECK YOUR RIGHT ARM AND GRIP

One-handed practice is hard to beat as a strengthener for the grip and arm. Here is a young man, who is almost a scratch golfer, showing a perfect right-handed action. This requires a lot of strength and control. He hit the ball very well and this was the first time he had ever tried right hand alone.

ONE THING AT A TIME

A new golfer taking a lesson cannot just yet remember everything. He has kept his head down, but forgotten to move his feet properly or to hold his left arm firm. Here a bit of individual arm-drill can help things along faster, but it takes time to learn to strike a golf ball accurately. Professional giving lesson: H. Giraud of Mougins, Cannes.

44

LOOKING AT YOURSELF

You look at yourself daily in a glass but, of course, the reflection is the 'wrong way round', so that when a player tries to analyse his swing before a mirror it is as though a left-handed player was standing facing him and playing the same way. This is the way a teacher sees his pupil. The Duke of Gramont invented an apparatus which corrected this situation, so that on looking into a mirror the golfer could see himself the 'right way round'. It was a bulky apparatus, and so was never a commercial success, but the idea appealed to me.

It is just this difference which makes it tricky to analyse one's swing: we do not always have the gift 'to see oursel's as others see us'.

I have never quite arrived, even after all these years, at being able to know *exactly* what I am doing; photographs and cine-strips have helped me, of course, but it is rarely possible to know exactly what happened in any one particular stroke, in actual play, unless a slow-motion camera was working.

One thing a golfer *can* check on readily is how his hands look viewed from above and how they look when he turns his head to the right to see the top of his back swing. He knows just how *his* hands look, but rarely does he get the chance to see what other players see when they look at their hands in these same positions.

I got Hilaire Giraud, the French professional at Cannes, to photograph my hands as I see them, getting him to hold the camera near enough to my normal eye position. Because my head took up the exact place the camera should have been occupying,

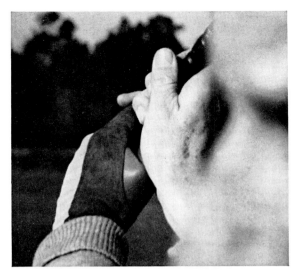

Looking at the grip from the front of the face at eye level.

the picture of the hands at the address position, viewed from above, was taken from the right side of my head and shows the right hand looking very much more over the club than it actually is; and the photograph of the hands at the top of the back swing is taken from just before my head, so again the camera does not quite view the position 'from my eyes'. Still it gives an idea and any keen student can get his hands so photographed and make a comparison.

When teaching golf, instructors very often do imitations of their pupils, staging the exact position at address or throughout the swing, in an endeavour 'to paint a picture' the pupil can remember. '*Oh, am I doing that?*' is the sort of surprised comment by a pupil on seeing more or less what he is doing — or failing to do.

During the past few years I have been working on my own swing to get the club, if possible, more upright, as I think with age one's swing gets flatter. I decided I had been going too much around my body, and when I asked just how upright was the last swing I had made, I found it difficult to believe it had moved so little from its old track, and yet it felt as if it had gone up over my head. Only a demonstration by Giraud convinced me that I was not swinging where I wanted to get! It has moved but little, despite my efforts.

The photograph of the hands at the address shows how the big muscle of the right thumb becomes prominent as the shaft is squeezed between the finger and thumb of this hand. This never shows so clearly from any other angle. The 'V' can

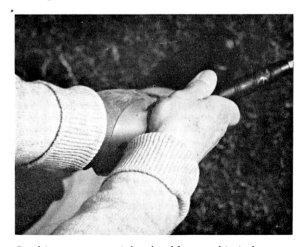

Looking over my right shoulder — this is how my hands appear. Note muscle of right thumb.

be seen pointing up the shaft, and the back of the gloved left hand is towards the hole.

In the 'top of the back swing' photograph, a pose which makes the swing short, the exact angle from which the photograph is seen by my eyes, the grip with the right hand 'club-shaft in the fingers' is clear.

So often I find golfers thinking the ball is, say, opposite the left heel when it is near the centre of the feet; just a slight step away with the right foot (as Fred Daly does) before beginning the back swing 'moves' the ball effectively, nearer to the left foot. I often wonder if Fred Daly began this trick or mannerism to get as far behind the ball as possible, or just to get his back swing started smoothly.

I find that the position of the club-face at address, especially with iron clubs — viz., open, square or closed — is always a problem, because it looks so very different from a spectator's position in front. I can get this problem straightened out with a mirror before the pupil, or by holding the club-face carefully to the ball, taking up the pupil's stance, and then asking him to take my place in front, and so see himself as another sees him.

Another point which is hard to 'see' is whether the hands are in line with the shaft or ahead of it at address; few players set their hands behind the ball. I have seen Hogan with his hands behind at the address, even for iron clubs. He claims it does away with the need for a forward press. It might be so for his game, but I know that experienced teachers would never dare to encourage it.

For most players the hands are in an ideal position when they are just slightly ahead at the address. This seems to encourage late hitting and a cocking of the wrists, and goes with a three-knuckle grip, as the left hand is set more to 'a back to the hole' position.

All the positions referred to in these notes are, in the end, personal ones, because they refer to the minor adjustments players make from time to time — but the whole point of 'Looking at Oneself' is to get the proportions right, and not to exaggerate.

A COMPARISON IN THE PITCH SHOT

Here are two photographs of the same shot, one played by Harry Vardon and the other by myself. The actions are almost identical, and the ball curiously enough has just reached the same spot in its flight to the pin.

There is the same easing of the knees and the steady head, while there is every indication that the shot has been played without the huge divots so common to-day in the play of many golfers, but really not necessary unless the lie is very tight. In my golfing costume, the bent right arm can be noted even at this point of the swing.

TELEVISION SHOT AND PUTT

In my book, 'This Game of Golf', is a photograph of myself playing a 'shot in a million' from the face of the bunker on the right-hand side of the 8th green at Sandwich in the 1934 Open. Here I am re-creating the scene for B.B.C. Television. It took some three hours on a cold December day to play this shot over again.

Here I am in position ready to attack the ball, which is plugged and almost buried overhead in the sandy face, just as it was all those years ago. I got the ball out on to the green in 1934 and with two putts collected a fortunate 4. I went on to do a 65 — still a championship record.

On the 11th green at the Temple Golf Club, Maidenhead, doing a putt for the television camera, when I made a series for the B.B.C. on golf. I am using my old square-shafted putter which I have had since 1936.

A LITTLE DIFFERENCE WITH A BIG DIFFERENCE

LEFT: *I am addressing the ball for a No. 2 iron shot with my hands slightly ahead of the ball. This, I find, makes me cock my wrists earlier and tends to keep much more weight on the left foot at the top of the back swing.*

RIGHT: *I have set my hands behind the ball. This seems to go with a wider arc in the back swing.*

These little differences creep into everybody's game and can have quite a big effect on the results. They are hard to detect, and that is why it is always good to have someone around, who understands your game, to ask. Do you mean to do this or that? Why not get the camera out and get something to study on paper.

This stance is narrower than I use for my big iron shots normally. I was just posing to show the differences.

AN EARLIER HIT

One always sees photographs of the crack golfers playing great golf strokes and so the average golfer with his vastly different physique sets out to copy them — often with disastrous results.

Here is a photograph of an 11-handicap player, Mr Jack Billmeir, playing a No. 8 iron pitch. It was a successful stroke. The ball was hit down and through and climbed correctly, as can be seen. The interesting point about his shot is that it was achieved with an earlier hit than is usually seen in the case of the powerful golfers.

This golfer could never achieve the pro.'s late hit, but he can get first-class results this way — given a decent lie!

TWENTY YEARS BETWEEN

Twenty years have flown (they simply do fly as one grows older) between these two photographs. What are the differences? Very few really. In 1937 my elbows seem a little more together, otherwise little seems to have altered with the passing years.

1937   1957

48

A COMPARISON WITH HOGAN

Here is an opportunity to compare the back swing of Ben Hogan with my own. Actually my club is at the very top of my back swing — Ben generally allows his clubhead to continue a little more — but they could not be more alike, viewed from this angle.

The angles of the legs, the right arm and wrist position, are identical. Hogan uses more body action than I do to-day — he is slimmer anyway — and so unwinds faster, but the similarity here is striking.

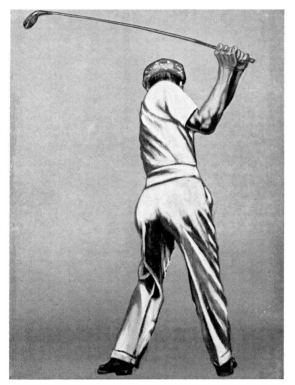

HOW NOT TO HIT ON THE TOE OF THE CLUB

When the hips unwind at the beginning of the downswing, there is a tendency for the back to straighten. The good golfer makes sure that the left hip moves back and 'the tummy is tucked in', as Sandy Herd used to say. It is not necessarily from standing too far away from the ball that the ball is struck on the the toe of the club. Stay down even after impact and keep the left arm going through.

49

D

NO INVENTION OF MINE

I am not inventing this grip you see — it was used years ago. This photograph of the golfer on the course shows a similar grip — the photograph dates from 1900.

I do not like it, but it can be used, and the old golfer on the right, Horace G. Hutchinson, was a champion — so it works. If the accepted orthodox grip does not produce results, why not try it? After all, golf is a game where the control of the finger tension is 'the great secret'.

TAKING AIM

Some players have been taught to stand behind the ball and point the club at the target as a means of impressing on themselves where they are going. Personally I have never seen the point of this, but never despise any such tips. Try anything, they say, once! This pupil of mine, Mme E. Visser, picked this tip up while golfing on the continent. I did not teach it; in fact, I do not see the value of it. But if it helps, why not?

50

THIS AIMING BUSINESS

ONE of the most difficult parts of the golf game for the beginner, once he has a reasonably consistent impact, is to aim his shot. This problem can be solved only on a golf course, and then really only on the practice ground. The value of learning the swing indoors in the initial stages of becoming acquainted with golf shows up to advantage, in my opinion, against beginning on the course, because the pupil becomes conscious of his swing and does not worry about where the ball goes. The extra problem at the beginning of 'why did that one go there'? — a question that cannot continually be passed over by 'Don't worry about that yet!' — wastes so much time and energy, during the first lessons, that much faster progress is made playing into nets, for the player can concentrate on the job in hand: that of swinging the club smoothly.

Once a pupil has got a sound, grooved swing and *can hold on to the club at impact*, the direction of the shot, which comes mainly from the correct placing of the body, can be acquired readily. This does not mean that the stance or the taking of aim is learned for good, for a trip round the championships will show players of the calibre of Snead, Stranahan, Hogan and Player, etc., playing endless shots on the practice-ground, some with a club lying touching their toes and pointing in the direction they wish the shot to go. They thus check up on their aim in this way.

I begin with my pupils by teaching them to stand with their toes parallel one to the other, and the lines across the toes parallel to the line ball-to-hole; and for a drive, with the ball on the inside of the left foot. This is just a simple programme to follow at the start. All sorts of adjustments come later as the player develops, these being made necessary by his own physical make-up.

The stance is important for two main reasons: it is the position of the feet from which the player intends to strike the ball, and it is responsible in the main for the aiming of the stroke.

Experienced players know that the hands have the final say, if they are strong and trained, for a club-face impact angle can be corrected sometimes if a faulty body action is leading it to the ball not in the position initially conceived; but to most golfers to aim wrongly, or to swing wrongly, means a misdirected shot. No players, of course, quite agree on what percentage the body plays in the swing, but that it has to aim the ball is generally accepted.

A club laid on the ground will help in aiming.

Abe Mitchell and George Duncan both impressed me as a young player by the way they seemed to fall into place, once they got up to the ball. There was no shuffling about, no fidgety movements. They gripped the club, put it behind the ball, and seemed then to line up to the hole, not to the ball.

Many of my readers will have read at one time or another the interesting test some of Harry Vardon's friends carried out when in search of 'why the Old Master was so devastatingly consistent?' Why were his shots so straight? They could have been fired from a gun. Did he have the knack of always finding exactly the same stance each time? Tests proved that in six consecutive perfect drives, with the ball always teed in the same place, and the ball driven between two trees, he had a slightly different foot position each time.

What does this prove, if anything? He was able to make all the necessary adjustments during each swing to ensure that the ball flew in the direction he had selected. Of course Harry Vardon was precise. He had a sense of 'where the ball was' that was exceptional.

Harry Weetman tries the harness for pitching. This strapping of the elbows to the body teaches footwork and body action in the shorter shots.

causing the player to repeat his best swing with almost monotonous regularity, do make a golfer aiming-conscious, as the rolling shoulder action of the body almost disappears and the arms go on, extended, to the hole.

All the same, most players do not pivot enough on the backswing, and although Bobby Locke has by no means a classical action — he exaggerates his closed stance — he is one player who really gets his back to the hole at the top of every swing; and this happens with him even for quite short shots. This is possible because at address his left shoulder points to 'long off' if not to 'mid-off', 30° right of the target, i.e., well to the right of the flag.

The left shoulder being well forward does help pivoting, and I think helps aiming, despite the fact that the open stance is universally recommended by instructors.

When a real beginner first plays on the course, he almost needs to be told at every shot how to aim, how to adjust his aiming; and that means how to stand to the ball. Someone has to tell him, for it is one of the most difficult things to adjust alone, for 'you cannot see yourself', and it is too late once the shot has gone.

One of his favourite tricks was to place a ball in the outside twigs of a small bush at a sufficient height from the ground to be able to get under the ball with a driver swing, and then hit the ball vertically up into the air as high as he could; and this would be done with his small-headed, shallow-faced driver, too. I have in my possession one of the actual clubs he would use for this trick. If you have any doubts about the skill required to do this shot, please try it next time you pass a suitable bush.

Getting back to this taking aim question, I recommend pupils to point the left shoulder at the hole and to hit towards the ball from the inside; for the long shots, that is. A narrower, open stance, where the hips partially face the hole, is best, perhaps, for the shorter shots, as in these more easily-performed strokes the body is best put out of the way. The arms and hands alone guide the ball to the pin. Some modern power players use shoulders and stomach for approaching — too much action, I think, for a small shot.

You may remember my advising golfers to try the harness and the swing-moulder idea, which holds the elbows together. Well, these straps,

Bobby Locke gets his back to the hole at the top of every swing. Here he is half-way back. Note how already his shoulders are well round — left shoulder pointing at the ball.

AIMING TIPS

*On taking aim — left shoulder forward and high.
Most low-handicap golfers look over their left
shoulder, at the address, to the target for full shots.
Point the left shoulder at the target, or to the right
of it, is a good tip.*

*Note Henri de Lamaze, H. Archibald of Paris
and myself all follow this plan when taking aim.*

PRACTISE CAREFULLY

*This golfer had every intention of playing for the
caddie, but stood carelessly, and so the ball finished
well wide of the mark.*

ON TAKING AIM: A DETAIL

Some golfers do better when they aim their feet at the hole, even for putting (2), others prefer the parallel stance as in (1). The main thing is to know what you are trying to do. Abe Mitchell told me, when I was a young professional and sat at the feet of this great striker, that he stood to the hole often in preference to standing to the ball and then 'aiming his stance'. Great golfers usually 'fall into their stance', they rarely shuffle about. Years of practice have done this, it is not a gift.

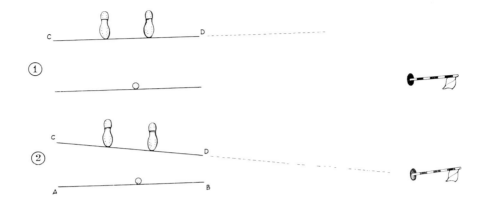

ON OVERSWINGING

One of the best brakes on overswinging is a tight-fitting jacket — but I have yet to see a golfer, male or female, of the present epoch who gets the club hanging down the back, who would ever bother to try this idea out. I can mention in passing that Abe Mitchell, one of my boyhood heroes, preferred a tight-fitting jacket for golf; he felt his swing was always under control.

← BALL

REMEMBER

The imaginary line to the hole — the clubhead stays on the line only a short time, but you must force the clubhead to follow along it. Put a peg tee six inches ahead of the ball and try to knock it down with your follow through.

JUDGING THE LAG

THE SECRET OF TIMING

Few handicap golfers, endeavouring to emulate their favourite star player by delaying the hit, really realize what it means. They try to get into a late hit position without having any hit to offer. I have chosen an old photograph, this time of Lawson Little, a wonderful golfer of pre-war days, who had the right fighting spirit and a dashing sort of game to go with it. Lawson always attacked the ball as though it were his worst enemy, and before the arrival of the fourteen-club rule he sometimes carried — or rather his caddie did — 24 clubs, including a veritable battery of pitching clubs.

SHUT-FACED ACTION

Lawson, like most long hitters, was at times wild off the tee, and as he used a more shut than open club-faced action, he needed to stay well behind the ball, to knock it up, as it were, for his wooden shots.

Here he is seen to have set his body ready to hit the ball in the back and while the clubhead is already moving fast — I estimate it will reach its maximum speed at the point marked X — it should be noted that the hands will scarcely advance at all until after impact; the clubhead will, in fact, overtake them. The dotted line shows where the arms and shaft will be in line at impact.

While there is no doubt that 'Swing the Clubhead' is an ideal slogan, in a basic way, once the question of applying the maximum power comes in, then, as this photograph shows, there is some evidence of the lever principle appearing. Lawson Little, like all top golfers, will not straighten his right arm till after impact.

WIDE STANCE

Another point which I recommend all golfers to study is the wonderfully wide base from which Lawson directs his operation. Not for him the narrow squatting sort of pose, but a wide, manly, solid width, in which he can use his feet and legs to the best advantage. Here is the hit past the chin *de luxe;* the braced left leg and the thrust with the right leg. His rolling on to the outside edge of his left shoe is typical of the way this foot often works when the big hitters let fly! In fact, many have been photographed while on the toes of both feet.

I find that very many what one might call ordinary golfers never realize, throughout the whole of their golfing life, that there is a sort of time-lag

in executing the commands ordered by the brain to the clubhead. That when the brain says, *now apply the power,* it is often too late to time the ball, and furthermore, in the great haste to give the maximum, the muscles nearer the headquarters of command react first — the shoulders, for example — and so throw everything out of line, including the arc of the swing.

SENSE OF TIMING

Children handling golf clubs from their earliest days instinctively assess this time-lag, and so grow

I think this photograph of Lawson Little (one of America's great golfers in pre-war years) is very instructive as it shows Lawson (in this younger days a colossal hitter) getting at the ball 'from behind'.

He has braced his body, his left leg is straight, his hips fully turned ready to flash the club at the ball. His shoulders are rotating under the head and the right arm will not straighten till after impact, but golfers must remember that already the clubhead is nearly at its maximum speed, which will be reached at the point X — before the ball, not at the ball. So many golfers, when they try for length, lean into the ball and do not get to their maximum speed till too late.

up with a natural sense of timing. 'Judging the lag', I suppose, is all that timing the ball really is in the end. We call it waiting for the hit—or 'just waiting for it!' — giving the clubhead a chance to catch up, by not letting any other part of the body get going too fast, too soon. This idea of the normal delay in the execution of the order from the brain is often tried on these car test-driving machines, which are set up to test a driver's reactions in applying, say, the brakes in an emergency. The delay is quite appreciable; seven-tenths of a second's delay means a good reaction.

ANTICIPATE THE DELAY

It is perhaps not difficult to understand this point which I have so often written about; but it is never easy to anticipate the delay and allow for it. That is why I have marked this photograph with an X some twelve inches before the ball, because I have proved many times that this degree of anticipation is just enough to make golfers get the hit in on time. Harry Vardon, I recall, often made his pupils aim an inch behind the ball in pitching to the green because this brought the hit in that

fraction earlier, gave a better timing to the stroke, and prevented that half-pinched or topped shot, the dread of so many handicap players, when the hit is just too late.

I find that with many little chips around the green this old tip is invaluable, and I can recommend it.

EVEN FOR PUTTING

Even for putting I find that any tricks which stop the hit being too late, such as addressing the ball with the clubface one inch behind the ball, setting the hands back a little at the address, aiming at the very back of the ball and not the top of it — all these help. Remember, timing is just judging the lag in the execution of the commands.

As a tip for helping the hands to get the clubhead moving fast without body interference, try 'Loose –Tight–Loose' as your slogan: Loose from the address to the ball, Tight at impact, then Loose to finish. This loose to finish is almost the secret of this particular golf operation. It often serves to get the tension out of the swing and to re-establish a free, fast swing.

SNEAD AIMS

Sam Snead practising at his home club, White Sulphur Springs. Note how he stands to aim for the caddie. Ben Hogan, practising alongside, picks a club from his bag. To me there is no doubt that Sam is aiming at the caddie. Photograph taken in 1948.

YOUR CLUBS

Do not forget that there is a shaft to suit your power, and a weight range for you, above or below which you will lose control or distance or both.

The grip size is of vital importance, get it right! Experiment! Better to scrap the beautifully neat celluloid ring at the bottom of the grip and rely on the old-fashioned string than persevere with the wrong thickness of handle.

Golf is a game of hands, so get new tacky leather

grips. You are seeking touch — they offer the best chance to find it. Get the right lie — this is very important. Every professional will have the necessary equipment to alter loft and lie. A too 'upright' lie on a club encourages pulling with irons — a too 'flat' lie will tend to push the ball to the right as the heel of the club in the first instance and the nose in the second case touch the ground first.

LEFT OR RIGHT SIDE CONTROL?

IT is, of course, accepted that golf is a two-handed game, and except in the case of those who play left-handed, or those odd few golfers who play with the hands crossed, as it were, the right hand is always below the left.

Most golfers, and I claim to be no exception, can swing the club with a beautifully free action with their left hand only. Perhaps this action lacks strength and precision, but nevertheless it has a sort of abandon which the right hand alone never has, and can never get.

The left arm hanging freely from the shoulder with a golf club at the end of it, a sort of continuation of the arm as it were, swings around the shoulder-joint like a windmill sail, but put the right hand on the shaft and everything changes. This is inevitable in a way, because now the same arm-plus-club, while still trying to swing from the left shoulder-joint, has a sort of brake on it, which interferes with its free-swinging idea. The reason is that now, if we take the arm and club as one unit, then half-way down the length of the radius, shoulder to clubhead, comes a power and a guide, ready to help the free-swinging left arm to propel the dead weight of the ball. And as the object of the game is to hit the ball in the desired direction and to a certain length, it is no use wishing we had no right hand in the action, because we should make a very poor job of the left hand only business.

Teachers and players of the game spend time showing pupils, and convincing themselves, just how the left arm works; and continually exercise this arm, hoping to develop the muscles thereby. But however much they attend to this arm, the manner in which it works, ultimately, must always be at the mercy of the right hand and arm, especially under pressure, or when forcing the shot as all players like to do.

I stress the right hand importance here, because even the very positioning of this hand on the shaft, ignoring the fact that a tense or loose grip can affect the swing, can alter the path in which 'the left arm swings' or wants to follow; and it can, if uneducated entirely, ruin a good swing made by the left arm.

It is clear that the influence of the right hand halfway down the length of the radius, shoulder to clubhead, must be dominant, and even with the best will in the world, nothing can be achieved unless the right hand and arm are educated to play their precise rôle.

So, when one talks of left arm control, it is

In the Open Championship at Muirfield in 1948. The left hand taking the hit — right arm bent at impact as usual. Wearing my sleeveless cashmere pullover outside my alpaca one, because I find it easy to take a layer off this way if needs be.

really wishful thinking for most golfers. You will have read of golfers with a 'floating' right hand, the club-shaft completely loose in the hand, or using 'an opening-up of the fingers' of this hand at the top of the swing, or allowing the lifting of the right elbow from the side on the way up — well all these happenings are not accidents in the case of champions. These players have found them essential, because, if they did not favour such happenings, their swings would not be serviceable; they could not maintain a correct balance of power between their two arms and a tension free action.

Players with a stiffish right wrist movement tend to allow this hand to go slack, because the hand cannot bend back readily as the cocking of the wrists takes place — if they try to hold on firmly, the swing becomes cramped and the clubhead gets thrown off the desired arc, or a snatch occurs.

That is why such players as Locke and Rees allow the club-shaft great freedom in the right hand — they cannot help themselves, as their joint construction dictates what they can do. My own right wrist allows a good bend back of the hand, but, having trained my right arm to stay close to my body, I find, if I am not careful, that my swing becomes flat, because the right arm pulls the club around my body when the right elbow is

BALL
ENDED HERE

5 FEET
FROM
FLAG

Stanley P. Morrison, a keen West of Scotland amateur, playing a perfect golf stroke. The right hand has come into the shot at the exact moment and the shoulders have not been displaced — they face squarely to the ball. If you can force a shot without your shoulders interfering you are already a golfer. Golfers who use their hands to this maximum as this golfer does, play past their body, not along with it.

determined to get to its place, near the right side, sooner almost than is necessary.

So when golf instructors say 'Let your left arm control the swing', they ought to add: 'If your right arm will allow it.' That is why an educated right arm is essential. Yet how many instructors teach their pupils how to use this arm and hand? It is often taken for granted, but it needs as much training as the left arm, because a golf swing is an unnatural action.

Older golfers will remember Irishman Jimmy Bruen, who really astounded the golfing world with his power and skill before the war. As a boy of from seventeen to nineteen years of age, he played fabulous shots, and really hit the ball like a 'horse kicking'. With his swing the clubhead went away up and finally forward, till it was almost over the ball at the very top of the back swing. Many old pros. prophesied that he would not be able to 'hit his hat' before long, with a swing like that. But the more I played with him the more I realized how sound it was, because he did everything right, only

'a bit more so'. He allowed the club to swing up freely, and as far as it wanted to go, the right hand just following passively until it was ready to give the ball that 'wicked whip' in the hitting area.

He had that gift of being able to swing the club as his left arm wanted, with no right arm interference, and few are the players who have even done that. I think his right shoulder-joint must have been extra mobile.

Jimmy Bruen damaged his right hand in 1940, and even to-day, after numerous surgical operations, he cannot hit a golf ball without great pain. This has been a great loss to golf, because he really contributed something worthwhile, and if he can stand the pain of the impact, he still 'knocks them a mile', with the same old swing which so many said would not work.

One teaching professional in America shows his pupils what he means by left arm control by scarcely touching the club-shaft with his right hand, only using it to steady the shaft at the top of the swing, but I know this pro. would be happier if he could arrive in the same position with his right hand placed normally on the shaft.

Showing Jimmy Bruen how the left hand goes through and the left leg resists — taken during a session together at Royal Mid-Surrey Golf Club, where I was professional from 1946–52. Note my 'back of the left hand to the hole' action, and Jimmy's thoughtful 'I used to do that' expression.

If the present general system of teaching golf was entirely sound, players would only need continual swinging of the club with left arm only to succeed, but while this arm forms the swing, it is powerless in most cases to carry out its intentions once the right hand is in position and begins to operate. Each player has his own problem to work out in the shape of his own body, and therefore the actual angle at which the right arm comes on to the shaft is important and needs to be studied.

One instructor states that 'the golfer who lets his right side overpower his left will rarely ever pro-

One-armed golfer, George A. Wilde, plays right-handed, fore-handed. I personally hit the ball less well this way, but can make a decent show when I get the arm warmed up. I find that when I try to play a round of golf with just one hand, I need to use my right hand fore-handed for all short shots and putting. I use my left hand for my big shots.

With Jimmy Nicholls, a one-armed American professional, who plays beautiful golf left-handed, back-handed. He can play around scratch, given suitable lies. Once he gets into trouble his results are bound to be affected. He puts on a fine exhibition, and his great shots often embarrass his two-armed colleagues. He has no right hand problems!

gress beyond the "fairly good" class', but as I have already said, it is a bit negative to think in this way — far better that the right arm be educated, because it cannot and must not be ignored to succeed. It has a major part to perform, an instinctive part, too — that of attacking the ball.

So do not think that endless swinging of the left arm is the answer to all problems; it helps, but watch the right arm, educate it.

HITTING AGAINST THE BACK OF THE LEFT HAND

The left hand and impact positions that handicap golfers seek; there is no club-slip here, beginners note.

THE FULL TOP

A top occurs because the clubhead makes contact with the ball above its centre.

Here is the end of a swing with the ball completely topped; the ball, which can be seen, in fact finished up only forty yards from the tee. The body has straightened up too soon, as the head has gone with the stroke, and with the ball. Where it is seen here, a mere ten yards from the spot on which it was teed, the head should still be down. I have seen it quoted that a full shot should travel at least thirty-five yards before the eye picks it up. Does this happen when you drive? A sort of 'Wait and See' is indicated, like ''it and 'ark' for putting.

BALL

LOOKING AT THE BALL

Alec Fox, one of our coming young professionals, really does look at the ball — ideal for him, but perhaps too long for some players, especially those of the wide-shouldered breed.

WATCH YOUR STANCE

This golfer either stood for a hook deliberately or took very poor aim. Her feet 'go' well to the right of the target — see arrow. This shot was mishit, so I could not quite judge, but the point that stands out is the way the hips have acted as a brake on the entire action. Clearly the shoulders have started the down swing, but the feet have not played any worthwhile part at all in this action, and the head has followed the ball! I am sure a spell playing barefooted would teach this golfer a lot.

FLAG

ON NOT STAYING DOWN TO THE BALL

Here are photographs of a golfer who has not used his hands at all, who has allowed his arms to bend and his shoulders to do the work his hands should be doing.

This is a weak position in every way; it is not possible to stay down to the ball properly, and, as can be expected, no clubhead speed is created. The best way to alter this situation is to improve the essential muscles and the shortest way is with a heavy club plus individual arm and hand hitting of the ball.

The bending at the elbows is a sign of weakness in the hands and wrists.

No hit past the chin here.

USING THE RIGHT THUMB

Unless a golfer has very flexible wrists he can rarely afford to press on the club with his right thumb as James Bruen is doing here. The effect of this thumb pressing directly down the top of the shaft is to give a sort of extra firmness to the right wrist — a tightness almost. I use it when I want to cut the ball.

Here James Bruen is practising some shots in the garden of his home in Eire. His property lies on the banks of the Cork River, seen in the background, and skippers of passing mail boats always give Jimmy a 'toot' when they see him doing an early morning spell of pitching.

61

PLAYING YOUR GOLF THE EASY WAY

WHEN you come to analyse your golf, one of the things to avoid is overstressing any factor, good or bad. I know because I blame most of those short shots which go left of the target to staying down too long or to what I call hanging on to the ball and pulling it off the line.

Now Harold Callaway, professional at Pinehurst, North Carolina, where he is one of the game's most successful and hard-working teachers — he is out with pupils all day long on Maniac Hill, the name of the hill-top practice ground there — listed some common faults he had noticed.

Callaway begins by noting this staying down too long of mine, which is, of course, the direct opposite of looking up too soon. So, as both are wrong, clearly there is a happy medium in this section of the swing. As an additional fault, apart from this dragging the ball off the line, comes hitting behind the ball and blocking the follow-through.

Too much inside-out stops the hips turning correctly and can cause either a hook or a slice.

Left arm too stiff brings tension into the swing, and I think does not help rhythm or clubhead speed.

A too-tight grip with the left hand, especially if three or four knuckles are showing at address, tends to stiffen the whole hand action, and so the right hand can never deliver the hit in time.

Back swing too stiff is more common in America because there many of the so-called modern school believe that wrist action as we know it — where the wrists open and close the club-face — is out of date. They are very wrong.

Many practise like wooden dolls with braced arms and dead hands. My regular comment on this is that it is a strong young man's method, and few humans can get enough speed into the clubhead at impact without using all the power available, and that means letting the wrists work naturally.

Finally, by having too wide an arc, Callaway claims that the correct inside back swing is impaired and causes too much sway — and he is right here.

Pupils whose long game is successful often fail in their short game, however, because they accentuate getting a wide back swing. They keep the arc too wide, when an earlier cocking of the wrists is called for, especially in approach shots.

Thus this balancing up of things so as not to exaggerate any one point is really the whole golfing problem. Often comments by a golfer, devot-

You do not have to push at every ball — you can play many pitch shots the easy way. Here I am playing a half No. 9 iron shot with the minimum of strain and effort. The blurred ball can be seen.

The action of the left hand, which I always seem to have used, was seen in a similar shot on the front page of 'Golf Illustrated' away back in 1931. This is not scooping the shot, for the ball is hit down and through, but with the minimum of divot taking. The left wrist hinges, keeping the blade square.

ing his time to teaching golf, mean more than 'How I do it' by a top-grade tournament player, who never gets on to the practice tee, except to hit balls himself.

Swing the clubhead as freely and as fast as possible, delivering the club face square to the line of proposed travel at impact — that is generally all anyone needs to do when driving. And luckily there are many ways of doing it successfully.

Do not hesitate to play the easiest way. It is more likely to be right than any other. So many modern golfers seek to complicate their swings, but the old champions who remained fine strikers of the ball all their lives played the easy way.

AT THE ADDRESS

Unless this golfer sets his head correctly, chin nearer his right shoulder, and begins with a drag back with the hands, he will find himself at impact with his hands far ahead of the ball, and because of his type of grip — all the knuckles of the left hand showing — he will be unable to hit past his left hand and so the ball will generally be pushed to the right.

Only by using a very lofted club and hooding the club-face can he get a straight ball, and then it is squeezed.

I suggested that because he had small fingers, an overlapping grip was a disadvantage, that he would get more control with a double-handed grip — hands apart, that is. It helped!

ILLOGICAL

This ball was hit very near the top edge of the club, as can be seen by the flight of the ball. The tee was too high, but this narrow stance for a drive is illogical, while the bent left arms mean weakness at impact.

Here is a case for the need for a wide back swing, with the left arm extended all the time. Alas, the golfer is well over seventy years of age. Should he worry or not?

MUSCLE MEMORY

I have no less authority than Seymour Dunn — one of the golfing Dunns, who went to America from Scotland generations ago, and successfully taught golf for some fifty years there himself — for supporting an idea I have not tested out, that if golfers learn to hold their top-of-the-back-swing position and then their finish to the point of fatigue on both occasions, counting up to a hun-

dred or even more, their muscles get trained to these positions and when the club is swung to and fro they find these poses. This may be wrong, but no stone should be left unturned in the search for success in golf.

I think the overswinger particularly could benefit from this training — but what an effort! However, I pass the tip on as a suggestion.

TENNIS ELBOW

THERE are some unfortunate golfers who suffer from 'tennis elbow', and all sorts of people have asked my advice about getting rid of this distressing ailment. I sympathise with the sufferers, but, of course, I can add nothing to the best medical advice.

However, I do know that players using a three- or four-knuckle left-hand grip are more likely to strain the delicate left elbow joint than golfers who, like myself, use the two-knuckle grip. The picture shows me at the address with the grip I have used all my life.

A sixty-year-old Yorkshire golfer, asking for my advice, said: 'I still have a handicap of three, but for a year I have been troubled with pain in the left elbow'. (One knowledgeable golfer told me he is sure tennis elbow is caused by a nerve in the neck-shoulder area being pinched. I pass this on). In reply I suggested he should seek medical advice and *change his grip to the two-knuckle variety*.

I once knew a golfer who suffered constant pain in his right wrist. This persisted for many years, and only by bandaging his wrist was he able to play at all. The cause of the pain was eventually found to be rheumatism. As soon as some uric acid was eliminated from his system, the pain disappeared, and he was able to use his right hand effectively again.

PLEASURES OF THE HUNT

This game of golf: Pleasures of the hunt.
Hunting or fishing — all in a day's golf!

W. T. Twine

Cyril Tolley

LOOSE — TIGHT — LOOSE!

When a crack player is trying for a special sort of all-out recovery from a heavy lie or deep soft sand, he has to give the ball all he can; and as there is considerable resistance from the grass or sand, the full finish is out of the question. What happens is that to get the maximum speed into the blow he knows he must finish 'loose', and often the end of the swing looks as it does in the four action pictures.

In three cases the left hand has stayed put, the right has come away, but in Bruen's case he has relaxed the left hand.

James Bruen

Myself

65

E

JUDGING DISTANCE

With the passing years the muscles of one's eyes tire, and those who get to the stage when 'your arm is not long enough' for reading without glasses will have noticed that there is a delay of some seconds in changing the range of focus. I have noticed this in recent years in switching my focus from the ball to the flagstick and back to the ball again.

I think anyway that it is a good idea to take a long look at the flagstick and wait for the eye to focus on the distance; a hasty glance as you get older does not help much. That is how the fluorescent flag idea came about; it is so much easier to see, it 'blazes', it is much easier to pick out.

I am sure, too, that it is more difficult to hold the focus, as is often required in putting — one is inclined, after so many seconds, to let the eye wander off the ball.

This might add value to George Duncan's old slogan: 'If you are going to miss them, miss them quickly.' There is much to be said always for the mechanical swing because that permits the player to have his eye on the ball and his mind on the distance. This is why approach play really needs much training and why competitive practice is the best training, better often than aimless chipping of hundreds of balls. Chip for money — even for a penny a time: it makes you try.

HOW?

How would you explain away this result? Here is what appears to be a perfectly normal sort of down-swing. The body is well placed and already the clubhead has 'fallen back', ready for an 'inside to out' attack on the ball — yet the ball finished short of the green well on the left of the target.

There are only two possible explanations — one that the club-face slipped round completely in the hands and the other that the ball was struck on the top edge of the blade.

Scene: the 1st hole, Cannes Country Club, Mougins.

WHAT VARDON SAID

Harry Vardon said: 'Uncocking of the wrist is quite automatic — there is no time in the minute part of a second occupied by this part of the swing to alter what comes naturally.' This will make many golfers think, I know. Here is the old master in 1932, aged 62, studying the line of a putt. He had putting troubles as the years went by and found the 'holing out' putts very trying to make. An uncontrollable nerve in his right arm would cause a jerk in these delicate strokes and the ball would miss the hole from two feet, often by inches, on the right.

A CHAPTER FOR WOULD-BE CHAMPIONS

I HAVE never stopped outlining how I think golf can be best played or how I have played it now for over thirty years, and while I have altered my ideas at times, basically they have remained the same, mainly because I 'came in' at the right door and did not lose my way in the building.

The only big mistake I made early on — and, looking back, it could be called a 'clanger' — is that I did not learn how to eat. I never attached enough importance to food and meal times. I thought meal times were wasted times. 'What, no golf practice?' So I often cut them out, making do with a bar of chocolate or a bun, while playing nine holes or practising.

I was never told what to do, or maybe I was and did not listen. Alas, the effect was the same; I cracked up after a fashion.

In those days vitamins were being talked of, so were calories, but they had not got written up into simple readable chapters for the layman. The medical profession already knew the answers, but I do not think there were many understandable books about on diet.

Even to-day in these more enlightened days of studying 'weights and measures', balanced diets and slimming cures, no time is given at schools to educating children on this vital topic. Should sex

Brussels, 1933, my staff. Left to right: Henry Cotton, Jules Swaelens (now pro. at Ghent), Bruce Thorpe (asst.), now out of professional golf, and W. J. Cox. D. Swaelens, son of Jules, is one of the best young professionals in Continental golf.

education or religion be taught in schools? Or in which class? Yes, these problems hit the headlines; but the one of learning to eat or eating to live, this is not touched; and yet it is one about

LEFT: *Another team of mine, this time at Royal Mid-Surrey Golf Club. Left to right: Oliver Wynne, Max Faulkner, Henry Cotton, Jack Knipe; in addition there were Keith Hockey, Peter Knight and Douglas Smith.* RIGHT: *I saw Ben Hogan hit twenty successive balls onto this green with his brassie. This was as great a stretch of consistent striking I have ever seen. It was in 1957, when he was already finding scoring more difficult, but it was not his long game which was at fault. Here he is beginning his back swing for one of the twenty great shots. Taken at The Greenbriar, where Sam Snead is professional.*

which there finally is no choice — you can choose or alter your religion, but you have no choice of stomach, just the one for all your life.

All later ills, nerve troubles, rheumatism, etc., can come through environment, but they generally come through eating incorrectly. If you plan to be a golf champion, please listen to me and learn to eat properly, because golf is a hard game and you need a long-term policy. It is no use burning the candle fast, try to nurse it and keep the flame going steadily by not using it too much — this means feeding your body and your nerves normally and not relying on dope.

Normal feeding, as I see it, means following a balanced diet. Learn to eat the things which are good for you and which suit you. Learn about your body and the functions of the various parts. It was not until I became ill, and got into the doctor's hands, that I began to learn about my digestion, my liver, etc.

If I had only known — the trouble I would have saved myself, and probably then how much better I might have played!

Now it is a bit late, but I hope I have got my metabolism right at last. I do not propose to put here a list of all the right foods, or those to avoid, for anyway this can be a question of opinion; but there are so many good things to eat that it is a pity to eat rubbish. Those who play tournament golf regularly, and who eat too often in the marquees erected near the clubhouses, know that what they get to eat is rarely right 'to work on'. It is enough to get through the day on, but must be supplemented by first-class steaks, fruit, and fresh vegetables, to give that vital energy.

As a final word to young would-be champions — *any money you spend on eating is an investment, not an expense;* and you can never do better in life than to invest in yourself. I have told this to many of our young players in recent years, and if they read these words they will recall my advice, I hope with gratitude.

THE DAILY DOZEN

FRANK Stranahan from the U.S.A. thinks that his competitive weight-lifting programme and his 'daily dozen' have contributed to his golf success. Frank has handled such commendable poundages as 300 pounds clean and jerk, 400 pounds squat, and more than 500 pounds dead lift. Training during the years, he played his best golf with the heaviest weights.

He did tear a lumbar muscle at Royal Lytham and St Anne's in 1958 with his weight-lifting. He tried to qualify but failed — his back was too painful — but not long after he was competing again on the summer circuit back at home.

I do not think that this top-grade weight-lifting programme is the ideal golf training, but I am sure that a muscle-building programme outside just swinging a golf club is essential to all young men aspiring to major golf honours. Many of our young golfers are too soft; just to shake their hand give me 'the creeps', when a 'wet fish' instead of a vice-like grip is extended to me. Golf muscles can be built by general exercises.

Young Gary Player, on my recommendation, set out to make himself tough, and does among other 'drill' daily press-ups on his finger tips. He improved the value of this with a big suit case balanced across his shoulders.

I remember one of the U.S. Walker Cup team players telling me that Stranahan, when a member

Frank Stranahan was a top-ranking amateur — he won the British Amateur Championship in 1948 and 1950 — before turning professional in 1954. Frank's game seems to have fallen off a bit in the past year or two. He is not 'hungry', of course, but I was always afraid that bulging muscles might not be best in the long run.

of their team and crossing the Atlantic on the liner to play in Britain in 1947, used to do his daily press-ups with a member of the team lying across his shoulders, just to make it more interesting!

LEFT: *Here the lie has been near the face of the bunker and in soft sand obviously raked there, because where I am standing it is firmer. I have skidded my 'sand blaster' through, but have gone in well behind the ball. This is not a spot from which one seeks length; 'get out' is the operative order.*

RIGHT: *Head down and feet well down in the sand — W. Lees, snapped in a tournament, has also not forgotten the rule about looking at the ball.*

PLAYING FROM THE SAND

PLAYING up to a flag on a green surrounded by deep, soft, sandy bunkers, ready to swallow up an erring shot even to the point of burying the ball, has always been a strain; and frequently I have elected to play a long, low shot in case, should it be off line, it will merely run into the sand, and not plug overhead in it. This seems a small point to many players, but I can assure you that it does not escape those in the running for top prizes; they have to see everything.

In the last twenty-odd years the sand iron has been one of the golfing blessings, and this broad-soled niblick, with the back edge riding below the front edge, is at its easy best in powdery sand, which is still frightening for users of the old thin-edged niblick.

I believe also that bunkers are generally easier than they were thirty or more years ago. They are raked in these days, even between couples in Championships now, and except at a few courses — St Andrews Old Course, for example — they are now so fair that to find an 'impossible' position in one is the rare exception. A number of the steep-sided bunkers at the 'Home of Golf' are coffin-like in shape, and at times one is pleased just to have a chance to play out anywhere, so long as it *is* out.

Unraked bunkers are really tough, for then it becomes a mere question of how deep is the foot-mark one is lying in. Pine Valley — that valley of despair in the U.S.A. — has vast areas of sand hazards which are never raked. That is one reason why scoring is difficult — the lies in the soft sand are always terrible. The broad-soled sand wedge, which does not bury itself in the sand but which skids through under the ball, if given a chance, is to be found in every worthwhile golfer's bag.

As the sand can be thumped hard, almost nonchalantly, players have found that a 'full-drive' swing, regulated to send the ball various distances by striking into the sand at varying lengths behind the ball, is the safest method. What golfers who panic inwardly do, when they see their ball disappear into the sand, is to rush in and hit at it quickly.

A recovery shot from sand is a precision-stroke

69

LEFT: *This is a typical 'sand blaster' stance — the player is aiming carefully at the spot behind the ball where he intends to make contact with his clubhead. The club just skids through under the ball. The actual distance behind the ball will vary for each shot, and the texture of the sand must be studied.*
RIGHT: *Here I am cutting the legs from under the ball — using a No. 9 iron with blade laid back, as I was not sure how hard the sand was under the ball and I considered I had a better chance to get near the hole. The ball ran to the back edge of the green — the lie was softer than I had calculated.*

— not a wild blast at the ball. The clubhead must be aimed carefully at the chosen spot behind the ball, so that exactly the right amount of sand is collected on the club-face between the club and the ball, in order that the ball will be thrown on to the green with just the right force, the trajectory being regulated by the way the blade is held at impact.

This type of stroke needs a firm base from which to swing, and it is essential to sink the feet well in the sand. This is important, not only because an accurate hit is needed, but, almost more vital still, because the stroke has to be played to a lower level. If the player stands on the sand, then it is necessary to dig down, say, two or more inches, into the sand by a special effort, steepening the hit or dropping down the shoulders at impact. This is hard to judge, so it is more simple to wriggle the feet into the sand so that the soles of the shoes come to the level of the bottom of the ball. Then an ordinary swing aimed at the back of the ball will take the clubhead automatically down to the level required to get under the ball.

The placing of the ball at address is important, of course, but the actual positioning will depend on the lie of the ball and of the type of shot wanted. A forward-driving sort of ball, such as from the back of a wide bunker with the flag well back on the green, can be played from near the

right foot. A sort of 'flop-out' from just under the face, with the pin very near, needs to be played off the left toe with the face laid open.

No one can give any hard-and-fast rules on this position at the address-point; the only way to learn this is to get into the sand with a bag of balls and keep playing shots till you know. The best players practise; so should you if you want to take the terror out of sand. Once a crack golfer knows the consistency of sand and the holding properties of the greens, he can get the ball repeatedly very near the flag. There is no trick — it is just knowing how, and practising to make perfect. I usually swing more upright, as I am often playing these sand shots with the club-face held open at impact, and find this easier to do if I come across the ball from outside to in, cutting up the shot. This cut causes the ball to hop to the right on pitching on the green, so this has to be allowed for in weighing-up the shot.

On very soft greens with a nap on them against the stroke, the ball can be made to come back off the pitch even several yards, especially if there is a favourable slope as well. The ball comes back off the second bounce, because on the first pitch the ball is spinning too fast to grip the turf. It first cuts out a groove; this reduces the spin, and so on the second bounce the reduced spin is enough to make it roll towards the player.

70

THE EXPLOSION, 1913

WITH the coming of the thick-soled sand irons and wedges, the bunker shot from soft sand became a simple matter. It just meant hitting into the sand, or swinging into the sand, behind the ball and skidding the back edge of the club along. But when the sand is hard and wet, there is as ever the problem of getting below the ball, especially if the ball is lying badly. Then the old-fashioned explosion, which Harry Vardon in 1913 demonstrates here, is still invaluable, and the best club is a narrow-soled niblick — a No. 9 iron to-day.

It is interesting to note in this action the way the back of the left hand is placed at impact — it is 'the latest method'. That the sand is hard can be seen by the fact that Vardon's feet have not even made an imprint; he is standing on the sand. This is in fact a push shot with no follow-through, a very definite sort of blow.

CLEAN OR BLAST?

THE Marquis of Bolarque, President of the Spanish Golf Federation, takes one cleanly from the firm sand at his home club, The Royal Golf Club, Madrid (RIGHT).

This is a dangerous stroke even when played by an expert. I like to see the ball blasted out as professional Bob Kenyon has done in the other photograph — a real head-down effort.

I stood in the bunker to get a close-up view of the shot, as he was not happy about his recovery shots from the sand and sought my advice. The left arm has done very little work in this shot, it has crumpled up, and there has not been much hit past the chin here.

A BUNKER VERSE

Little Willie, home from school,
Lifted his head against the rule.
The ball half-hit, the result of a snatch;
And so Little Willie lost his match.

BLAST IT!

This golfer has forgotten to hit past her chin and to look at the ball. She has been afraid of the sand! Remember to hit against the left side — left arm firm.

If in doubt, blast it before — not afterwards!

No golf stroke is a scoop. Down and through is always right. From hard sand play the ball as if on a hard lie on the fairway.

RIGHT UNDER THE FACE

There are not too many such bunkers about to-day — this one is at Felixstowe. Other places which come to mind where these turf 'walls' can be found are St Andrews, Muirfield and Troon. The only way to get elevation is to open the club-face very much and cut across the ball.

Note that here I have aimed to the left of the flag to allow for the slice spin which will take the ball to the right on landing.

UP AND DOWN

Walter Hagen forgot to look at this ball. Here can be seen a real head-up, but there is no information whether the shot was good or bad. The ball is just up from the sand and yet his eyes are on the flag. Alongside is the perfect head down with the clubhead skidded under the ball, played by Mrs W. F. George. So you can trust your swing even in the sand!

Here Frank Stranahan is playing from a bunker on the 10th hole at Muirfield in the 1948 Open. This awkwardly placed ball has been successfully played, because he has taken care to stand to the ball comfortably and solidly, despite the unusual positions his feet had to assume. There is no question in this shot of the body playing its usual rôle in the action; it is all 'hands and arms', for balance must be maintained to achieve an accurate hit.

If necessary sacrifice length, play to get out first.

THE AWKWARD STANCE

This shot, although it is only a comparatively short one, to the green in front of the trees in the distance, is not easy to play well, because the feet are considerably higher than the ball.

There are no rules to follow to guarantee success except that the head must not move till the ball has gone and the body must be placed so that the ball can be reached. The eye must really be glued on the back centre of the ball, not just at the ball in general. If the body does move forward with the pull of the club gaining speed, a socket is more than likely! I know no better spot from which to expect 'one off the socket' — which has now become in the latest pro. slang a 'Lucy Lockett' or a 'Davy Crockett'.

The golfer in action is Rex Harrison of stage and screen; he is well placed to attack the ball, and he did well with the shot, I remember.

The lady golfer has a little chip down a bank to a green below, but the ball is too far on the left foot — it cannot be hit a descending blow. It was in fact hit off the sole of the club, half topped, but the result was far better than the quality of the stroke. If the hands remain where they are, they would then be ahead of the ball, which should be at point X, an ideal position.

THE SUPERB COURAGE OF BANTAM BEN

BENJAMIN William Hogan was born in 1912 in Dublin, Texas, a town appropriately named because it was full of Irish settlers. In fact, one whole block was peopled with Hogans and Gallahers. Ben maintains that his small stature is due to keeping late hours on the news stand when he sold papers, after a full day at school, to help his widowed mother.

When the family moved to Fort Worth, where there was a golf course, Ben began caddying instead of selling papers. He was then twelve years old. The first golf club he ever possessed was a left-handed one, and that was how he learned to hit the ball, from the 'wrong' side of it. Later he turned round when the professional gave him a right-handed club.

About this time Hogan first met Byron Nelson, who also started as a caddie at Fort Worth. On one occasion these two tied in a Christmas Day caddie tournament.

Hogan was a glutton for practice in those days, and his slogan has always been: 'If you can't outplay them, outwork them.'

It was not until 1941 that Hogan's maxim began to pay the biggest dividends, although he had made a name before that. Between 1931 and 1940 he won only one tournament. But he became leading money-winner in 1941 and 1942, and when after the war he beat Nelson, the pride of America, and known the world over as 'Mr Golf', by seventeen strokes in the Portland Open, he remarked with a tight smile: 'I guess that takes care of this

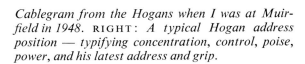

Cablegram from the Hogans when I was at Muir-field in 1948. RIGHT: *A typical Hogan address position — typifying concentration, control, poise, power, and his latest address and grip.*

Mr Golf business!'

The story of his amazing recovery to health, strength and playing skill after his car accident in 1949 was the subject of the film, 'Follow the Sun'. His wonderful come-back to the top fired the imagination of the sporting world as an example of unequalled 'guts', and he was an even better golfer after his accident than he was before.

Hogan's record is fabulous. He has won the British Open Championship, four American Opens, and tied for a fifth in 1956.

His wife Valerie has been the perfect companion for him. When Ben is playing she can usually be found in a comfortable niche at the clubhouse, knitting socks for him.

I first played with Ben in 1948, before his accident, but I saw a lot of his play in 1947. He has really great golfing hands, so immensely powerful for his weight that he can almost be said never to let the club-shaft slip round in his fingers accidentally.

We played again in 1957, and I noticed he was still hitting the ball as squarely as ever. He does not possess an elegant swing in perhaps the Snead or Jones style — it might even be called flat — but he is the master of it, he knows exactly how to control it.

After building up his game from a natural draw, which caused trouble in his early days, to a controlled fade shot, he has now again reverted to a straight shot tending to draw; but now his left hand is in a safe place, showing a maximum of two knuckles. When putting he keeps his chin tight to his chest. He says this prevents him looking up too early.

There has been no golfer quite like 'Bantam Ben', 'Battling Ben', 'The Mighty Atom' and 'The Hawk' — and he is still the biggest draw in America. It will be a sad day for the game when he decides to give up, but many professionals will, I know, raise a silent cheer.

Ben and Valerie in 1956.

THE FIERY DEMON WHO PERFORMED MIRACLES

JOHN Henry Taylor, the smallest, but only in stature, of the Great Triumvirate, is still with us, and at the ripe old age of 88 lives in happy retirement at Northam, North Devon, his birthplace. He takes a lively interest in all modern golf matters and he still contributes excellent articles to golf magazines.

'J.H.', as the world always called him, has been a great leader and has set an example to the profession he still honours. For many years he was the spokesman of the P.G.A., which he helped to create, and he realised more fully than his colleagues that golf was going to be big business.

J.H. also had a commercial swing to go with his commercial brain. He possessed a powerful forcing action and acted relentlessly on his two principles: 'There are no hazards in the air', and 'What's the matter with the middle of the course?' He always attacked the ball, and I can still see him now, giving everything as he thumped into the back of those mashie pitches to the green, fairly rubbing the paint off the ball and giving an expressive sort of grunt at the same time.

J.H. could have been a politician, for he was never at a loss for a word. His diction had that schoolmasterish clearness, and the arguments were always well-reasoned and forcefully presented.

In 1921, as a schoolboy, I went with my father and brother Leslie to Royal Mid-Surrey Golf Club, where J.H. was professional The idea of the visit was to play with the great man and for him to give my father a report on us. In those days we had not yet thought of becoming professionals, though we were crazy about the game. J.H. thought I would become the better player because I had that extra bit of determination and concentration. My brother Leslie is professional to the Reading C.C., Johannesburg, South Africa; he is a renowned teacher.

J.H. constructed golf courses with his partner, Hawtree, and manufactured golf clubs with another partner, Cann. He travelled widely, and contributed articles on golf to the *News of the World* for two decades. When he retired in 1935, I replaced him. In addition to creating the P.G.A., he wrote books about golf and helped dozens of young pros. on their way.

He must have had many proud moments in his life — five British Open Champion titles came his way among other honours — but I doubt if anything could have pleased him more than when his son J.H., now a headmaster, captained Oxford University at golf.

LEFT: *John Henry Taylor, stiff collar, white golf jacket and 'Sunday' bag. No caddies on Sundays then; hence the name.*
RIGHT: *As a young man. J.H. and his head down. A typical finish with his spade mashie, the modern club of his day, held well down the shaft.*

J.H. lacked the phlegmatic calm of Braid or Vardon. He was a fiery little man, but he harnessed that fire to produce miracles. He could get cross with himself during a round and use that 'burning up' feeling we all know to play more devastating shots, just as Bobby Jones did years later. With cap pulled right down and chin thrust further out, he became a demon to beat. He was never so much to be feared as after a bad spell of holes.

I always admired the way he holed-out the difficult four-foot putts. There was no hit or miss about him. They had to go in. Method was second; will-power came first — and he got them in. They were willed in, in fact.

In 1924, at Hoylake, when he was fifty-three, J.H. nearly achieved another magnificent victory in the Open. So well did he play that he would have won had the two qualifying rounds as well as the four championship rounds counted. The rougher the weather, the more solid his stance became and the more punch the ball received. Alas, young golfers will never see him play, but they can take my word when I say: 'He was some golfer.'

STILL THE SAME — OR DIFFERENT?

IT is only necessary to pick up an old golf book and read through it to find that the golf swing has not changed fundamentally. As I study these old volumes I realise that I am inclined to dwell on the dress of the day, the coats the players wore, their small-diameter caps, their cycling breeches and hickory-shafted clubs, and my eye tends to brand the action as old-fashioned, before I have even studied the swing itself.

I often wish I could dress up some of the old champions in the modern sweater and slacks, and then ask golf students to say what era they represent and from what country they come. This difference would be even more marked in the female ranks, for the ankle-length skirts, heavy-looking headgear, and blouses or long coats, would soon be replaced by the knee-length skirt and short-sleeved sweater with an eye-shield instead of a hat.

I know that golf clubs have changed most of all, and Charles ('Chick') Evans, writing in 1914 in a golf magazine in which he was interested, said that it took him four years to collect together a set of iron clubs which balanced up and which pleased him. I wonder what the modern golfer would think of this extra problem if it existed to-day! It was, of course, a reason to go to every pro.'s shop, hoping to find *the* club missing from one's set or maybe to find a better and more steely hickory shaft, which would be an improvement on what one already used.

'History repeats itself', runs the old adage, and when one reads that in pre-war days a serious, successful golf-ball manufacturer declared that finality had been reached in the distance a golf-ball could travel, then it is amusing to think that there is quite a firm opinion to-day that the limit has been reached once again.

The thicker grip of some fifty years ago, necessary because of the cushioning effect required to deaden the sting of the impact with the non-resilient gutty ball of the day, made the position of the hands on the shaft look agricultural by our standards, when a sort of finger-grip is a natural, because of the thinner grips in vogue to-day.

I have proved to my own satisfaction by my own experiences, and from encouraging others to use the two-knuckle grip (where the back of the left hand is facing the hole at the address), that if this hand is so placed on the club, a lot of latitude can be allowed in the positioning of the right hand. This means that it can be set at any angle, even palm-upwards, and good results can come. It can

even be a complete palm grip with the shaft lying in the 'V' between the first finger and thumb.

I start out by teaching the two V's up the shaft as a classical approach, but if I find it heavy going, then I will settle for a free, fast hit-through with the right hand in any position, stipulating only that the left hand stays put.

I have come across a photograph of one of our greatest old-timers, John Ball, who had a terrific championship record: he was a lightweight too, and yet played the testing Hoylake course, his home ground, better than his contemporaries, using a double-handed grip, with a perfect left hand position and the palm grip with the right hand. To succeed as he did is not entirely a question of method, for a good nerve and a courageous spirit are almost as important; but, whatever the method, it must be one that is tension-free under pressure.

I have an idea that the main value of a palm grip with the right hand is that it allows a non-cramped top-of-the-swing position and permits the club-head to be thrown freely at the ball on impact. No tightening of this hand is really possible if the fingers are kept out of it. We have had many champions since John Ball, using the palm grip with the right hand, and I created a very surprised and contented pupil only a short time ago by 'selling' him such a grip, when he had been persevering, not too satisfactorily, with an orthodox overlapping grip for a long time. It comes as a real shock to a conservative frame of mind golfer to find an experienced teacher asking him to forget all he has learned in the way of hand action, and to begin again to swing the club with this most unusual and ungainly form of grip — for it does not look elegant.

There is one definitely encouraging aspect to such an experiment: it feels so different that any open-minded golfer must say to himself: 'At least, *this* I have not tried. It must open a new world of experiment for me.' The throwing about of the club-shaft in the hands during the swing is a very frightening thing to players educated to hang on all the time; they feel at first that it cannot be right, and only the results begin to persuade them that perhaps it will work after all.

To-day one never hears of a push-shot, yet all the low-flying shots to the pin are played in the same way as they always have been, the loft on the club-face being diminished by the action of pushing the hands forwards in the impact area. The common wedge shot of to-day is actually a

George Heliopolos, who takes the 'bank' at the big 'no limit' baccara tables at Cannes and Deauville, is a useful golfer. Here he is practising with his 'other chips'. These are simple stiff-wristed push shots, a very safe method. ('Chips' is a name for the 'jetons' used in casinos.)

push-shot with a heavy, broad-soled niblick. In golf played with the bigger ball, even the thick top of the blade in iron clubs is designed to contribute towards keeping the ready-to-fly-high ball from achieving too high a trajectory, and so not being progressive enough in flight. The push-shot gives a more forceful, low-flying type of ball; one which goes to the pin by the shortest air route.

The interesting part about these lower-flying strokes is that they can also be produced by a controlled wrist-rolling action, and this has always been a popular way to play them. But it must be acknowledged that this action gives a more running type of ball, for the ball is not squeezed as much as in the square-bladed push-stroke, for it is hit down but with a combined up-and-over action of the wrists.

So, taking all in all, everything is still much the same in the general action of striking the ball; golfers have only altered their action a little to cope with the different peculiarities of the ever-improving equipment, golf-balls and clubs.

IMPROVE YOUR GOLF — WITH BASEBALL!

Ever since my first visit to America in 1928, I have firmly believed that baseball, with its horizontal throwing and batting actions, is the best preparation if one thinks of other sports as good training for golf. Look at the baseball hit finish in this picture and you will recognize the finish of the golf swing. The player here is none

other than that great golfing hero of years ago, Walter Hagen, whose first love was, in fact, baseball. At one time he even toyed with the idea of becoming a professional player.

For developing the action of the right arm in striking a golf ball, there is no better exercise than the throw. I always liken the way the right hand and arm operate in a golf swing to the ricocheting of a pebble on water. The skimming of the stone on the smooth surface of a pond can only be done with a bent right arm and a well-timed flick of the wrist.

Older golfers are advised to get back on to this throwing game as soon as possible. Once school-days are over few people ever throw at all, except those who continue to play cricket. But start by throwing gently. It is very easy to tear muscles and do damage to all parts of the shoulder and arm structure by beginning with a violent throw, 'showing off' as it were.

I have yet to see a good thrower who was not also a long hitter of a golf ball. Those who practise in a net will find it is a valuable muscle-building exercise to throw golf balls into the centre of the net, overarm first, and then horizontally, aiming the ball at a target in the net. Remember that successful golf can be played only with trained muscles. So get throwing right away — you can throw a soft ball into the curtains as a start!

THE LEFT FOOT ACTION

CONCERNING the action of the left foot in the back swing, there is always very great individuality to be seen. This must be so because, while it is accepted that a full pivot in the back swing (left shoulder pointing to the ball) is essential for a powerful blow to be delivered, how this is obtained depends on the flexibility of each player. In the pictures in these pages of some of our leading professionals, the various left-foot positions during the back swing can be seen.

Christy O'Connor uses the inside edge of his left shoe and seems to be pressing much more lightly on his foot than many players. He seems in fact to pull his weight more on to the right than is usual. This gives him more chance to flow into the ball, which is a distinct feature of his game. Ted Ray, the interesting old champion in the days of the Triumvirate, claimed this pull away was essential to his game; he gained power this way.

Players who allow this pull away have always less weight on the left foot — the left foot rides on the inside edge of the shoe and the top of the body comes away from its original address position — but nothing is usually encountered quite as pronounced as the way Fred Daly has moved away in his swing. Daly has a most individual and, if I might be permitted to criticize such an illustrious player, dangerous shoulder-roll on the way back. He pulls the top of the body away from the address position as if he is trying to keep his lower part only level with the ball, and so gets the weight all on the right foot at the top of the back swing. This means that he is much lighter on his left toe and, this being so, he gets his left heel well clear

of the ground, so that he is almost completely on his toe at the top of the back swing.

The photograph taken with the club still going up shows very clearly how Daly's head, too, has come away from being over the ball as it was at the address. He uses a 46-inch shaft, and the great distance he is from the ball can be seen. His arms and wrists are particularly powerful for his size, and so he can whip his long, heavy driver through the ball to send it a long way. The danger in this 'up-on-the-toe' position is that there is always a chance to sway back too far and get ahead of the ball at impact. Good players like to stay behind the ball as it is struck.

Harry Bradshaw, another stocky type, gets his flexibility into his action from his grip — he overlaps the left hand almost completely with the right hand and this enables him to get a full wrist cock at the top of a three-quarter back swing. He is almost at the top of his swing in the photograph. His left heel is normally well clear of the ground. He, too, uses the inside edge of his shoe and presses with the ball of the foot in the classical manner, and gets a full, free shoulder-turn. I know that slimmer, and perhaps younger, men can do a full back-swing with the left heel raising but little, which must be a safer action, but not all golfers are slim and young.

Harry Weetman, one of the power players in the game, hits some of the game's longest shots with both feet nearly flat, and in the photograph here, when over half-way up in his back swing, it can be seen how little the left heel has so far lifted. He uses the ball of his left foot to swivel on. Gene

Christy O'Connor

Fred Daly

I PRESS WITH THE BIG TOE LIKE THIS

Harry Bradshaw *Harry Weetman* *Myself*

Littler, in a recent quote, considers that the left foot is best kept on the ground — it suits him, I guess. Naturally flexible and in the mid-20's, Littler is considered a possible future champion of the U.S.A. His swing and golfing temperament are outstanding. He was working on a stiff-wristed theory. I did not like the idea much, but I think he has changed recently.

In my own back swing I use the inside edge of my left shoe, and like to feel I am pressing with the big toe; that is why I have always liked shoes which flex. I know that at present there is a tendency, due to the craze for larger and longer spikes, to have stiff, thick soles on golf shoes, but the added foot freedom with a supple shoe is, I consider, too important to be ignored.

In my own case the more I lift my left heel, the more I tend to sway into the ball, and I know I am not alone in this fault, because the higher the heel is lifted, the longer time it takes to brace the left leg on the way down and ground the heel.

I have studied the method, used in the U.S.A. by many players, where the left toe points outwards quite a lot, and I find that it makes my left knee work too much outwards and causes me to dip my left shoulder down too much going back. This may suit many players, but I dislike the little twist I feel in my left knee on the way up.

The whole left foot action fits in anyway as part of the whole swing and should be unconscious, the club should be free to swing uninterruptedly to and fro, and, if you dance on your left toe, it is because you would feel anchored down if you forced it to stay close to the ground; but, as usual, it is good advice to say: 'Don't exaggerate!'

LEFT FOOT COMPARISON

Mr and Mrs Paul Summers from White Sulphur Springs have classical back swings with interesting left foot action. Mrs Summers, who can break 80, has weak-looking leg work here because her stance is too narrow. She can swing the club successfully from this narrow base, but loses the chance to deliver a solid blow. A wider stance would work better as it would cut down excessive body twist.

Mr Summers, who plays in the middle 70's, uses the inside of his left foot correctly, but his chin should point behind the ball.

80

ARE YOU LEADING YOURSELF A DANCE?

WHEN you go to the top of your back swing, does your left foot behave like mine in the picture? Do you use the inside edge of the sole of your left shoe or do you dance on the toe? Perhaps you play 'flat-footed'? There is no rule about this. The actual way the foot works in the swing depends on physical make-up, particularly on the flexibility of the joints.

There are players who are so supple that they can get into the correct top of the swing position with their left foot flat on the ground. Others need to get well up on the toe of the shoe to ease their body round into the classical top-of-the-swing position. Horton Smith lifts his heel very much to get even this far back towards the top of the swing.

The old idea of always cracking down hard on the ground with the left heel, as if to break a nut, is sound *only if the arms and hands are very fast.*

Many golfers get the hips well started, but are not able to check them enough to allow the hands to overtake, and so they get their bodies ahead of the shot. Good golfers have strong legs — walking round the course keeps the legs strong — and I realise that once my legs go, my golf will go, too.

For those who can walk only a little each week, either from lack of opportunity or inclination, it is important to study the timing or the dropping down of the left heel.

Eric Brown: *Horton Smith:*
left heel barely lifted   *heel very much lifted*

I find that in winter, when wearing more clothing, I tend to lift my heel more. I have to watch that I do not sway into the ball on the way down. In order to check dropping the heel too early, I press more on the ball of the foot. In this way I check the unwinding of the hips too far.

I have several friends who play in tennis shoes so as to use the toes of their feet to the maximum advantage. Francis Francis and Tommy Goodwin are fine golfers whose names come to mind. They both can afford golf shoes, but prefer ordinary tennis shoes!

Both play in Nassau, where the climate favours this procedure, but they do it solely for the reason that their foot action is at its best when they can really feel the ground with their toes and control their weight-transfer to the maximum. Both are around the scratch mark, too!

To be a good golfer it is not necessary, as some golfers think, to copy the youthful power-players of to-day and barely lift the left heel — as Eric Brown from Scotland has done.

J. H. Taylor, one of the all-time great golfers, did lift his left heel well clear of the ground, but all the same this swing looks firm and free. Note the short handling of the club and full pivot.

All right, go ahead and dance a little, but remember you must not be in a hurry to snap the heel down. Get the hips started down without dropping the heel — then you are all right. *If you try to drop it after the ball is hit,* then you will be just about in time.

I press more on   *J. H. Taylor:*
the ball of the foot   *heel well clear of ground*

F

USEFUL NOTICES

LEFT: *This notice at the Westchester Country Club, N.Y., is a very usual one in America, and it is a good idea to stop the inevitable hold-up on a crowded course at the longer short holes. I hope some home Greens Committees will try this out. It works, I can vouchsafe, and the players like it. This hole is between a No. 3 iron and a spoon length during most of the year.*

CENTRE: *At the Seminole Golf Club, Palm Beach, Florida, one finds soapy water in the ball washers and clean towels hanging on the post. The length of hole from tiger and ordinary tees is clearly indicated. Ben Hogan has been made an honorary member of this exclusive club, and takes a golfing holiday there every year to work up his game for the Masters' Tournament in April at Augusta, Georgia.*

RIGHT: *There are notices explaining the rules, too, at Seminole. On the 10th fairway near the green on the left is an encroaching pond. There is no doubt where to drop when a penalty has been incurred. The flag can be seen at the right of the photograph.*

PRACTICE DE LUXE

LEFT: *I like the ball 'Picker upper'. I find it fun to drive one of these jeeps collecting the balls from the practice-ground. Drivers are protected by a wire grill so that collecting in the firing line can go on !*

RIGHT: *Golf practice* de luxe *at the Indian Creek Country Club, Miami Beach, Florida. You take a wire basket from the pile on the left and fill it up from the bin, which is full of good-quality golf balls. Sign your name on the sheet attached to the box and hit away to your heart's content — in glorious sunshine, what is more.*

Myself: filling a basket on this golfing paradise where the members split the deficit in the club's finances at the end of the year!

ON SLOW PLAY IN AMERICA

WHEN in America, I took the opportunity given to me in tournaments and in friendly games to study the reasons for the further slowing up of the speed in playing a round of golf. I am sure it takes longer, every succeeding year, to play a round of golf on a normally crowded course there, and I can assure any American, who lives for golf, that he can fit in more rounds per month in the remainder of his golfing life, if he plays in Britain — but one must add 'weather permitting'!

Two rounds a day is long a thing of the past, and this very slow play tempo has not escaped the notice of U.S.G.A. But their plea to 'step on it and not to forget others on the course' has little hope of pushing down the time taken for eighteen holes. Many players go out for the whole day for their one round, and pick up a substantial sandwich and a drink at the ninth hole, because five hours on the course is almost a day's work, and some sustenance is required to 'make it', but they enjoy every shot they play, even to the tiniest putt which finishes out the hole. No matter how many strokes they take — they record the score.

On a crowded course, it is obvious that the slowest four-ball match dictates the speed of play, rather like a few slow pedestrians on a crowded pavement, or a big lorry on a narrow road. There is little to do, except stay behind, and it is often, in the first place, sheer ignorance which causes this sort of situation on a golf course, and bad manners in the second. 'To blazes with them, I'm all right!'

On municipal or public links, where there is no way of restricting a real beginner from holding up the rest by his continuous excursions in all directions (though on the American military golf courses in Germany, military personnel who cannot play decently enough to keep their places are given their money back by orders of a motorized golf course ranger and told to play on the driving range first), playing round is a desperate business. And in some localities rules are now being made to stop strangers from playing at all, and to permit only the local ratepayers to enjoy the amenities. This will give the local controllers of the club a chance to get at their own beginners and advise them to learn to play before spoiling the pleasures of others.

The new 'leave-the-flagstick-in' rule has helped slightly to speed up play, and it does save a certain amount of walking around the hole. It is, generally speaking, a help. The longer and longer courses, even when beautifully manicured, still mean more yards to walk, and that alone takes time, so until

A typical scene during a family four-ball match at the Indian Creek Country Club, Florida. The golfers and their wives and friends follow the play, taking turns to ride or walk round the course.

courses are much shorter again, no time can be saved in the walking.

At one time, the next tee was usually right beside the green and so it was possible to get on with the job. Now there are frequently quite extensive walks to the next teeing ground, and quite often tiring climbs to elevated tees.

Four-ball games are the rule in America, not the exception; and if players are lucky enough to be able to afford a caddie, the latter has to 'tote' two bags, which slows him up, while he chases from side to side of the course to hand his other patron a club; all this wastes a good thirty minutes per round.

Looking for lost balls is, to-day, a very small part of the five hours taken to play, because most courses have their rough well trimmed. The Stableford Competition, which has a growing place in our golf, is not unknown in America, where it is called a 'par points' tournament, and it follows the same principles; but with all players religiously putting out anyway, it saves little time on the average medal round.

Electric buggies, it is calculated, hasten play, for the older members have a chance to keep up with the younger element as they ride round the course, but again all is regulated by the speed of the slowest foursome.

Golf is an expensive game anyway, and the effort to get to the course, to change completely into golfing clothes, and then to wait for a starting time to get off, all means that there is no point in hurrying. 'Enjoy your day to the full!' And that means playing out every hole; the ball has to go into the cup. I spoke to an old golfer in New York, aged eighty-four, whom I had previously met in London during the war, who still plays regularly, and is so supple yet that he can lie on the ground and swing his legs up and touch the ground with his toes behind his head. I enquired how this golf game was going. 'Oh, I shoot now between 100 and 125', he told me. That takes time, he knows, but he can play at the quiet periods during the week — this he does, as he realizes he is a slow player.

At many crowded courses, players stop for half an hour at the refreshment hut, eat and rest, and then just go on to the next tee and continue; those making the full round non-stop have no more rights than they have. I do not think much can be done to alter the time taken to play a round in America. Slow play is there to stay. Efforts are being made, by special films and the written word, to spread the etiquette of golf at public links, where citizens acquire a set of clubs and go straight out to play round the course, without even knowing how dangerous an erring golf ball can be to their fellow-golfers.

At Vittel, in France, where I go to do my cure annually, quite a number of young American Air Force men come to play from the air base at Chaumont, sixty miles away, and these lads start off without caddies, to find their way round the course. It might conceivably be their first game ever. They scatter the balls in all directions, and on one hole our foursome asked to go through the 'beginner foursome'; clearly they had never heard of such a thing, for they continued to play along with us, and it was getting dangerous, so I had to explain briefly the situation and the etiquette. This could have been embarrassing if the members of the passing-through foursome had not been able to speak English, but they were very happy to learn and were most apologetic.

The marking of score-cards in four-ball matches with no 'gimmes,' and all the lifting of the balls, must of course make for slow play; and on a sizzling hot day (much of the golf played in America is in hot weather) it is almost pleasant 'to stop and smell the flowers' even if it means almost starting off all over again at each hole.

I have chatted about this slow play question with various U.S. golf officials, and they can see how the game has adapted itself to American ideas, because the old Scottish pros. and their direct disciples spread a different idea of the golf game when they crossed the ocean. Perhaps because ordinary life there is so hectic, golfers like to take their time playing the game. They must ease up and slow down at some time in their lives, so they do it on the course.

The only visible solution — a floating golf ball and shorter courses. A floater will not go more than 220 yards unless there is a following wind, and even then it has to be flighted; then a championship length course could be under 6,000 yards.

I do not know what would happen with a floater on a day such as there was for the Amateur Championship final at Troon in 1956, when even the small ball was blown off the line on the greens, but I suppose on such days one could, as one does in other athletic pursuits, wait till it stops! There are many pros and cons for this idea, but just to have to walk fewer miles must make playing a round a faster affair. Do you see any other solution?

I LIKE — AND I LIKE

In a country where golf goes on somewhere in top gear all the time, it is difficult to keep track of the game, but by getting about and meeting people and reading all the available golf information, some sort of idea can be obtained of what is continually happening. In the United States to-day golf is big business; it has never been bigger business, and with so many millions of educated people thinking hard about 'how to beat the game', it is not surprising to find that very many fine golfers are produced and that many new ideas on and around the golf game are evolved.

It seems entirely wrong that the tourist traffic is all one-way, because there is nothing that golfing enthusiasts at home would like more than a tour of American golf courses. I wonder if I shall live to see it and maybe organize it? I see little hope of this, alas, while the present 'sterling–dollar' situation exists, but it is something to strive for in the future. I have made a point of getting myself in the mood to see America as a tourist, and not just going around all the time as a privileged sort of visitor for whom the golfing red carpet is readily and generously extended. But because of golf commitments and the many friends I have there, it is not always easy to follow out my 'tourist' programme. I seem to get bedded down in great comfort in one spot.

At the end of my fifth visit to America in 1957 — my first was as an enthusiastic young professional golfer of twenty-one in 1928 — I must say that I was more sold on American golf than ever. This does not mean that I would prefer to spend the rest of my days golfing there, but that the general status of golf in national life has won me over. The vitality of those interested in golf, to go ahead and develop the game, just leaves us standing, as it were, at home while the promotion of the game in general is magnificent. Their easier-all-round tax situation, I must admit, helps greatly.

We still are linked with a tradition, which golfers who have been brought up with the game hope never to see broken, but there are some ideas from America which could be copied with advantage. We in Britain have never quite got away from the basic fact that golf is just a game — 'fortunately', many will add. It helps business men to get distraction, relaxation and amusement, and to make social and commercial contacts, but over there somehow it is big business and it is treated as big business, the sporting side runs about level with the commercial side.

A golf club annual membership subscription is a legitimate business expense, and so, being a charge on the business, the actual figure paid often makes little difference. Nobody therefore makes an issue of a slight rise in the subscription to keep up with any increased costs, and while annual sums of 300 to 600 dollars a year seem very high to us, when calculated at 2.80 dollars to the pound, to Americans — the dollar is still five to the pound for

A four-wheeled single-seater job; these are not so popular as the two-seaters, but are really fun to ride around in. The clubs fit in the front behind the bumper. This is taken outside a pro.'s shop in Augusta, Georgia.

them — in assessing values, it is only our money which has been officially devalued.

After all, to play golf at a Country Club, where caddies are available and first-class restaurant service is provided, for extended hours during the day, must be expensive. To use new top-grade balls is costly; 1.25 dollars each (American-size balls, too, are even more expendable than the smaller-sized British ball); lunch can run the golfer into four to five dollars; and sharing a caddie

LEFT: *Piping Rock Club, Long Island, New York. Enjoying a drink at a fountain.*
CENTRE: *A Driving Range in Massachusetts, U.S.A., which has a 9 holes short golf course, Sports Shop, 16 Bowling Alleys, and a Buffet. There are thousands of these in America, many not as elaborate as this particular one, but they all help to develop the golf game.*
RIGHT: *The little box of score cards on the second tee for those who have forgotten to take a card. Mr Bruce Coffin, an active American senior golfer, stands by the box.*

Toots and I enjoy our golf at the exclusive Indian Creek Country Club at Miami Beach, going round in an electric buggy on this occasion. They are slow to come to England, although one was provided for President Eisenhower for his games at Turnberry, Ayrshire, when he was over in the summer of 1959.

carrying two bags generally another four to five dollars per bag. As the pace is slow caddies only do one round a day and insist on carrying two bags. The practice range at the club, where a bucket of balls can be hired for one dollar and lessons taken in comfort, is an asset to any golf club, and really is a necessity. I like the free peg tees, the free pencils, the soapy water in the ball washers, which are to be found on every tee, and the clean towel attached to the post, the washing-off of the iron and wooden clubheads with a special solution, after every round, in the pro.'s shop, to clean off the grass and earth, and the excellent shoe-cleaning departments in the locker rooms. At The Greenbrier Hotel courses, White Sulphur Springs, West Virginia, the coloured locker-room boys clean up to 400 pairs of shoes a day in the season.

I like the little weatherproof box on the second tee, full of cards and pencils, handy for those who have started off without a card. I like the seats on every tee, and often a special rail for the caddies to rest the bags against. I like the rakes in every bunker, so that every golfer following can get a good lie in the sand (your caddie is *obliged* to carry out the chore of raking out the footprints; you

are expected to do so too). I like the general policy of repairing pitch marks on the soft watered greens, and the sandwiches, hamburgers, and drinks of all sorts in the rest-houses at the 9th hole.

I like the free salt tablets and iced drinking water; spring water, too; not that beastly chlorinated liquid from the tap we usually get in Britain. I like the numerous drinking fountains round the course and the receptacles for the empty paper cups, when spring water is supplied, all appropriately placed.

I like the electric buggies, which have come to stay; they really are fun to ride in and make senior golfers play those extra holes each day; and what a pleasure they are to use to watch your friends play — real armchair comfort.

I like the proper asphalt car parks, well illuminated at night, while at many clubs the uniformed attendant will put your car away for you and bring it to you when you leave, a real luxury on a wet night. I like the idea of changing your clubs regularly for the latest model and being able to get a 'trade-in' on the older set, according to its age and condition, a bit like changing a car.

I like signing for everything at the bar, green fees for guests, meals in the restaurant, purchases in the pro.'s shop — and then writing one cheque for the lot at the end of the month. I had no cheques, alas, having no account and no dollars, but I appreciated the idea!

I like the 'hole by hole' score boards at tournaments, which give full particulars of the play of each player, not just the 18-holes score. I like the starter calling the next players to the tee from the clubhouse bars and locker room, over the internal loudspeaker system, so that there is no need for players to hang around the first tee awaiting their turn — a simple idea but so practical, and golfers cease to be impatient.

I like the practical golf clothing for hot weather; it seems startling to the visitor from the Continent of Europe, especially as the colours and designs are so daring. I am not sure that I like to see all women golfers in shorts, but I am told they are the most comfortable form of dress for hot weather. Many men favour them, too. I think they look hideous.

I do not like the always lush, moist-watered, clovery fairways, nor the spongy teeing grounds, but they seem to be favoured by the greenkeepers and Green Committees. The always-holding greens are, of course, easier to play to, and the top players are inclined to protest if the ball 'does not come back off the pitch', but some golfers, I find, still prefer a green that requires skill to stay on it.

These are not all the points which please and displease by any means. Many home golfers may even know of others, but golfers everywhere look up to America as the leading golf country to-day; and our definite superiority ended when we lost the numerical advantage, golfingly speaking, some years back.

I honestly do not see what can be done to beat consistently this golfing colossus again, but to keep on trying is a 'must', and we should not be disappointed if we do not succeed all the time, but we must send more and more young golfers on extended visits there, to see what they have to do to keep up with the world's best. More and more courses are being built, and driving ranges spring up by the hundred, soon to be crowded with customers, golfing far into the night; and where both beginners just learning to play golf and old golfers trying to improve their swings crash out thousands of balls. What a sight that is! What entertainment too!

With the *Comet* bringing the American Continent just a very few hours away, perhaps one day we can plan to have a week's golfing in America as readily as we plan a week at Sandwich, Kent.

Do not please run away with the idea that I have sold my golfing soul to America. I am still British through and through, but my life has been dedicated to golf and while our traditions and customs mean so much to us all, I know that there are such things as 'keeping up with the times' and 'not being too proud to learn'.

CHECK YOUR ARC

A self-check on your arc. Swing back with the left hand only (LEFT) — then add the right hand (RIGHT). You can easily see if it goes on the club comfortably.

I find it difficult to swing naturally quite as upright as this. I get too flat, if I do not watch it, and then lean into the ball as I pull down with the left arm — because my right arm always wants to glue itself to my right side.

DOUBLE TIMING

A T The Greenbrier Club, White Sulphur Springs, West Virginia, for twenty-odd years the golf headquarters of Sam Snead, I again ran across a young American professional, Walker Inman, whom I had met for the first time the previous year.

Walker is a keen golf student and has lots of ambition to become a great player, but has to watch his budget, as to play tournament golf only moderately successfully costs a lot of money. So this particular winter he went to work as an assistant Club professional in Florida so that he could collect enough cash to 'do' the extensive summer tour.

The summer tour is considered easier than the winter circuit by many of the top players, because the courses are better and the competition is considered less fierce. But as all the tough players are still there, I think there is nothing in it from this angle.

Walker was telling me that not only did he do well in Florida, but he learned a lot about golf, as this was his first proper extensive experience of teaching the game. He said that he had realized that the best way to acquire deep knowledge of the golf game is to teach it. This applies to all subjects, one can add.

Having been mixed up with both the playing and teaching sides of golf for many years now, I can appreciate that one's pupils can often teach one things about golf and make one aware how real are the problems of the less gifted people trying to get pleasure from golf. People who have to make do with the muscles they have, because they have no time or inclination to work at the game — they just want to play it — provide many original problems. It is no use suggesting a method requiring several hours of practice a day; they want to play golf quickly and easily; and few, if any, will relish a long-term programme by the teacher,

LEFT: *Walker Inman practising at Augusta. Note left arm and hand position and half-shut club-face — this action suits youth and the larger ball and is the action I use to begin a push of the ball.*
CENTRE: *Sam Snead has already arrived in the 'good golfer' position. The body is already placed for the lash by the wrists. The clubhead is well on the inside and now with strong, alive hands the ball can be given a strong blow. Poor golfers can get somewhere near this position, as I have so often seen in photographs sent to me for comment, but their hands are not strong enough to complete the job. In the photograph of my swing (page 90), taken from in front, my body action is similar to that of Snead's at an almost identical point in the down-swing.*
RIGHT: *Harry Vardon's top of the back swing position is interesting to me not only because of its obvious lack of tension but because of the way his right elbow has left the side. This is considered to-day to be far from the body, but 'Chick' Harbert from U.S.A., one of the game's really colossal hitters of a golf ball, allows his right elbow great freedom. Many long hitters do.*
The right elbow from this position must go directly to the right hip as the down swing begins.

such as might be proposed to a player with more than average potentialities.

Every instructor likes to see each pupil succeed to his maximum, and he advises accordingly, but the great majority of those taking up golf are anxious to get on to the course and play in competitions.

I have one golfing friend from Chicago, who loves his golf, who likes practising more than playing, because he gets the maximum pleasure striving to hit perfect shots. He gets far more pleasure seeking academic perfection on the practice ground than producing a score on the golf course made up of a succession of obviously mis-hit shots. Such a golfer is rare, but it has been an education to me to get to know such a person, because however much I have wanted him to play on the course — and, as it were, see where his practice had led him — he has more often than not resisted because he felt his percentage of satisfactory shots is too low.

All this is fundamentally a personal question, and beginners can soon be seen making up their own minds as to where to 'aim their sights'. They can be influenced by their golf associates or just make up their own minds.

Many golfers visit prominent teachers, hoping to have a magic wand waved over them and to set out for home having seen the light — and with all their troubles behind them. This frequently happens, if only in a temporary way, because often the difference between playing very well, and just mediocre stuff, is very small, and a simple tip can do the trick. But these tips, through over-accentuation, usually 'wear out', and the chase is on again. That this is true is, I feel, proved at any big championship, where few of the acknowledged capable contestants ever produce, in that particular week, the form of which they are capable.

Why is this so? It seems as if it should be simple enough to learn to hit that little white ball where one wants to, but so far there has not been discovered a method, *the* method, if you like, of doing this. I am always interested in the so-called latest methods exposed, whether by old champions 'discovering' something different, or newcomers working on their own particular lines, but to me it is the same old swing with a different dress.

I think that Ernest Jones, in his little back room on Fifth Avenue in New York, with his time-worn exhortation 'to swing the clubhead,' is expounding the oldest yet the latest thing. The point that Ernest makes about 'Paralysis by Analysis,' to use a phrase of his, is in part true, but it does not satisfy all golfers to be fed with 'simple truths', as Ernest

Copying Harry Vardon by lifting the left heel a lot more than usual. This photograph, taken before the Ashridge Golf Clubhouse in 1938, shows me experimenting with this action. I found that in wintertime with a thicker sweater on, I sometimes worked in a freer action this way. I think the big lift of the left heel more difficult to handle — I find myself leaning into the ball if I am not careful.

calls them; they like it 'complicated', if only later to get a 'brain-washing' and simplify it.

Years ago we had Harry Vardon with his statuesquely graceful swing, an absence of tension most marked in his whole action, as the ideal model, and golfers were content to let their left heels lift readily on the back swing and then to allow their right heels to come well clear of the ground in the follow-through — a poetry of motion, and very successful motion, too.

Now the trend is to glue the heels down as much as possible, to twist the body to the maximum without freeing the heels. This is an action suited to the young athletic types (or the double-jointed exceptions, like Jimmy Adams), but I regret that it is poison to many. There is naturally a limit between 'dancing' on the toes and a flat-footed action favoured by, say, Harry Weetman, and I am sure that thousands of golfers would do better if they just got the clubhead to swing without using their feet as brakes.

LEFT: *Myself, half-way down the swing. Compare this with Sam Snead's action on page 88.*
CENTRE: *Good foot action is incredibly fast yet unhurried. Tommy Bolt in action — the double timing in evidence. Note foot position 'miles' ahead of the arms — timing!*
RIGHT: *James McHale, who played in the American Walker Cup team in 1949 and 1951, driving. Although his hips are back in the address position, the club-shaft is only just beginning to descend.*

I have seen more than one prominent golfer stating in print that the swing originates in the feet, and it might be true at one particular moment, but I do not think it is the right place to put the spotlight permanently.

You see, good footwork never seems to be noticed. It just happens. Good footwork is fast, smooth and inconspicuous, yet one can tell a beginner by the clumsy way his feet operate. Your whole body-balance depends on the foot action; the weight distribution may be regulated by the swing of the club itself, but your feet must be alive to respond. I have found that when taking raw beginners along, from zero, in golf, once the main arm action has been acquired, the action of the feet (unless it has come really naturally) is the big stumbling-block.

If you teach in a net, and your pupils wear soft-soled tennis shoes or casuals, the use of the toes in the swing can be seen and felt, and I think pupils become more aware of the way feet work — but in those heavy thick-soled, long-spiked shoes, the feet seem to me to be blocked and less alive. I have thought for many years that a golf-shoe should be really flexible to help golfers, but many still prefer something like an army boot, *to anchor them*, I have heard it said. The feet do not need long spikes to anchor them to the ground if the toes are used; there is such a thing as double timing.

'Double timing? Now you really are complicating things', you will say. Let me put it this way: there is 'Beginner's timing', where the feet work after the arm swing, the club pulls the feet into position, as it were, going up and down. Then there is the timing where the feet are working ahead of the swing on the way down, placing the body correctly for the attack on the ball by the arms and club. This double timing, the feet for a time leading the clubhead (that is until the left heel is down and the right heel freed), is always seen in a little caddie boy's swing; he has got it from intuitive copying, but in a grown person learning golf, it is conspicuous by its absence.

Good foot action is incredibly fast yet unhurried, and I always could see so clearly in that old golf hero George Duncan's swing the perfect double timing — that slick, smooth foot-work, a feature of the play of the great golfers, because the feet move quickly while the arms seem to be taking their time. There is no jerk and no haste in this double-timing swing. Just look at James McHale driving; his body work, part one, is over; the hips are already as square as they were at address — and look where the club-shaft is still.

It is this double timing which is the thing the good golfer has almost naturally; the rabbit is a rabbit because he rarely acquires it.

NO ONE WAY TO PLAY GOLF

GOLF is not an easy game to teach. Those who have never tried to impart their skill to others will never realise this, for I do not consider teaching a person with almost inborn natural gifts a great feat, because it almost amounts to this: 'You could not stop him from becoming a good player.' I admit that the reputation of a teacher, and his fortune for that matter, can come from being lucky enough to have had a hand in creating a 'star'. The real teaching of golf becomes tough when the pupil has no ability, no muscles, and no burning desire to play — he or she just doing it to oblige the doctor or the family.

So many teachers look for a standard method which will apply to everyone and, given a class of young, strong boys, a method might succeed with 75% of them. But, taken throughout the year, I do not suppose that as many as 15% of the pupils the average professional takes on have any natural aptitude for the game. So the rest have to be taken as individuals and their cases really studied, to help them to get the maximum from their limited ability.

The stock platitudes have some value, but the clever teacher varies them as the need arises. The talk of the fundamentals can be confusing, as even these are difficult to define; for just taking the opinion of two successful professionals, in material I have before me, one speaks of three fundamentals and the other tabulates a list of twenty. The most satisfactory way is to simplify the instructions as much as possible, but I have never found that the most simple phraseology, however much repeated, is guaranteed to sink in. It is only by trying all sorts of phrasing that one can register in the pupil's mind the action required. This is obviously because such words as 'Swing' or 'Drag' have different interpretations for different people.

A natural golfer is one who is adept at learning and mastering the essentials of the game — he just plays, never having perhaps seen the game before, as though it were born in him.

The U.S.P.G.A. Teaching Committee, a body which tries to standardize teaching and to raise the standard of skill of instructors, has got to naming five fundamentals: grips, stance, arm action, wrist action, body action (pivot). But then, of course, the whole matter is turned over to the instructor to interpret these, *via* the player's own physique and using his own terminology to put 'it' over.

Those who watch golf will have noticed the varying actions of modern top-rank players.

Power-golfer Harry Weetman in a 'hair raising' shot: photograph by Pierre Canivet of Paris at 1/2,500th of a second. Compare this with Bob Hope's action — the direct opposite. Here is the open to shut method. Weetman's No. 4 iron shots are as long as my shots with my No. 3 wood.

The one and only Bob Hope remembers the rules, but he has got himself a bit locked here somehow, holding the face open. He comes from very shut at the top of the back swing to open, as can be seen. I dislike this method and always have. The scene is the Golf Club of Samaden, near St Moritz, Switzerland, a heavenly place in midsummer.

There is Charles Ward's lightning swing — no slowly back here; Arthur Lees's flat-footed, three-quarter swing; and Bobby Locke's long, flat swing and left hip forward. What of Dai Rees's double-handed grip and his ducking action of the right side; Sam King's flat-footed short back swing and shorter finish; or Harry Weetman's fast flap with his wrists, with right heel down? And so on — a host of actions, all different. All successful, all personal.

What then are the things which impress the golfer who studies the game when he sees these men drive off? The speed of the clubhead — at times he may be distracted from realizing this by glueing his eyes on a mannerism: but this club-head speed is there in every swing, this flash through of the 'square to the line' clubhead, at impact.

To achieve this flash through, the hands must be strong. I think that this is essential to success. I like 'essential' better than 'fundamental'.

To 'make do' with the limited power the average person has in his hands gives the instructor all sorts of problems to solve, in order to make up or cover up the weakness in this vital section of the swing. For the rest of the body plays too big a part, and it is in this fight to correct the balance of power that the skill of the teacher is seen. To get somewhere near the proportions I consider to be right, – viz., hands and arms, 85% of the power; body, 15% only — many poorer players, when doing their best effort, are doing a 50–50 job.

I know that if a gentle swing is taken, it is possible to achieve a good 150 yards stroke with the right percentages of power, but how satisfying is this? The answer is — *not very!* Some players, with a very placid disposition, can get some satisfaction in just lazily hitting the ball, because if the wrists and hands are weak they cannot *take* a strong hit anyway. But the majority are not happy to take this weakness lying down — they want to do something better, and even if it (the 'something better') comes off only now and then, the risk is worth it. This is where the instructor gets his problems. Everybody wants to 'kill' the ball.

A coach in other sports — football, cricket, rowing, lawn tennis — can generally discard those with no aptitude; in golf, the instructor has no choice, he must take on the fat, thin, short, tall, weak, muscle-bound, neurotic, placid and indifferent. The object of the game does not change, even if the rules do, but the details of the methods employed do alter, as the clubs, balls and courses have changed.

I think that the test of a basic method of teaching is that it will work for every type of golfer. I do not claim that my particular way is the *only* way, but I can see that more and more players are coming to the grip of the club I have always used and to my hand action, which I have always had and which I have written about regularly since 1929.

My grip starts with two 'Vs' up the shaft, the back of the left hand facing the hole. I consider this an essential. I allow a slight variation up to three knuckles, according to arm and wrist structure, but then compensations have to be made all round, when the 'Vs' no longer point up the shaft.

My essentials: to swing inside-to-out and to hit *past* the left wrist with the head of the club.

COMPARISONS

IN my book *This Game of Golf* I put on page 73 a photograph of Jimmy Demaret taken in Florida in 1947. The photograph, reproduced here, shows Demaret's left-wrist action for a middle distance iron shot. Since Ben Hogan began to write about and demonstrate in his own play the high left-wrist bone, as being nearer to the hole than any other part of the hand at impact, great interest has been taken in his action.

The value of this action is that it prevents what is known as the fatal reverse cock of the left wrist (as occurs when a ball is scooped). This forcing of the left hand to bend back, as it were, instead of trying to get the left arm in line with the straightened arm at impact, is not new, but the accent, rightly or wrongly, is on it at the moment. I think that Ben Hogan's left-handedness, for he is left-handed naturally, has now brought him to this method since he changed the position of his left hand on the shaft, from three to four knuckles to two knuckles showing at address.

Now that he pronates, opens the club-face going back immediately on starting away from the ball, he finds himself in the hitting area with his club-face open, left palm down, so to get the face square he must, as must all golfers, supinate with the left wrist, and so get the palm facing slightly upwards after impact.

Some instructors talk of this as the high left wrist, others call it crowning the wrist, or even arching the wrist (I use arching the wrist in another sense). In these photographs of Bobby Jones and myself taken by Mr Brownlow Wilson around 1930–4, a comparison can be made of our impact positions; the left hands have behaved in exactly the same way, but we are whipping the ball more, while Hogan is inclined to push his shots a little more. Hogan, despite his accident, continues to use a bigger degree of body whip than either Bobby Jones or myself, for example, ever did.

While all this sounds very complicated, it is in fact a sort of double guarantee for a late hit. Demaret, for example, is doing what our fathers would have certainly called a push shot, an extra late hit if you like. It is, therefore, not everybody's cup of tea, because many golfers never hit early enough to succeed — they never get the clubhead to catch up to the ball in any case.

There are so many avenues to explore, all giving hope of a glorious end, that no golfer should give up hope of improving until he has ventured down them all.

I find that I often meet golfers who think they have already finished their explorations and turn to me in case there is still something left to try, some avenue to go along. I can usually set the explorer off again.

I think that the work put into that great contribution to golf by Ben Hogan, Herbert Warren Wind and Anthony Ravielli in their book, *The*

LEFT: *Jimmy Demaret, seen arching the left wrist.* CENTRE: *The fatal reverse cock.* RIGHT: *Hogan just after impact. Here can be seen his usual action.*

93

LEFT: *Bobby Jones, 1930.* RIGHT: *Myself, 1934.*

Modern Fundamentals of Golf, is first-class; nothing better has ever appeared, and it gives a great picture of Ben's latest method of play; he has modified his methods with the passing years.

But students, when delving into this textbook, this analysis, of one of the greatest of all-time players, must appreciate that the golfer under the microscope is a very powerful physical specimen with a natural gift for this difficult game and a natural left-handedness, rather like Sam Snead, who can break 80 with left-handed clubs, with very little practice, at any time.

It is a bit unfair to the average golfer that few champions have ever made their swings and built up their game from nothing; most, if not all,

began half-way up by starting off into golf because they had natural talent. This means they had exceptional natural gifts, and so golf was always easy. I think that my understanding of the game has been helped by the fact that while I could play golf decently as a schoolboy at fourteen years of age, I was no infant prodigy. I just thought golf would be a fine career, and set about trying to develop whatever gifts I had.

This caused me to put the accent on muscle-building early on, but without any guidance. There were no data available for me to follow; how I wish I could start again with all the knowledge I have since acquired. This, alas, can never be, but I can at least pass on to others some ideas.

Ben Hogan and myself. My left-hand action and attack on the ball have been unchanged over the years. The photographs on this page of myself were taken in 1934 and again in 1959. The back of the left hand is driving towards the hole.

94

1.   *2.*   *3.*

THE BACK OF THE LEFT HAND

THERE always seems to be a danger, in the play of the golfer with untrained muscles, for the club-face either to stay open, or to 'smother over', as the critical impact position approaches. Many golfers, feeling as they can instinctively on the way down that the club-face is just not going to arrive square at impact, often add a bit of shoulder action to their hand action in their endeavour to make a square impact.

From the position in photograph No. 1, where I am making my backswing, I continued to lift my hands to the height of my shoulders to the point marked X. My shoulder and hip turn being already completed, I then began to come down. The hips start first and then, when the hands get to just about waist-level, the back of the left hand is turned down towards the ball gradually and then on to face the hole. The trick which puzzles most handicap golfers is how to get the club-face square at impact without rolling the wrists violently

and throwing the clubhead off the correct arc to the ball.

From the normal top-of-the-swing position the club is pulled down by the arms, and the club-head falls back, moving from A to B, as seen in photograph No. 2, as the hips unwind first and the end of the shaft points to the ground. It is from this particular position that the average golfer can still go wrong. He continues to pull down, or tow down, the club without being able to bring the club-face square to the ball with the hands only. You can see that my hand is turning the club in the photograph.

I have always seen from my very earliest days, when I began to practise madly, hoping to become a champion one day, that with a one- or two-knuckle left-hand grip I could really turn the back of my left hand to the ball more freely, with no danger of overdoing it, and that furthermore the right hand could really be allowed to 'pour' its

LEFT:

Ben Hogan nearing the top of his back swing with his brassie. No slackening of the vice-like grip here. Note that he holds the club well down the shaft, not at the very top.

RIGHT:

Ben Hogan playing pitch shots— opening the club-face more as he now rolls his wrists going up. How ready the back of the left hand is to play its rôle and turn down to square up the blade and pinch the ball.

95

power into the shot without doing any harm. Now this action, seen in photograph No. 3, has always been the part which many students of golf miss when analysing the swings of their favourite players. The value of a strong left arm can be seen in my swing as shown here. My arm is held straight by the muscles, not by the locking of the elbow joint.

I know that at first it seems to be an impossible action to acquire, but it can be made part of every golfer's swing with practice. Ben Hogan has made a feature of this hand action in his great book. In fact, since he changed to a two-knuckle grip a few years ago, he has become more aware, I feel, of this particular way to deliver a square blow, and he has by his usual thoroughness made the back-of-the-left-hand-to-the-hole a key feature of his present swing. One might almost say that he has even exaggerated the turning-down of the back of the hand from the position in the right-hand photograph (page 95) to impact, for he shows in some illustrations that his wrist even sticks out towards the hole, bending his hand back.

This exaggerated bend-back of the left hand would have been classed as part of a push-shot in the days of the old masters, who had to employ this type of stroke very often in the period of few clubs and the pressing need to have to make up shots, when there was no club to fit exactly. Many golfers still fail to see the value of the two-knuckle grip. They experience a feeling of power when they put their left hand well over the shaft, show many knuckles and 'lock their arm at the elbow'. But, alas, at impact this position is not the best, because not only does the arm stay rigid but the wrist gets rigid, too, and prevents the club-face from being squared up *gradually*. It is almost jerked to square at impact and so rarely arrives twice alike in the impact area. From position No. 2 the left hand can be trained to come up square to the ball gradually.

There is the key-word — 'gradually' against jerkily. My swing is often referred to as being smooth and my hit disguised. I believe, if this is true, that it is because I have always used my left hand in this way. It is not new. I have photographs of Bobby Jones doing it, and he did it from the normal 'old-fashioned' left wrist under the shaft at the top position. If it was good enough for him I beg you not to overlook it, for the club-face must be brought squarely to the ball at impact if a straight shot is to result.

HOGAN'S CHANGE OF STYLE

Few top golfers reorganize their game during the height of their careers as Ben Hogan has done, and in these two pictures the big difference between his methods of 1947 and 1957 can be observed.

In 1947 (LEFT), *he used a wide stance, drove with a lofted club and had the two 'Vs' pointing to the right shoulder. Now he uses a narrow stance, 'Vs' pointing up the shaft, and so his right shoulder at the address becomes higher. If the hands were completely overlapping one on the other, the shoulders could, of course, be level, but with one hand below the other the shoulders must tilt to varying degrees according to the grip of the club.*

The left-hand 'V' up the shaft offers greater scope to the player

and, of course, gives a wider choice of right-hand positions. Ben now has his right hand well over the shaft, rather like the position I have always used. Note the way the right elbow is placed with the change of grip — the elbows come more together.

The drawing of Ben, by Anthony Ravielli, is from his great book, The Modern Fundamentals of Golf.

A. Maura (LEFT), *Spanish Amateur Champion, in the hitting area. He has his left hand working in this way because of a three- to four-knuckle grip. The back of the left hand is not going to face the ball or the hole later; it will go through almost edgeways. This means that the right hand just whips to the point when the arm is straight and then pushes the entire arm through.*

Baron Guy de Rothschild, on the right, because of a two-knuckle grip, is whipping the ball with his right hand against his left, the back of the hand facing the hole.

SPATULATE THUMBS

IT was not only yesterday that I became aware of the key importance of the position of the left thumb in the type of golf grip which I favoured, the Vardon grip, where the club is gripped strongly between the index finger and thumb of both hands. I always knew that, in my programme of intensive practice, I had to take care and see that my thumb did not get so worn that it became sore and tender, for it did a lot of my work. Many top players plaster up their precious thumbs before playing at all, as often their skin will split if they do not do so.

My practice was interrupted for a few weeks in 1931, when I had a bad boil on the back of my neck on the left side, and I did the maximum to get rid of it, which meant, in those days, holding hot compresses on it for as long as possible; I suppose to-day some penicillin or like drug would alter the treatment. Anyhow, the repeated dipping of my hand into very hot water softened up the skin on the front of the hand, and when I could begin golf again the skin was too delicate to stand up to the practice, and the incessant hitting of shots caused a water-blister to develop, not only on the outside but near the bone. This most painful condition caused a wasting of the muscle, and finally the pad of the thumb had to be opened. Since then my left thumb has never been as fleshy as the right one and has to be taken care of. I learned to value this thumb the hard way.

The left thumb is a sort of fulcrum for the swinging of the club, for at the top of the back swing quite a lot of weight is carried directly on it, especially in the method where a two-knuckle grip is employed.

The actual position of the thumb, whether it is bunched up or extended, depends on its shape. If the thumb is a 'spatulate model', as an Australian reader of my articles in *Farm and Country* told me it is called, then the making of an orthodox back-swing *à la* Sam Snead is a simple matter. My correspondent said how much he would like to borrow 'Slamming Sam's' left hand for a round or two. He explained — and necessarily so, too, for I had not met the word 'spatulate' before (it comes from *spatula*, of course) — that it meant 'pronounced', and suggests that players with such thumbs have advantages from delicacy of touch and added power. My dictionary covers the word 'spatulate' thus: 'shaped like a spatula: elliptical'. Anyhow, the point he made was that it is easier to play with such a shape of thumb. I am not aware that it is possible to train one's thumb to bend back more; I should say it might grow that way if one began golf early enough, as the body is forming, but the huge variety of grips used by champions indicates that not only are their bodies different shapes, but their hands also — and the thumb is the key.

Golfers who interlock, thumb outside, or use a double-handed grip, usually do so because their left thumb does not make a firm left-hand grip, and a free full-length swing, possible at the same time, or it has been damaged. Most short back-swing players have limited left-wrist flexibility and

97

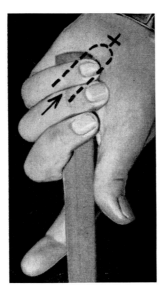

LEFT: *My left hand on the putter. I often have the left hand on the club like this. A doctor friend of mine from Cardiff thinks the ring finger should touch point X, to give the perfect 'hinge'. I do not disagree with him, simply because I find it awkward to do, but I pass it on as an idea — it might be easy for some hands to do.*

RIGHT: *Harry Vardon's left hand grip. The shape of his thumb can clearly be seen here and while it does not bend back like that of many other top golfers, there is still that sort of golfing bump and the bulging muscle seen on the hand of many modern champions.*

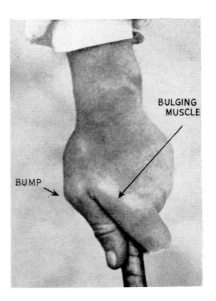

a not very flexible joint at the base of the thumb or in the top section.

My Australian correspondent had studied photographs of most of the stars, and he lists some with those spatulate thumbs — viz., Snead, Mangrum, Boros, McSpaden, Von Nida, Vardon, Hogan, Faulkner. His quoted exceptions are Hagen, Duncan, Locke. He is not sure about myself or 'Babe' Didrickson Zaharias. I think my top joint bends back quite decently.

He is right, in the main, with the names given above. My own left thumb goes back well, but I could have used (I have felt, advantageously, too) an extra degree of 'bend-back,' at the joint where the thumb joins the hand, because my swing has been shortish, due to the limitations of my left wrist action.

The left wrist cocks so much easier, and the grip can remain solid throughout, if the thumb bends back well. Hogan, though, has never had quite the same left thumb movement as Snead; he used to extend this left thumb down the shaft, almost getting it parallel to the shaft itself for its full length. As everyone studied this genius, it was soon called 'the long thumb', and it was suggested as *the* thing — but it turned out to be a

Hogan-personal-model-grip, because his thumb is extra long.

I am sure that the old golfers who used a palm grip, when everyone was holding the club in the fingers and thumbs, did so from necessity; their left wrists could not function properly when they used their left thumb and index finger as vices. They did not play less well, though, for 'Sandy' Herd won the Open Championship with this grip and went on to complete four rounds in a major tournament in under an average of fours when nearing his seventieth birthday. This would indicate that he was losing little flexibility in his hand action. A study of the left hands of some of the players mentioned by my correspondent shows how the thumbs vary.

Thoughtful golfers will immediately look at their left thumb to see if it has a Sam Snead shape. If it does not want to bend back, then it is worth while investigating to see if it is cramping your action, when it is squashed on to the shaft by the over-lapping of the index finger of the right hand.*

*A worth-while step might be for parents, anxious to see their babies become golf champions, to make sure the left thumbs are well bent back while they are soft and the bone is forming. I take no responsibility for any results arising from this suggestion (unless they are successful!).

SETTING THE HANDS

Students of the game will have noticed how some players have difficulty in setting their hands on the club, especially with iron clubs. I can understand their problem and I think that there is something in lining-up the club-face with the right hand alone, before placing the left hand on the shaft. The iron-head is made to line up the bottom edge of the club-face at right angles to the line to the hole. Many golfers are doubtful on this point.

98

WEETMAN'S KEY

Harry Weetman's left thumb is the key here. The club shaft is riding on the end joint of the left thumb, which is shaped like Harry Vardon's, and the right hand has opened slightly. This extra freedom in the right hand helps Harry to get that frightening lash at the ball, but if the closing snap of the right hand is misjudged, errors can creep in.

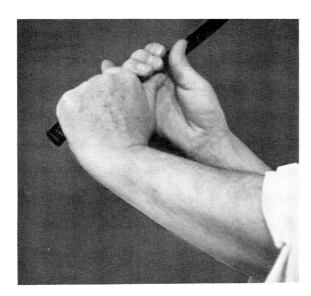

INSIDE THE HAND

This shows, with my right hand purposely opened (ABOVE), *how the left thumb lies on the shaft. You can play golf very well, opening the right hand like this. Former English Champion Frank Pennink* (RIGHT) *does, but the club-shaft* must not turn, *the hand must just open and close. Frank does this because of a stiffish right wrist joint giving limited flexibility in this part of the swing, where the right hand is usually bent back.*

DICK MAYER'S THUMB

Here is former U.S. champion, Dick Mayer, doing his daily chore. (Note nice big heap of new balls.)

He is experimenting with a reverse overlap for this series, but all the same his left thumb is clearly visible at the top of this swing position. The shaft rests well on it. His left wrist is flexible and his thumb bends back better than mine; this makes a full swing easier.

HANDS AND THE
GOLFERS

America's Lloyd Mangrum and I on the first tee at Walton Heath, 1949. I beat Lloyd that day to enter the final of the News of the World *(P.G.A. Match Play) Championship. Note the different shape of our hands. Lloyd has very strong hands but shorter fingers. This is the grip he uses. Unusual because he 'interlocks, left thumb inside'.*

OPEN TO SHUT — OR VICE VERSA

Swinging the clubhead naturally away from the ball, the club-face opens gradually and no effort is made to stop the natural result of the left shoulder pointing to the ball as it goes under the head. Myself in Cannes, 1956.

BELOW: Tommy Armour seen in his great golfing days in the 1920's and 30's. Here his strong hands, with left wrist under the shaft, have placed the club-face fully open, the nose of the club pointing to the ground. This is a great position. His left hand has relaxed a little to get a full wrist cock, but there is no danger of the shaft turning with such fingers — like steel grips they were. If Armour could relax here, others can!

BELOW: Ben Hogan, 1956 edition, when he had already reached his 'cocking of the left wrist more' period, putting this wrist well under the shaft and almost opening the club-face fully. This I try to do — and it is the way many other successful players have always also preferred, so I have noticed in my golfing life.

This interesting photograph shows the successful American professional Lew Worsham using the shut-faced action. Lew has a flat back swing and the club-face faces the sky — completely shut, that is. This is a strong man's action; and fast body action, almost exaggerated, is required to get the club-face back to the ball square. I find users of this action vary very much in their play.

Three golfers from the shut-faced school who have the club-faces of their drivers looking at the sky.
LEFT: *Lloyd Mangrum, a great golfer and former U.S. Open Champion, has been snapped here with his left hand and forearm in line. The cottage in the background belongs to Bobby Jones and is at the Augusta National Golf Club, Georgia, where he is Club President. Mangrum is driving from the 10th tee.* CENTRE: *A powerful six-handicap amateur who could not have his club-face more shut. The ball is sent a long way, often, but the danger of a smothered hook is always present.* RIGHT: *A tall thin American professional, Harry Todd, uses the shut-faced method. He uses a big body unwind to hold the face square at impact. Dangerous, I have always found.*

Christy O'Connor clearly coming on to the ball from the inside. All is correct, but this particular tee shot on the 3rd hole at Walton Heath, Old Course, was pushed slightly to the right, as the body was a little too much ahead of the hands, which did not succeed in bringing the clubhead square or even slightly turned in, if a hook was expected. Note the bent right arm seen in all class golfers.

Here can be seen clearly the difference, at a half-way stage, between 'open' and 'shut' hand action. (LEFT) my arm swing; (RIGHT) Bob Hope in action. Bob breaks 80 regularly.

We are using different clubs, I know, but the action of my hands is the same for all clubs. I have the nose of the club pointing down — the nose of Bob's iron club is pointing to the front. I find it difficult to use my hands with his action or to hang on to the club, as the club itself seems off balance and wants to twist.

LEGS AND THE GOLFER

As I have often recalled, one of my boyhood idols was Abe Mitchell, as neat and powerful a striker of a golf ball as ever lived, and particularly of the old, small, very heavy ball which needed 'getting up'. He never liked the big American ball or steel shafts.

Abe, who taught me lots of things (one was that a driver must have loft on it; it cannot be putter-faced), always stressed that a golfer was as good as his legs, and that in his own case it was his legs which 'went' first. This is true, because as one gets older one walks less and the circulation is poorer anyway; any excuse not to walk is sought for and, besides, there seems to be no time to walk anywhere. There is no doubt that hitting hundreds of balls is the best way to get your swing into shape, but playing round after round of golf on the course is the best practice for golf and for the leg muscles, plus a daily spell of skipping; even fifty skips a day keeps me going.

Have you noticed that when you see a small person play golf you hardly ever notice his knees; his knee action is very inconspicuous. As I write, veteran Gene Sarazen's forceful action comes to mind. I can see his arm action, his grip, the way his feet slew round after impact; but his knees — I simply cannot place the action of his knees. Yet there is that other great American striker of modern times, Sam Snead, a big fellow whose wonderful back-swing always seems to me distinguished as much for its amazing wind-up of the body as for the prominent left-knee action. The left knee seems to be in the picture all the time.

I have satisfied myself that the very tall players look more awkward playing golf; they have to get out of the way of themselves — and many golfers will remember that I once put the cat among the pigeons when I came out with the statement that 'you can be too tall to play golf well'! There are the usual exceptions to this rule — but I did not mean it as a rule, just a statement that the larger arc of the tall golfer can become unmanageable.

Looking simply at the action of the knees, the player who can make a nice free back-swing with the minimum lift of his left heel must have a better chance of repeating this movement exactly than the player who gets right up on his left toe like a dancer. Players who lift the left heel very much generally do so to facilitate their pivot, but they can be said to make their top of the swing position weaker, because it lacks that tight sort of body wind-up, which is released, like a spring, as the down-swing is created.

Players who are inclined to shift the weight to the right laterally often call on a forward push of the left knee — i.e., towards the ball, or to the left of it — to get their hips to turn. At various periods great champions like George Duncan and Tommy Armour have dwelled very much on their left-knee action, and I recall having seen both of them actually raise the heel before moving the club away from the ball, or of timing the lifting of the heel movement so that it gave this impression. This forces the maximum hip turn, as does the right toe pointed outwards at address.

You can perhaps think of players who seem to press very lightly on their left toes as they reach the top of their swing, the heel very clear of the ground; but their swings are usually of the slack variety and they have to fight against a sway into the shot.

Sam Snead in his usual top of the swing position. Sam still keeps his form despite the advancing years and his powerful, flexible, athletic body gives him a great advantage over his contemporaries.

He blocks his hip twist by a squatting action. This gives a very personal-looking position — which one writer described as 'all knees and elbows' — but to me his swing has great rhythm and great poise, not forgetting the power. There is a spring in this pose — the toes are alive, and this ball will be sent 'a mile'.

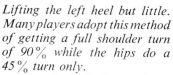

Lifting the left heel but little. Many players adopt this method of getting a full shoulder turn of 90% while the hips do a 45% turn only.

Here the U.S. Open Champion of 1958, Tommy Bolt, is seen in action at Greensboro', North Carolina, in 1956. Bolt has a particularly supple spine and a powerful pair of hands.

Tommy ('Thunder') Bolt, although reprimanded regularly and occasionally fined for his club-throwing activities, is a wonderful golfer with a classical swing, and when 'hot' he can play the most devastating golf. He is an amusing companion, and confines his outbursts to the course.

Rolling very much on the inside edge of the left shoe suits some golfers and can be recommended, but the ankle must be very supple. This action is more powerful than it would appear. M. George Rey, seen (LEFT) in play, is a Swiss hotel director from Zürich and plays in the middle 70's. I am clearly pressing with my big toe (RIGHT).

A high-handicap golfer finishing his swing, compared with my own action. It can be seen how his left arm has collapsed and how badly he has used his legs. This is one of the cases where golf muscles are needed to sort out this action and make it produce better results. No aspirin will cure this ill, a regular treatment is essential.

The golfer on the left plays steady high-handicap golf, even with this action where the legs are not used except to stand on. That his length is limited is not surprising. There is not the slightest inclining of the trunk here — this is unusual. Compare this photograph with that of Richard Chapman (RIGHT).

Richard D. Chapman, of Pinehurst, North Carolina, has been one of America's keenest and most successful amateur golfers for many years. Dick is a real lover of golf and a great student. Here he is practising during a visit to this country. Note the correct position (in my opinion) of his left wrist and arm and club-face.

This photograph of Douglas Bader (LEFT) just about personifies the famous fighter-pilot.

Standing on his 'tin' legs. Head cocked professionally to the right. Pipe and club gripped firmly. Brow furrowed with concentration and determination to give 'that' ball the best possible.

Stanley Holloway (RIGHT), one of the world's great character actors, has what one would call a 'jolly good idea of the game'. His footwork is not classical, maybe, but 'With a Little Bit of Luck' he can get the ball away well.

Many of the game's top players who are thickset of build prefer to use a narrow stance and little footwork rather than risk 'dancing about', as they might need to do if they used a very wide base; this is, of course, very general in the shorter shots.

I have always had great admiration for those players who are able to roll on the insides of their feet. It is perhaps safer than the left knee forward technique, but very flexible ankle joints are needed for this action. As I have got heavier I have used the left knee pushed forward more.

Weight transference is loosely talked of as being from right to left, but this was really debunked many years ago, when Bobby Jones was asked to play when standing on scales with each foot on a separate balance, the weight movement being registered on dials behind him. This really opened the eyes of the golf students, and made some golf books obsolete. The weight never left the left leg, it was seen, despite the loose talk of transference of weight, which still continues, I think, only as an instructional exaggeration. The action of the right leg in the hitting area is one of thrusting and often it is straight before relaxing for the finish with the knee bent.

To get rhythm into the mind of a raw beginner, many instructors will teach a balancing action where the legs are instrumental in transferring the weight really from side to side, but this is not easy to use when there is a ball there and later has to be corrected. It is used to get the body to follow the clubhead in the early stages of learning.

The weight is never so far back on the heels that the toes are not able to move into action and keep the body balanced during the attack on the ball. Good golfers never lose the grip of the ground with their toes.

Wartime photographs of an old friend, the late Sir Arthur Elvin, boss at Wembley Stadium, London, for many years, who loved a game of golf. Arthur was not a golf stylist and certainly never worried about correct foot action. He had not forgotten his cricket strokes — he demonstrates a 'sweep to leg' action in the photograph on the left. LEFT TO RIGHT: *Sir Gordon Craig, Lyn Hart and myself made up the foursome at the Hampstead Golf Club in London.*

In the other photograph he has tried another 'step', but such details did not stop Arthur from enjoying his golf and the company of his friends on the links.

LEFT: *John Panton, from Scotland, a leading golfer for some years now, has earned his place in the golfing history by his iron play and general polished finishing out of the holes. He has in recent years driven poorly, and I have always been puzzled about this, for his action always seems sound. In the photograph he is driving, but here seems to be leaning into the ball as though trying to reach it. His leg action does not seem to fit into the picture — the ball looks too far on the left toe.*

RIGHT: *This shot of Panton was taken after impact (the shot was a good one) so it is not fair to make a direct comparison with the other photograph. There seems, however, a firmness about this particular leg action which will be missing when the swing in the left-hand photograph is completed.*

LEFT: *The Earl of Lisburne, a keen golfer who lives on the Wentworth Estate, Virginia Water, Surrey, is caught here by the camera at the end of an iron shot. The stroke was not unsuccessful despite the fact that the hips have not joined in the action. The shoulders and arms have done well, but the anchored right knee has caused the right side to stay back. This action could be improved with faster foot action. Some regular hip twisting with the shoulders held still in a door frame, for example, would help.*

RIGHT: *Here in my own action can be seen the very points I appreciate in the swings of others. The definite hit past the chin, the resistance by the left leg to the thrust of the right leg, and clubhead overtaking the hands.*

106

Eric Brown (LEFT) *stays behind the ball.*

R. T. Boothby (RIGHT), *an old-time St Andrews golfer, leaning into the ball.*

GOLFERS, DON'T LEAN INTO YOUR DRIVE

EVERY golfer who sends the ball a long way from the tee stays behind the ball when he hits it. In other words, the successful driver is the player who does not lean into his shot. This sounds very elementary, but just watch the driving off on any first tee at a week-end.

It will be enough to show that, even if many players know my statement to be true, few are able to organize their swings so that the ball is *hit from them* and *not with them*. Your head is the centre of the swing, and it should not be allowed to drift forward on the down swing. The hips can go forward, but the head never.

My picture here of that long-driving Scot, Eric Brown, shows him in the correct position. He is giving the ball that distinct thrashing with the right hand which all good golfers manage to supply at the right moment.

The golfer (ABOVE, RIGHT), photographed nearly sixty years ago, has got a good-looking arm swing, but he seems to have got a leg action which does not fit. I should say his excessively wide stance has made his foot action so slow that he has been obliged to use his left knee in this curious way to finish his swing — but unlike Eric Brown he has gone with the ball and not stayed behind it.

Many women golfers are frequently caught by the camera up on *both* toes at impact, as the hips check to permit the hands to bring the club-head squarely and in time to the ball, at the maximum speed. An earlier hit, necessary for weaker golfers, who cannot leave their final acceleration to the last sector of the down swing, is responsible for this hip check.

So bear in mind that you can play longer off the tee if you stay behind the ball, as Byron Nelson is doing here. Do not fall back on the right heel, but even that is better than leaning into the shot with the top of the body. Remember the hammer and the nail. If the nail is sticking out from the bottom of the tee box, you must have the hands in line with the shaft to deliver a square blow.

Mrs Ian Cowper on her toes just before impact.

Byron Nelson: hands nearly opposite the ball and wrists just beginning to apply the missing 85% power — he is well behind the ball.

107

HERE'S HOW THE LEFT HAND WORKS

Y<small>OU</small> all know the old golf axioms about 'hitting past the chin' and 'letting the club-head do the work'. Both are golden rules, but many people have never seen a picture showing exactly how the left hand looks when these axioms have been translated into action.

In the particular stroke shown above, a pitch with a No. 7 iron, I have played well under my head. I have allowed my right knee to ease as the left arm follows on and have let the left wrist hinge to ensure the clubhead can continue on its way.

Many golfers hesitate to take the strain of the shot on the back of the left hand, with the left arm held straight. But there is no danger in trying to hold the arm straight, if the grip used is of the 'two-knuckle' variety (which I employ), because if the arm is not strong enough to stay straight, the elbow-bend acts as a safety valve.

One sometimes hears of golfers suffering from 'tennis elbow'. This is often the painful conse-quence of using a three- or four-knuckle grip and then trying to whip the ball. The elbow joint locked

by the grip of the hand receives a jar if any resis-tance is offered by the left arm and hand.

The only grip with which a maximum whip through with the hands can be employed is the 'two-knuckle' type. As can be seen here, my left wrist and arm have played their rôle exactly in helping the right hand to thrash the ball as the face of the club is brought up square at impact with the left hand.

The point where the actual hingeing of the wrist takes place will decide the flight of the ball. An early hingeing will give a high floating shot, a late hingeing will produce a low flying wedge-type flight — the old push shot, in fact. There is one essential — your left arm must be strong *and educated.*

This is where you can get the full value of a strong left arm. My left wrist position here is ideal. I hope you can all do it.

A COLLAPSE

Here we have a 'let go' of the club-shaft in the hands, as can be seen by the angle of the club at impact. The result was that this ball was smothered to the left. The left arm action is poor, but if the club had not slipped in the hands a fair result would have been obtained, even with the elbows so far apart and the bent left arm. Even a pair of gloves does not cover up entirely a weak hold on the club.

ACCENT ON THE LEFT ARM

Have you ever stopped to consider the impor- tance of improving the left arm in your golf swing? Most golfers know that they must go well through the ball to achieve satisfactory results, and this only becomes easy if the left arm is allowed to play its full part.

It forms the back swing, when the club is moved away from the ball, and the good player, even if the arm is relaxed at the address, keeps it straight, once the swing away from the ball begins, right to the top of his back swing. Then on the way down, and until the stroke is completed, that arm remains straight. It should not bend until the ball is well on the way, unless for a special reason.

All right, you know all this, but apart from a few casual one-handed swings at a daisy with your driver now and again, do you ever try to improve control of your left arm?

You cannot cheat and cover up this weakness, but there is one solution to the problem: Learn to strike the ball properly, not necessarily a great distance, one-handed. Simply guide the clubhead to the ball, then when you try using both hands you will notice the difference. Your shots will benefit enormously.

Little space is needed for this drill, not even a real ball for a start. It is the training of the arm to receive the hit which counts, and that is why daisy-swiping does no good. Teaching the muscles to resist the blow is essential, just as striking a punch-ball or -sack is essential for boxers, in order to train their arms and hands to take the punch they are throwing.

In my picture here I am practising with a No. 4 iron, and though my arm is not quite as strong as

Where the left thumb lies, viewed from the side. Practising one-handed at Westchester Country Club, Rye, New York. The shape of my thumbs can be clearly seen here.

it was a few years ago, I can still hit the ball around the 140–150 yard mark — but not quite every time, I admit. I try to position my left hand on the club in the way that I do when I use both hands, but may go down the grip a little to shorten the arc.

When I say arm, I do not mean shoulder — remember that. Make the arm and hand do the drill and add the body later.

THE SAME SHOT

LEFT: *Heel down — classical hit past the chin action by the hands, with the left hand low and clearly helping the right hand.*

RIGHT: *Left heel up — wrist action stiffer; hands have lifted and so club-face is held more open, a much weaker hit, because the left hand has 'frozen'. It has been pushed through by the right — it has not helped in the action to advance the club- head.*

109

PROBLEM OF THE PLANES

THIS title sounds extra topical just now, but sticking to my own subject, it is quite interesting to study one's own back swing, to pick up a club in the house and do a few swings and notice exactly where your hands are half-way up; and at the top of the back swing how the club shaft lies, while looking into the mirror.

Golfers can observe for themselves, when they make a change in the position of their hands on the shaft; they can check up, too, any change in the position of their feet at the address, but the change of the plane of their swing is often an unconscious one and difficult to check when in play on the course.

Actually it is possible to swing up in all sorts of planes and still be able to pick up the right track as impact approaches. Good players can do this quite easily and instructors often do it as a demonstration, but in the ordinary way it is accepted that the plane or angle of the back swing has a distinct bearing on the plane of the down swing. Incidentally, it is accepted that the golf swing is not a 'circle' and that the paths of the clubhead up and down do not coincide — i.e., their paths do not overlap, they cross.

Golfers began to get puzzled when the slow motion camera showed that in the swings of the leading golfers, when viewed from behind — following the flight of the ball, that is — the clubhead went up on one path and down on another.

The clubhead makes curious designs when its path is traced. There are swings which begin flat around the body and arrive back straight on the line ball-to-hole, or which begin on the line ball-to-hole and arrive back at the ball at impact, definitely coming from the inside. Golfers are classified by their back swings — flat, medium flat or upright. In this part of the swing much experimenting is done and all seek to improve, of course, their stroke production.

Myself, I am about medium flat. When I try to go upright, I pivot less, of course, and I never seem to get into a powerful position. I wish to recommend that players, who are not getting their usual results, should get their professional adviser to imitate their swings so that they can see the path they follow as they go up from the ball. This often provides a shock in golf; that is why you frequently need a talking mirror — your professional is as good as anyone.

While the actual arm action will decide on the path chosen to go back with the club, the action of the hands has the final say in this all important action. Speaking again, in a general sense, I suppose the old Scottish style consisted of a long flowing, loose, double-handed action carried through on a flat plane. Harry Vardon is credited with beginning the overlapping grip, combined with the upright swing, which took the clubhead to the top of the swing on an upright path, a plane approaching more to the vertical.

From my own experience I feel it is quite easy

W. Sharp, a scratch amateur   *Ben Hogan*   *Al Besselink*

to drift unintentionally into another plane of back swing, which for a time, perhaps, passes unnoticed, because unless the down swing plane changes, too, the results do not give away the alteration at first, but eventually bad shots will reveal this unwanted change.

In 1929, when I began to work on hitting the ball from inside to out, I found I needed a very flat back swing to keep enough on the inside of the ball on the way down; previously my swing had been very upright and I had faded the ball. This flat back swing is still used by many players, but it is not possible to say that the very flat swingers are better than the very upright swingers or *vice versa*, though I suppose a medium flat swing is accepted as classical to-day for players of average build.

All long drivers, whatever the actual length of their back swings, do a full shoulder pivot and get their hands high, but the upright swingers get their hands higher than the flat swingers and their right elbows are in consequence further from their bodies. Actually, the very solid, thickly-built players seem to swing flatter than the tall, wiry fellows, but this is from necessity.

The terms flat and upright are very rough expressions really, as there are limits to the planes which are usable, for although vertical and horizontal are obviously the theoretical limits, the actual planes or angles followed fall into a comparatively small range. It becomes, too, difficult at times to say into which category a player falls because, unless he is at the extreme end of the range, he becomes just an average — between the two, a medium flat swinger.

Although my back swing is quite flat to start,

Myself

for I take the club well away on the inside, I arrive medium flat at the top.

Tall golfers usually swing more upright than smaller ones. Opposite is American professional Al Besselink ('Bessie' to his colleagues), with his upright back swing, his club-shaft almost on his neck. He is *really* swinging under his head. Mr W. Sharp, a scratch amateur, uses an upright swing — elbow well away from the body. Compare this with Ben Hogan's flatter swing where the shaft lies below his right shoulder. Yet all will get into the same plane as the ball is struck. My swing is a little less flat than Hogan's, as can be seen.

TO IMPROVE THIS SWING

Here is a swing which would improve if the left elbow pointed more to the ground at this stage. The elbows are too spread, and with a much raised left heel, the return of the body to the right position will be slow, and may be too late for the ball to be well timed. The body angle here is too upright; the trunk should be inclined and the head bent down. This would solve the angle of the left elbow. I often tell women pupils: 'Get lipstick on your shoulders.'

111

MORE PLANES

Seymour Dunn had the same idea thirty years earlier, but had the clubhead touching his canvas frame. This had to happen because the clubhead has no option; it cannot weave about, the canvas holds it. The object was to show the angle of the swing.

I do not think that these ideas help very much in teaching golfers what plane they must follow, but they do indicate how much study has gone into trying to analyse the swing, through the years. I think that my bird's-eye view — looking down on the golfer, where the actual path of the clubhead has been traced, showing its relationship with the direct line ball to the hole — is as educational as these more complicated efforts.

My 'Picasso' is outstanding! It is not meant to trace the exact path of any known swing, but is drawn to show the general attack plan on the ball by the clubhead in my case. The clubhead loops backward as usual at point 1, crosses the up-path at points 2 and 3, but still stays on the inside of the line ball to hole, so that the hit is inside to out.

The clubhead can loop in all sorts of ways, and does in actual play, but this is a general plan.

Sᴇʏᴍᴏᴜʀ Dunn, who has made many fine contributions to the golf game, is seen standing inside a canvas frame he made thirty years ago, to show the actual path of the clubhead during a swing.

This frame just shows the general track of the clubhead but, of course, cannot trace the actual track, as the clubhead weaves about in the air. It loops as it changes from up to down.

In Ben Hogan's book, *The Modern Fundamentals of Golf*, scribe Herbert Warren Wind and artist Anthony Ravielli have tried to expand on this question of the arcs, but it is difficult to give a two-dimensional effect when working in one plane, on paper. They have not succeeded any more than I have here with my drawing (opposite) or Jim Dante has done with his light in the dark (page 114).

Ben has been drawn with his head poked through a huge inclined pane of glass, which goes from the ball to behind his neck, and then he has shown that his club stays all the time *below* or beneath this pane of glass. I show this with a lady golfer.

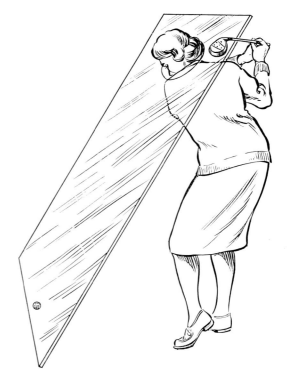

This is a drawing of the path taken by the club for every golf stroke. The width of the arc in the down swing at the point A can be up to 12 inches or more narrower than the up swing, which to me always debunks the straight left arm as a must in golf. Harry Vardon and ex-U.S. Champion, Billy Burke, were two notorious left arm benders who did not demonstrate the wide swing going up. They could argue, 'why trouble to stretch out the swing when you are going to narrow it anyway coming down?' So if in trying to hold your left arm rigid your game is suffering, have another think.

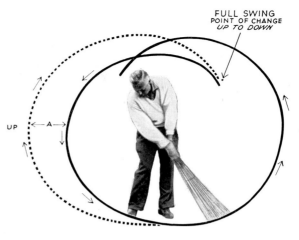

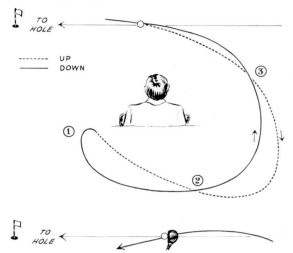

My 'Picasso' shows how the clubhead attacks the ball. The clubhead loops backward at (1), crosses the up-path at (2) and (3), but stays inside the line from ball to hole. The slice action crosses this line, coming from the outside.

A LIGHT IN THE DARK

ON the next page can be seen the path of the clubhead in the down swing. A light on the clubhead and a light on the handle have produced white lines on a dark background.

The change over of the clubhead from up to down in seen in the little loop in the big white arc. The white line near the body shows how the hands work as they come close to the body.

This clubhead arc is much narrower than the arc made in the upswing — the clubhead arc going up would go right off the photograph. I have shown this width going up in the drawing-photograph of myself in action, in a similar plane (ABOVE RIGHT). It must interest many golfers to see how much narrower the descending arc really is, but it flattens out, of course, at the bottom in the hitting area, to attack the ball in 'the back'.

LEFT: The end view (looking after the ball in flight) of the lighted clubhead attacking the ball shows how the slice swing looks — an outside-to-in hit is taking place. The ball will be pulled if the club face is held down (or turned in) or sliced if the face is square at impact.

Note, too, how Jim Dante, the American professional who does these demonstrations, has allowed his right shoulder and his head to come up. This outside-in action is difficult to show when photographed in this plane but seen in the horizontal plane, my 'Picasso' (ABOVE LEFT) shows much better the path of the clubhead. The slice action crosses the line coming from the outside as in the smaller drawing.

Any golfer trying to avoid slicing the ball would have to keep his shoulders facing the front — line ball-to-hole, i.e. — and allow his hips to work separately from the shoulders. The faulty action of the shoulders ruins most swings; golfers use their shoulders because their hands and arms are weak.

113

YOU DO NOT NEED TO WEDGE EVERYTHING!

Here is a little pitch with a No. 7 iron played from a good lie on the fairway to a wide open green, with the flag well back. A simple shot, played the easy way. There is no tension here, no risk of a 'skinned one', a straightforward swinging of the clubhead with the hand doing the work. You see a wedge is a pushed stroke; some do it easily, to others it is unnatural.

If you do not push the ball readily, do not desert your No. 7 iron; it can be a real friend. I find I use it too little. Give yours a try, as an approaching club from all distances.

OR CHIP EVERYTHING!

When you see that the Championship record total for St Andrews gets lower as the years go by — it is now 279 by Bobby Locke — just remember that nowadays all bunkers are raked after each player leaves. They have no real terror any more and at the famous road hole — the 17th — the road is so smooth and the bank so angled that you can easily putt off it — which is what I am doing here! In the old days the road was full of pot holes and there was a steep grass kerb to the pavement and the bank, too, was uneven.

UP WITH THE TIMES

Away back in the early 30's — in 1931 in fact — that great golfing figure Bobby Jones (R. T. Jones, Jnr.), decided to become a professional golfer. He never became quite an active professional in the full sense of the word, but he broke the amateur code by earning money from the use of his name on golf clubs, so that he automatically lost his status as an amateur.

Bobby Jones (he prefers to be called Bob Jones) also made a series of films, instructional films with a sort of story in them, designed to help the average golfer. They were entitled *How to Break 90*. This modest title implied that a golfer could become better than, say, 18-handicap with a little guidance, and although Bobby Jones wrote many sound instructional articles, I do not think he ever taught golf extensively — if at all.

In Ben Hogan there is a parallel of another of the very greatest players, who never teaches but who has made films and produced a series of articles, *The Modern Fundamentals of Golf*, for *Sports Illustrated* (later made into a book published in England by Nicholas Kaye), in which he

audaciously said: 'Play my way and break 80.' So we have two champions, a quarter of a century apart, thinking of a ten-stroke improvement in the value of their advice to the golfing world. I think a sales angle inspired the 'break 80' line.

As I see things, it will be harder to break 80 '*à la* Hogan' than '*à la* Jones'. Why would I say this? I am not merely trying to stick up for the hero of another generation, though I think Jones might still rank as No. 1 on total championship achievements (and after all he did retire aged twenty-eight!), but to point out that his method is the easy one, the natural way, as it were, to play this trying game.

Hogan's method to-day — he had had several since he broke through in 1948 — is quite a complicated one and requires more than normal physical strength and flexibility of body. And even he himself needs incessant practice to play as well as he wants to.

The older method, as one is inclined to call Jones's, is still *really the latest thing*, because while it is classical, it is topical and still modern — like the straight bat in cricket or the straight left in boxing — and so will live on for ever.

When I studied photographs of the swings of champions of nearly sixty years ago, I found much evidence of the Jones type of swing; but there were, curiously enough, examples of this Hogan action, too!

There is in golf, one can truthfully add, nothing new under the sun, but the significant change has been in the mental outlook. The 'break 90' has become the 'break 80' and, who knows, in time

Still correct to-day — they cannot swing better than this. Bobby Jones in his heyday.

someone may come out with a 'break 70' slogan; the public expect it!

One cannot say that the standard of play is much better all round in golf just because millions play now where thousands played a few years ago. But there is no doubt that there are more good players to-day, because of tougher competition. This one has noticed in all athletics. I put much of the responsibility for any real improvement noticed in golf on the great improvement in the equipment, balls, clubs, and even wearing apparel, and maybe tonics and stimulants — as well as the smoothing out of bunkers by greenkeepers in championships after each couple and the filling in of pitch marks and cleaning of the ball on the green. The steel shaft, made by one big company here, which has millions of pounds of capital behind it, and a research department ever striving to perfect it and improve production, has made a great contribution to making golf easier to play.

People sometimes ask me why there is no competition in steel shafts; one firm has nearly all the business. The answer is that it is difficult to improve on the best and any other firm would be obliged to make a next best, or so it seems to me.

I think that since Jones's day (steel shafts became legal here in 1929; he retired in 1930 and won all his honours with hickory-shafted clubs) every golfer has had the same chance to acquire a first-class golf club. Before that, super-quality hickory shafts were 'rare jewels' and the profes-sionals and makers of clubs sorted out these gems and held them aside for their friends.

Whether steel shafts can continue to improve, I do not know. It seems as if the manufacturers have almost reached the height of perfection, but as research continues something yet might turn up which is in some slight way better. Golf-ball makers are still trying to improve their already 'perfect' article, but the rules of golf limit their scope. All the same, golfers get the benefit in the end.

I must get back to my swings. In a brief comparison, Jones, as Vardon did before him, stressed the full cocking of the wrists, clubhead forward at the top of the back swing, and the full rolling over of the fore-arms in the impact area as the clubhead was swung freely.

Hogan's methods, as his first significantly-titled book *Power Golf* indicates, are power methods. A swing, surely, but somehow tighter and more forceful; less graceful, too, in a way, and demanding more strength, than that of the older masters.

It is this accent on strength, so apparent even in his latest book, which shows that golf the Hogan way is a strong man's way, and that means one needs incredible power in the hands, arms and back. I question whether we all have that strength, and to me good golf for the average golfer is easy golf. Do not miss reading Ben's book, but read it with the knowledge that the writer is a very strong person with a grip of steel.

Harry Vardon: no tension here; left wrist under the shaft, like Jones.

Bobby Jones and Glenna Collett (former American Ladies' Champion) seated, with myself on the verandah of Bob's cottage at Augusta National Golf Club, where he is Club President.

RURAL ENGLAND

A beautiful golf picture of part of the Municipal Golf Course at Rickmansworth, near London — with the Sandy Lodge course in the distance on the right. This is a great London district golfing area.

Here is park golf at its best. Note the bracken in the foreground; real lost ball country. These built-up greens on slopes must be hit with the approach shots if a good score is expected.

TELEVISION IN THE U.S.A.

Television cameras behind the 18th green of the Oak Hill Golf Club, Rochester, N.Y., during the U.S. Open, 1956 (Cary Middlecoff won this championship).

Note the caddie in foreground wearing his 'U.S.G.A. Open' vest and the shirt-sleeved gallery. In June the weather is usually very hot, and these Open Championships are a test of stamina. Note the periscopes in use in the background by the spectators.

ARRIVING FOR A WEEK

Why we do not travel by air! We started one American trip with twenty-one pieces of luggage and here we are arriving for a week's stay with friends in Florida. I think they were a bit surprised to see this pile — it just filled the hired station wagon, but we were away from home for three months!

PENNIES FROM HEAVEN!

A Red Cross match, and the crowd obliges with silver on the green. The organizers and players pick up the coins, and the 'inevitable small boy' gives a hand.

WHAT I FOUND AT BOCA RATON

Twenty yards from the front door of Sam Snead's pro.-shop at Boca Raton in Florida grows a thorn bush. I had never seen such cruel thorns before so I simply had to photograph them. My friend Fred Perry, ex-world tennis champion, who showed me the bush, took the photograph of me by it.

A GLENEAGLES VIEW

Not a Turner landscape, but an actual scene from the window of a first floor room at Gleneagles Hotel, Perthshire, our national Golfing Show Piece. The famous Glen is in the centre and the 1st green, King's Course, is the small enclosed light strip just above the trees on the right edge of the photograph. Pity it is not in colour. The story of the Glen and the weather in this area of Scotland, which is notorious, goes like this: 'When you can see the Glen, it is going to rain; when you cannot see it, it is raining.' It is still Britain's golfing paradise — turf out of this world!

TO VENICE FOR GOLF

The Doge's Palace, Venice, taken from the Car Ferry to Lido Island, 1955. The scene that artists from time immemorial have loved to paint. The golf course in Venice (RIGHT) is interesting and quite testing. I enjoyed playing it very much. The City of Venice is really beautiful, unbelievably so, with canals for streets, and as the American tourist said on seeing water between all the buildings: 'This really must have been some place before the floods came.'

119

FIRST CLASS SPECTATORS!

Lord Rosebery and Lady Carr with my partner Sir William Carr and myself spectating at Gleneagles after we had been defeated in the Gleneagles Tournament in 1957. We were sitting behind the 14th green — that exciting long one-shotter.

THE GOLFING COP

A golfing cop looked in on my practice at the Westchester Golf Club, N. Y., one morning. The cop, a scratch golfer, who has several brothers in the golf profession, often brought his patrol car through the club grounds to see who was playing. He loves the game, and it did him good just to watch the ball being struck. 'Made my day', he said. Between us is Colonel J. B. Kaine, from Chicago, a golf 'nut' if ever there was one, someone who really loves golf.

ETIQUETTE

Some years ago I went to see the French Open played at St Cloud Golf Club, Paris, and caught Max Faulkner driving from the 18th tee. His long back swing and very closed club-face can clearly be seen, but what is more interesting is to see his partner, that charming but impetuous Italian, Aldo Casera, already 'halfway to the green'!

Golf etiquette says: 'A player must not move when his opponent is playing' (but supreme concentration can beat that.)

120

OUR LADY

On the golf course at San Remo, on the Italian Riviera, by the side of the sixth fairway, is a statuette of Our Lady, which must surely be the only one on any golf course in the world. I opened the wire mesh door, which protects the statue from flying golf balls, for the photograph. The statue was obviously there long before the course was built, and must certainly be the only one in the world watching and listening to the passing golfer from so near at hand and, I hope, hearing their prayers. My partner, Mr Arpad Plesch, pauses while my caddie takes the photograph.

A 'PROFESSIONAL' PRIEST

'Toots' with Father Len Scannell, an American Roman Catholic priest (attached to the U.S. Air Force), who began life as an assistant golf professional and then went into the Church. Father Len's second love is golf, and what a good player he is, too, for a casual golfer, still around the scratch mark. He must surely be the only golf professional to enter the priesthood.

GOLFING PRIME MINISTER

With Harold Macmillan and Lady Dorothy Macmillan by the 18th green at Nairn, on the north-east coast of Scotland. Mr Macmillan naturally does not get much time for golf, nor is he such a keen player as his American opposite number, Mr Eisenhower, who made time to play at Turnberry, Ayrshire, during his short visit to this country in the summer of 1959.

BLACK AND WHITE

LEFT: *In a New York street with my camera, May, 1957, a study in light and shade. This is about 50th Street, looking East from Fifth Avenue; just an ordinary sized row of buildings.* RIGHT: *Park Avenue looking towards Grand Central Station, New York City, 1929. Note old-fashioned look of the cars, then the latest thing, of course.*

WITH THE STARS

Left to right: Toots, Leo Genn, Victor Saville, Richard Todd, his wife Kitty, and myself on a yacht in Monte Carlo harbour, when producer Victor Saville was making the film 24 Hours in the Life of a Woman *with Merle Oberon. The yacht was used for scenes in the film.*

SURPRISE BET

WHILE practising for the Open Championship at St Andrews in 1955, Ed. Lowery, that old friend of mine from San Francisco, U.S.A., a great golf supporter and a scratch amateur with a wonderful aptitude for finishing 'when the chips are down', said that he would take his friend, Byron Nelson, as his partner, and play me and 'another' the next day for a respectable bet. 'O.K.' I said. 'You are on.'

I thought I could do no better than get Fred Daly in my team. When I walked on to the first tee of the New Course at 10 a.m. as arranged, alone — you have to know both courses at St Andrews (as both are used in the qualifying rounds) — and met them there ready to go, I left them guessing for a minute or two who I was playing with, having told Fred to hide behind the starter's hut.

I think Ed. was a bit surprised when I produced Fred, as the latter proceeded to do the first nine holes in 31 strokes on his own ball, which put us well up, and we went on to win comfortably.

Ed., of course, did not mind losing, as he is a good sport, but he is one of those golfers with a deceiving style, being a much better performer than he looks. But he cannot handle the small ball anything like as well as he does his American-size ball, so he has never shone here.

This same Ed. Lowery, now a prosperous American business man, made the headlines at Brookline, U.S.A., when as a ten-year-old caddie boy he carried the clubs of nineteen-year-old Francis Ouimet in the American Open Championship in 1913, when Francis beat Harry Vardon and Ted Ray in the play-off for the title.

Ed., playing truant from school and knowing the school attendance officer was looking for him to

The ten-year-old Ed. Lowery, playing truant from school, carries for Francis Ouimet in the Open Championship, when he beat Ray and Vardon in the play-off in 1913.

Here is little Eddie and his nineteen-year-old hero. This victory by Ouimet is considered as the beginning of the end of British domination in golf.

take him back to school and punishment, let another boy carry Francis's clubs off the first tee — he was already hidden in the bushes somewhere down the first hole. When the officer had left, he took on the bag and carried his patron to victory. This was the greatest day ever in American golf history and was the end of an era in a way, because an unknown American amateur had beaten our best golfers. Francis and Ed. have been great friends ever since that day.

LEFT TO RIGHT: *Ed. Lowery, Henry Cotton, Byron Nelson, Fred Daly.*

MAC'S MEDALS

I was invited to present Macdonald Smith's trophies and medals, bequeathed by his widow to his old golf club at Carnoustie, Scotland. This was the club from which he played as a young man, before setting off, as so many Carnoustie boys have done before and since, to gain fame and fortune in the U.S.A.

This was a sweet thought. Since this day James Braid's two sons, James and Harry (both successful business men), have presented their father's Open Championship medals to the Royal and Ancient Golf Club of St Andrews.

SIR WINSTON CHURCHILL ON THE LINKS

Sir Winston played golf at Cannes on the Riviera in 1913 with Miss Maxine Elliot, a beautiful American actress, for a partner. It must have been tricky keeping such a big hat on during a golf swing and finding somewhere to hang the handbag!

OUR GOLFING HOPES

Dolores Hope, 'Toots' and myself with the inimitable Bob at St Moritz, July, 1955. Bob's wife is a fine golfer with a lovely style. Bob arrived at St Moritz that year driving a 12-seater bus, full of baggage and his teen-age (adopted) children!

A MODERN CAMERA

I usually remember to take one of my cameras with me as I travel around, because I do enjoy having visual souvenirs of happy days. The days and the years pass so quickly that we finally have just memories. Photographs refresh these memories and give pleasure to others. Here I am using a Polaroid Pathfinder Minute Camera, which can take up to speeds of 1/400th of a second and develops the photograph right away.

PEEK-A-BOO!

The peek-a-boo finish by Humphrey Ellis, a natural golfer who was in the top amateur class at the beginning of the century. This is unusual to-day, but the hands are certainly high. Mr Ellis lived at Rye and played much of his golf there, and I remember when I was an assistant there, around 1924-25, seeing him still play quite beautifully and most consistently.

SUN IN YOUR EYES

The hardest situation to master in the game for any player! There is no trick I know to solve this problem. You either look down too much to avoid the sun getting in your eyes or you look up too soon to follow the ball — one is never at ease. I do not know the real answer to this problem. I hate the sun in my eyes. I find it difficult to swing naturally — I am uneasy. As a film title said, *The Sun is my Undoing*. This is not only true for me, but it goes for all other golfers too!

Here the warm afternoon October sun in Barcelona, right in my eyes, has cramped my spoon shot finish. I have stayed down too long, it looks — I forget where the ball went. I suppose horse-blinkers would be a solution! Still it is bad enough to play like a horse in these circumstances without looking like one!

125

LEARN YOUR GOLF SWING IN THE NETS

I AM satisfied, from my own experience, that beginners learn the golf swing faster when playing in nets. All golfers know that practice makes perfect — no teacher has to sell this slogan — but many have no idea how or what to practise. It is not enough to do thousands of swings to become a champion. If only that procedure was necessary, then the competition would be really fierce.

Few good players, in fact, know how to practise. When learning in a net a golfer can concentrate on his action, building up his muscles without worrying all the time about where the ball went.

Naturally when a player has a swing which 'works', which sends the ball regularly on its way more or less as nominated, practising on the practice ground is important — to learn to aim and to play from different lies — but a limited amount of practice only can be done. Fatigue soon sets in, errors creep in as the golf muscles tire, and then the other less tired muscles begin taking over — and time is wasted seeking corrections for errors which are normal ones.

In a net a golfer can usually hit more strokes per hour than on the course and so give his muscles a better work out. So do not despise the value of learning golf in a net. It is not to be regarded merely as a substitute for the real thing — it is an essential part of golf training. I have a net in my back garden in the heart of London.

INSIDE AN IDEAL GOLF SCHOOL!

LEFT: The inside of an ideal golf school I built in Monte Carlo, on a spacious, well-lit floor above the big cinema in the Place du Casino.

RIGHT: In my own net can be seen:

The bench for the teacher — most essential.

The automatic ball-teeing machine.

The basket for the balls.

The short and long weighted clubs — muscle strengtheners and looseners.

The long pincers to re-tee a ball which falls off the rubber tee, to save stooping.

The harness for the elbow-spreading pupil — saves many words.

The series of charts to explain theories better — they often save endless explaining.

The illustrated golf books on the table — again to endorse your opinion with doubting pupils.

Assorted clubs with different grip thicknesses and lengths of shaft — most necessary.

A screen, to show stills and to project films, my own and those of pupils — not fully appreciated.

A mirror, full-length, very necessary to all teachers.

A large thick coconut mat — these are costly and very expendable, but not better than rubber.

A long-shafted wooden hammer (to keep heads down!) to demonstrate with for the knocking in of the nail, and to illustrate to those who have never realized that a teed golf ball is *hit along and not always pinched with a downward hit.*

IT'S A DIFFERENT JOB TEACHING WOMEN

I SUPPOSE 50% of all golf lessons are given to women and their physical limitations complicate matters for them and call for a different approach. As a young professional, I spent some time experimenting with balloons in my jersey to see if I could understand the female golfing problems! I found that my swing burst the balloons, so that taught me a lot!

Their weaker arms and wrists, more supple bodies and looser joints, add further problems, as there is an overswing to fight against in most cases. I think the wider hips and smaller feet make a difference, too, in the matter of balance.

There is no left arm close to the body for the 36, 22, 36's — the shoulders have to turn first going up and down, which makes the swing look different, to me, at least. Muscles can be built up with exercises, but most women do not want big muscles. They will practise golf, but do not like to do exercises which may help them to progress faster.

Those with a long swing should learn to wait, because it takes a long time to get a clubhead hanging down the back, at the top of the back swing, into the hitting area.

I think women are slower in learning to play golf than men — they have less ball sense. Most women love competing (hence the success of the casinos!) and many dash off to compete for prizes long before learning to play properly. This slows up learning to groove the swing.

I have found that a pair of tight-fitting leather gloves does help women players to hold the grip more firmly, that a double-handed grip is a good idea for those with small hands, and that long nails must be cut.

Another point that women hate to hear is that a softer compression golf ball goes further for them. They *will* buy the hardest-to-compress pro. ball, on the ground that 'if it is good enough for the pros., it is good enough for me'. Women who cannot drive 200 yards should not use a straight-faced club from the tee — a club with loft is wanted.

THE PROFESSORS

Robert Halsall, the Royal Birkdale professional, and myself in the indoor school I built in Monte Carlo. We thought we would look the part for once! Note hammers and tweezers! These are part of the teaching and torture chamber equipment (that's what the pupils called my net). A half-hour's lesson, treated as golf muscle building drill, is more than most golfers can stand.

If an attack is made straight away by the instructor, the muscles naturally begin to tone up. I claim to be able to tame the strongest young lions in my golf net by making them do 'golf gymnastic' exercises.

TEACHING INDOORS

Showing a pupil how.

Teaching in a Dublin department store in 1928. The P.G.A. later forbade all P.G.A. professionals to teach in stores on penalty of expulsion from the Association, but now pros. can have their own golf schools, if they do not sell golf equipment. Crazy world, isn't it? Elsewhere in the world pros. can teach in shops or department stores or anywhere; and in the winter this means an invaluable source of regular income. In Paris, for example, French pros. make a fine living all the year round.

I had my first experience of the damage a golf ball can do in the very net seen here. I walked into the bottom of the net to collect the balls just as a powerful pupil hit a full drive, not realizing I was there. The ball hit my calf muscle and made a rare mess of my leg for a time. Luckily for me I was facing the right way, for such a blow on the shin bone might have done permanent damage. It is interesting to note that the 'cloche' hats in fashion thirty years ago were back again 'à la mode' last year.

WHO SAID THE STARS CAN'T TEACH?

Here is Sam Snead teaching at his summer club, The Greenbrier in White Sulphur Springs, West Virginia. Sam is a fine instructor. He usually teaches from 8.30 to 11.30 each morning. In the photograph (LEFT) he is teeing up the ball for my 'Toots', who loves having lessons from different professors, and in the other photograph watching a pupil who already seems to have an idea of what a good swing should look like. He then practises himself for half an hour, has lunch and is ready to take on anybody for money. I have seen him give lessons at his club the morning of the Annual Festival Tournament in which he plays. Nothing seems to worry his swing — he did a 59 in one round when winning the event in 1959.

DEMONSTRATING MYSELF

I always feel it is important for the instructor to be able to show his pupils, not only just to tell them.
LEFT: *Here I knock off a line of balls left-handed for keen pupils in Dublin, 1958, at the Elm Park Golf Club, right in the centre of the city. And in Belfast (RIGHT) I hit some drives for another class, at the Belvoir Park Golf Club.*

MAKING THE LEFT ARM WORK

Here the pupil tries to copy the master. Dublin, 1958. He can swing the club back very well, but can he attack the ball with any degree of control? That is the question — but practice will make perfect.

YOU CAN'T TEACH STANDING UP!

How like Cotton to say a thing like that! I can imagine many saying this, but do not think I have not taught golf all day long, too, sometimes standing up all the time and in addition bending down teeing up balls for my pupils endlessly — because I have.

This is an exhausting procedure and unnecessary. It is of no value to the pupil for the professor to get physically tired, as once the legs go, the whole body is done, brain and all. The teacher cannot give of his best when tired and the pupil loses. I do not mean that I sit down all the time. I enjoy getting on my legs to do a demonstration to illustrate a point or even to strike a ball, but I have now learned that you can't teach standing up — all the time!

HOW I TEACH GOLF

As I can truthfully designate myself to-day an experienced golfer — for I have lived among golfers and thought principally on and around the game since my schooldays, and have tried to analyse and study the technique of the swing — I feel it might interest golfers to get some slants on 'how I teach the game'.

I have long since realized that each pupil is different and, although the basic problem may be the same, each pupil sees it differently, and somehow translates your same words into different feelings. The main problem of every pupil (there may be an odd exception) is to get his hands, and fingers especially, in control of the swing.

There is always the confusion to be fought in getting the pupil to forget what he sees and to listen to your instructions; this is the weakness of the initial lessons being out of doors on a practice-ground. Most beginners, anxious to get at the ball before they have acquired a swing capable of delivering a true hit, begin to fret straight away, because they do not produce the desired results — 'What did I do then?' 'Why did that one go out there?'

If the teacher is weak, he then begins to explain (often unnecessarily) why such and such a thing occurred, and if his pupil is difficult, disgruntled, the 'I-am-not-getting-anywhere' type, he begins to add tips to his instructions, little 'cheatings' to get results, knowing only too well they are temporary and wasting time.

Of course, there are fundamental laws concerning a golf action and there are fundamentals to be observed in 'doing the swing', but I think that if I insist on my pupils trying to get classical movements, when my experience tells me they will never get a swing like Sam Snead's, then I am not being entirely fair.

That this is so comes frequently before me, because I often get 'desperate cases' to look at — golfers who have been following the classical way and have arrived just nowhere. The fundamentals, as accepted by teachers and students in general, have not worked; there is no clubhead speed, no rhythm and nothing for the effort! What then? To give up? To continue playing as if hitting 'a mushroom with a croquet mallet'? To disregard the classical and try anything?

You see, golf is a game of the hands and fingers working in co-ordination with the other parts of the body; it is a game of two hands, not one hand only plus a passenger; and if body balance is acquired and the clubhead is swung in a free arc, then lots of the so-called fundamentals — straight left arm, braced left side, head still, full shoulder pivot — take care of themselves, they just happen. I have found that if a hit is made at an imaginary ball at eye level, every beginner gets his hands and fingers working properly, pivots well, and gets a lovely free sweep through of the clubhead. The baseball stroke in fact. Then, if the trunk is inclined slowly, often some of the hand action remains. It can certainly be felt.

Golf is a game where the teacher tries to 'sell a feel'. He has to put a sensation into words, which, as everyone knows, is nearly impossible. He can demonstrate what he wants, even imitate the pupil to get home his point, but he still has to sell *feel*. This the pupil gets from exaggerating — too tight, then too loose. Naturally, with very strong fingers, the effective range of tensions is larger, for there are many degrees between a complete 'let go' and a 'freeze solid'. With weak fingers it is often difficult for a player to hold lightly and yet have *enough* grip to stop the club-shaft from turning in the fingers — yet this is what most successful golfers are able to do.

Harry Vardon was right when he said, years and years ago, that the first fingers and thumbs of both hands were the parts of the hand with the most feel. Yet so many golfers pin their faith on the right grip with the last three fingers of the left hand and a 'loose' right thumb. Whatever sort of swing a player does, it is *via* his fingers that his impact with the ball is made, so I teach my pupils to know where the ball is, to trust their eyes and their feel. They hit balls without addressing them, when walking about, with little back swing; these little 'drills' are part of their education. I never like a pupil to stay in one place with his feet, while the balls are placed in the same place for each shot. I like him to learn to walk to the ball, take his stance without hesitation or measurement, and to swing without tension. So I often make each shot a completely new action. 'Walk a pace away and begin again'!

I always thought the secret of Bobby Locke's putting was his unfailing following of a rite — two little practice swings, replicas of the actual stroke he intended, a half-pace forward to the ball and then 'off' — no hesitation, no extra look! If pupils can be taught the George Duncan swing, fall into position, no waggle, then 'off', they learn fast. Hesitation, calculation and reflection often bring too much tension. Yes, I know beginners have to think hard of several things if they can, things which need monotonous repetition for them to sink in and become mechanical, but often there comes a point when the player must trust his swing and 'have a go'.

I get the desperate cases often — golfers whose teachers have given them a classical basis, but who are lacking in an individual interpretation; and they are so conservative that even when encouraged, say, to loosen up their hands, to sway their heads a little with the swing, to allow their shoulders to roll and weave, to fall away from the ball, all of which actions need not pull the clubhead off its path, but which may give greater speed, they are scared to develop a fault and look funny!

No two champions look alike, so why should I expect pupils to look alike? Yes, I know that with a two-knuckle grip, elbows kept together, the wrists fully cocked, the grip firm not tight, the left arm straight, left knee eased inwards, a shoulder pivot of 90°, a live hip action, a transfer of the weight, a delayed hit, head down, eye on the ball, a hit past the chin and a wide, high finish, all

these should add up well; but while that is the target, I will always settle for a satisfactory result with a bit of 'unorthodoxy'.

All golfers love experimenting — I still do — and that is, after all, the charm of golf, because if all the bits of your puzzle do not fit together in one way, there may be another way of arranging them, with slight adjustments. When one critic picked on me for writing in this way a while ago, I could not but feel sorry for his pupils, who were all taking the same medicine — some were sure to get 'sicker'! In the course of a few weeks I have advised one golfer to 'hang on' and tighten up the muscles of both arms as much as possible, and another to loosen up his hands at both the top of the back swing and the finish of his swing — and they are both getting greater distance than ever before — *pro tem.!* For they will one day exaggerate and then will need contras. It may be three months' time even before this happens, but it always does.

THE 'V's' MUST BE PARALLEL

I do not like to see the hands forced over the club shaft so that the 'V's' point to opposite shoulders; it is a sort of 'falsely strong' position.

In photograph 3 the golfer has tried to place his right hand correctly, but this hand will slip off its position on top of the other hand. The 'V's' must be parallel. My pupil got her right hand placed in photograph 1 so far over the club-shaft that all she could do was to push at the ball. Not until the hand was placed as in photograph 2 could she get an effective whip into the ball. The 'V's' are parallel in photograph 2; in photograph 1 they oppose. In photograph 3 the right rides high on the left — too high.

LINES OF COMMUNICATION

WHEN you take hold of a ping-pong bat, or slap somebody's face, no question ever arises that you are not going to deliver a square blow. Your hand will meet the objective squarely. You will not strike with the edge of the hand, with the finger tips nor with the heel of the hand. No matter from what angle you attack, your instinct somehow compensates in the matter and the hit is delivered squarely.

The lines of communication are not taxed because ever since you have moved your hands about you have this gift — everyone has it. Your brain knows exactly what to do to hit squarely.

Your golf club face is really an extension of your right hand and if you can remember this it does simplify things. There are several problems to be overcome and the main one is that your hand is extended by some three feet. You, in fact, are operating your squaring-up programme, often at great speed, at this unusual distance from your brain. Our instinct to do this squaring-up job is still good enough, but the prolonged lines of communication are unnatural.

Children growing up with a golf club in their hands, as young caddies used to do when killing time, awaiting their turn in the caddie yard, have acquired an instinctive anticipation of the delay in the action commanded by their brains. They think nothing of it — it comes as easily to them as juggling does to a juggler who has begun as a child to work the clubs or the balls.

Now a golfer beginning 'This Game of Golf' late in life, who has used his right hand 'direct' as it were — to write with, to chop, to play tennis with, etc. — has had no need to 'think three feet away'. His hand has done whatever he has asked of it. When he begins to play golf, the problem to solve for him is to allow for the delay between the command from his brain and the response by the clubhead; the long extension of his hand is unnatural. So often before the command is executed, there is an interference in the lines of communication, usually by the powerful shoulder muscles.

A golf club weighs a substantial amount and the centrifugal pull is considerable when it starts to move fast, so that strength is required, as well as control, to guide it to the objective, the ball.

The outside of a wheel, the rim, has to move faster than the centre or the inside of the same wheel to keep up with it, and this, of course, is so in the golf swing — where the shoulders are the hub and the hands are halfway down the spokes; the clubhead being the rim. Once the shoulders (the hub) get ahead of the hands (the rim) it is nearly impossible to catch up — the clubhead will arrive late.

I have found that many golfers never realize that their lines of communications are faulty. They are never adjusted correctly and no allowance

LEFT: *You slap the ball with the right hand to deliver the club-face square.*

RIGHT: *Just let the club-face turn away naturally — your instinct will always bring it square at impact if your lines of communication are right and you have the necessary strength.*

is ever made for the delay in executing the command given by the brain. When I tell a golfer to hit earlier, as I often do, because more golfers hit too late than too early, he is usually incapable of getting the clubhead alone to respond. That is why I stress so much 'individual training' of the hands, hitting balls with separate hands, so that they become able to work as ordered.

In timing tests of the human reactions when car driving, the time taken of the delay between seeing a danger and pressing the brake pedal is 0·7 seconds, with a racing driver. In a driver swing it must be an appreciable amount of time too, between the command given by the brain and its execution by the clubhead. It is to the hands, of course, that the order is given, but this extra three feet of arm as it were makes this a tough problem to solve. When I see a golfer get right down the shaft for a short pitch or a putt, he is only making his clubhead a shorter extension of his hand, and it must be a sound move because his lines of communication are shorter.

When you try to hit earlier you have to allow for a delay, so do not be afraid to go to what feels like an extreme action. It is unlikely that you will over-do it and, if you do, then you have only to move 'the hub' a little faster, which is easy to do, and all is well again.

In putting a simple movement of the clubhead is performed and yet those whose putting fails as they get older are really failing in their lines of communication — their reactions to square up the blade. As I have always realized that this instinctive squaring up is one of nature's gifts to us all, I have never seen any point in doing an action which is unnatural, such as trying to hold the club-face square, shut or closed purposely, to get it more square at impact. You cannot get a club-face or a tennis racquet face more than square at impact. To achieve this square position with the latter, the player never thinks of measuring its squareness on the way back; he just swings it back naturally, allowing it to open.

A golf club can be swung the same way. Let it go back naturally — it wants to roll open. You can bring it up squarely anyway and if you count on your right palm to face the hole at impact, as you would in slapping, say, a tennis ball hanging on a thread, then it is easiest to do, *if you have the right 'V' running up the shaft when you grip the club.*

REFLECTIONS ON TEACHING GOLF

THE teaching of golf is an interesting career; it is rewarding, too, not only in a financial way, but in the satisfaction it gives in bringing happiness to people who are troubled by the difficulties in playing the game — by helping them to play better.

Whether your pupil is a raw beginner, being initiated into the golf swing, or a champion seeking the missing clue to put him on his top form, the instructor gets the pleasure of achievement, if he is able to produce better results.

When beginners are taken along from their very earliest days, they are dependent on their teacher, they trust him and follow his advice as the way to strike a golf ball is unfolded to them, until they get wings and 'leave the nest'. They rely on his guidance. They might learn to swing the club in a net indoors, one of the best places, I find, to learn the golf action, but they can learn to play golf only on the course, and their first practical introduction to the rules and etiquette is most important. I have found that any time spent in introducing golfers thoroughly to this part of the game brings as much satisfaction as anything else to the pupil, as his golf career advances.

It is not necessary to be a champion to enjoy playing golf; everyone can play and enjoy the game. But to play and enjoy the game, the rules must be known and followed. One of the rules of life — to be grateful for all mercies — is, I find, often overlooked particularly by golfers, who take too much for granted and therefore often fail to enjoy golfing to the full. As I have grown older I have realized, I hope in time, that I have spoiled for myself so many days, by allowing a poor golf score or the result of a match to affect my life; on the contrary, I ought to have been grateful for the opportunity to play on a perfectly groomed course, with nice people about me, on a lovely day. In fact, even on *any* day, as it means I have been granted that day on earth!

All of this leads me to the difficulty the teacher often has with the good player who is off his game, who, not having found for himself the missing link, seeks the professional's advice. If the instructor can spot the trouble and so fix up the swing, all is well, but usually the main satisfaction obtained is only the financial one, because the good player feels it is some sort of reflection on his golfing knowledge to admit he had a tip even from the pro. But the really great champion is never too proud to seek help and acknowledge openly whence it came.

I recall that in the final of one Amateur Championship many years ago, that golfing idol of the American public, Bobby Jones, was down at lunchtime and playing very poorly. One of his staunch admirers put in a long-distance call to his old mentor Stewart Maiden, asking him if he could suggest something to help 'The Bobby' he had formed to play better. Said Maiden: 'Tell him to knock the Hell out of them — they have got to go somewhere.' This was all that was needed, and Bobby went on to win his match.

I have found that for every grateful pupil there are several who readily blame the teacher for their loss of form, or their inability to regain their top game after a consultation. On second thoughts, I do not suppose that the golf teacher expects gratitude any more than the doctor does; he only feels he is doing his job. But it does strike him, as I know from my own experiences, that there is much real pleasure to be gained from starting a golfer off into that unending maze, 'This Game of Golf', where at each turn of the path a new hope is kindled, that *this* path may really be the final one, and the end of the road to permanent success.

Every golfer should be grateful to his initiator in the game. The task of a club professional is more difficult than the task of the city professional teaching in a net, because his *clientèle* is in a way restricted. He may take some outside people, of course, but generally it is only the members who support him, whereas the city instructor draws from a vaster public. The fact of his *clientèle* being restricted, and that they all play together at the same club, can make his life very trying, as it only

needs a few ungrateful and unsuccessful golfers, ready to put the blame on his lack of ability to teach *them*, rather than on their own limited talent, to start a malicious whispering campaign against him, which can cause much unhappiness.

I have noticed that many capable but sensitive professionals have continually changed around, from club to club. I assume they cannot fight the clique of ungrateful pupils, who go around the corner for lessons and who will *always* go round the corner, because they have not realized that they are now playing their 'usual game', and it will always be poor. They think they are great golfers, held back because no one discloses the missing secret to them.

This malicious criticism of teaching methods used by any given professional often drives a capable teacher to rattle out a series of accepted platitudes which, when chewed over at the bar, are found to be indisputable. It is rather like a doctor giving everyone the same tonic medicine, whereas if a different, contradictory prescription is made, one often hears: 'He told me just the opposite; he must be nuts!'

Whenever I get on to the teaching subject I feel I can speak with some authority, as I have spent many hours teaching, both on the course and indoors, and have had great satisfaction helping along raw beginners and champions alike. I have suffered, also, all the hurts which come from remarks of thoughtless pupils, who, after all, I suppose, are only following the usual trends of life. It is a wonderful world and our golf game is a wonderful one, *and* I am beginning to enjoy it more. It is a pity that tournament golf is so tiring, but then, after all, that is only a part of life now, not all my life.

THE GOLFING DUKE

The Duke of Windsor is one of the world's keenest golfers. He loves practising and during the past forty odd years has played with and had lessons from many of the game's top players. I do not know whether his garden comes before his golf, but he loves both. When this picture was taken, we were spectating at the St Cloud Country Club, Paris. He is quite a student of the game and enjoys his practice sessions; he enjoyed learning to 'hit and stop' one day, as a way to building up impact speed.

THE PRO. AT WORK

Giving a pupil the feel of a steady head — this 'sells' a feel better than many words. The teacher is in no danger really, and especially if he has long arms and can trust the pupil to hit the ball and not his foot!

'From here the right hand brings the clubhead through — as the left begins to hinge.' Most pupils have not got this action naturally, but by holding the club as I do here and making the clubhead accelerate, the pupil gets the feeling. The left wrist does not just tow the clubhead along indefinitely; somewhere at a variable point with each player, and for various shots, it will help the right hand to whip the clubhead through. It gives a back-handed kick on its own.

THE MINIMUM AND THE MAXIMUM

I am not, in showing here a small golf clubhouse and large golfing centre, claiming to have found the smallest and the largest of their types in the world, but to me they are good extremes. I think the charming little country cottages, which are the clubhouse of the Piltdown Golf Club in Sussex, are unique and I adore the name on the garden gate. The course is very interesting to play and not nearly well enough known. The welcome is in keeping with the old English charm of these cottages. The big golf centre is at Boca Raton in Florida, where Tommy Armour was for two decades, and where Sam Snead now has his winter headquarters. This is a wonderfully equipped golfing paradise and the weather is ideal. Few British people, alas, will ever visit it, until our dollar situation improves, but believe me, it is fun to play there.

BLOW-ROUND-LOOK-THIRTY!

I HAVE been playing golf with a beginner; at least, with a golfer who, at the age of sixty-six, has decided to see if he can play golf decently. Although he has owned a set of clubs for years, he has not been on a course many times and he has had but a few lessons. This is the departure point.

Now this particular golfer — I imagine his medical adviser suggested that he should take more exercise — is not interested in hitting balls on the practice tee, and in this he is not unlike thousands of other golfers and would-be golfers. He wants to get out on to the course.

So the problem is to get him to observe all the essential rules of the good golf swing without suffocating him with advice. My pupil, an intelligent, reasoning person, soon began to evolve for himself a series of slogans, as he called them, from my advice. And to help him to perform the 'rites', he condensed them. This seemed very practical to me, and, I must say, in some degree original, because I had not previously put these condensed slogans to my pupils.

Luckily his grip of the club is good. This is always a big advantage, because it means that the swing can follow standard lines and the chances of delivering a square blow are increased. The swinging of the club backwards and forwards with the object of hitting the ball he had likewise grasped; his movement, in general, was looking like a golf swing. But he had been told to follow through at all costs, that the follow through was the life's blood of the swing, and he *did* follow through, but, alas! very slowly.

My immediate problem was to make his swing more business-like, to get some violence into the action, because the golf ball will not go a long way without receiving a good send-off at impact.

The usual right shoulder intervention, in an effort to increase the power of the blow, caused the inevitable head-up. *So 'look at the ball' was ordered.* This golfer, stocky, powerful, and thick-necked, had already acquired the habit of taking a deep breath prior to beginning his back swing, which caused tension and made the elbows separate. To play well the air must *always* be expelled from the lungs before beginning the back swing, so I tried to teach him to empty his lungs and to blow out the air. 'Whistle', I said, 'or blow like a whale.' He got this idea readily, but the point was to remember it along with all the other things. *Relaxation at the address was ordered.*

The arc of his swing was too upright; the club went too straight back from the ball and so his pivot was limited. The immediate correction of this was to swing around the body, to take the club on the inside. *A flatter swing was ordered.*

When this going round the body began to work, it was noticed that the club continued round the body on the follow through; it did not want to go towards the hole even for the essential foot or 30 centimetres after impact. *Throw the clubhead towards the hole was ordered.* These were the four keys at the moment to a successful shot, *when* they could all be remembered!

Not long after, I was intrigued to hear my pupil saying on the tee: 'Blow-Round-Look-Thirty!' He had condensed my advice into single-word slogans which appealed to him so that he could remember better what to do for every shot.

The big difficulty with teaching beginners is to get them to remember what to do; it is impossible to concentrate fully on more than one thing at once (hence the success of the stage and real-life pickpocket), and golfers usually have a lot of things to remember until they can become mechanical swingers. This idea of my pupil was brilliant. It certainly worked for him. It does not mean he is able, each time he strikes at the ball, to carry out his 'rites' and hit the centre of the back of the ball with the centre of the club-face as well, but he has a positive programme to follow and it works surprisingly often.

It does not mean, either, that these slogans, as he calls them, will necessarily be the operative ones for a long time — he will need to add or substitute others — but four seems about the right number: not too many, not too few!

The ideal is just to have one slogan, or 'peg to hang your hat on' when you play; every golfer, even the greatest champion, always has a daily positive thought, one tip on which he concentrates, which balances his action. This tip changes repeatedly and the trick is to find the right one for each day.

Norman Von Nida played some of his greatest golf, he told me some time ago, following on a chat with me when he first came to England. He came along to my flat in London soon after he arrived and we talked about Australia and his golf and I asked him if he had ever tried emptying his lungs before striking the ball. He said No! But he was not long in trying it, soon found it helped, and collected some big prize money. Fred Daly whistles his way round the course and goes on whistling even during the address. I have never asked him

137

if he does it for luck or because he knows it relaxes his body prior to swinging. I fancy the latter but it may be a semi-unconscious act.

My pupil is still making progress — his 'Blow-Round-Look-Thirty' is operating. *Blow*, to remind himself to empty his lungs (to relax, that is); *Round*, to remind himself to swing the club around his body (to pivot); *Look*, to remind himself, to see the ball being hit; *Thirty*, to remind himself to send the clubhead straight through to the hole after impact. (Thirty for 30 centimetres, as that is about a foot and he had been brought up in the metric system.)

These slogans are personal, but on saying them to myself it strikes me, as I write, that they might work for lots of other people, too.

THE AMERICAN INFLUENCE

Trying to look like Walter Hagen — a boyhood dream in 1921 when fourteen years old, with hair plastered down and wearing cricket shirt and bow tie. This is how I thought one of my heroes looked.

Then a few years later, aged seventeen years, when assistant at Rye Golf Club, looking very American! Black and white shoes, light-coloured plus fours and sleeveless pullover, with a driver I made myself.

RECHARGING THE BATTERY

WHILE so many of my friends, who go to the office for business and play golf for pleasure, envy me because I play golf for business (as well as for pleasure) and stay at home for the office, many overlook that fact that it is quite an effort of self-discipline to keep in the best physical shape, when over fifty, to be able to play one's best at, say 11.38 a.m. or some other awkward time on a given date some weeks away, when the starter says: 'Play away!'

The hard thing to do is to find a sort of happy medium where the necessary physical preparation can be undertaken without tiring the heart too much. Some few years ago I forgot I was forty-six years old and overdid things in my preparation, but I trust I have learned my lesson in time and now have found the right way to 'recharge the battery'.

I have become sold on the idea that 'it is later than you think' and that 'a *real* rest is essential now and then to every very active person'. I think that a main part of the rest is to be somewhere really quiet, where there is none of the usual every-day roar of the modern world and where nobody expects you to do anything other than what you want to do, or what you should do; nor eat anything but the things you like and which are good for you.

I was sent to Vittel, a spa in the Vosges, in France, some 200 miles from Paris in an east-by-south direction, where there is lots of pure moun-tain air and peace, and it is there that I now go annually to recharge the battery. There is a good golf-course there, too — that seems a necessary part of my life wherever I go — and if I do only a few holes daily and hit a few balls out on the spacious practice ground I feel I am not letting my golfing muscles go too soft, while following the cure and thereby getting a 'decarbonise and a battery charge'.

There are so few places anywhere in the world where one can find a hotel where the client can just please himself without feeling he is annoying the staff, by keeping the hours he desires, or where he can eat exactly what he wants without being thought eccentric, and where there is real quiet. Yes, that is it — the quiet, the silence, once so aptly described as 'awful' by a poet. Where do we find it? I have friends who sleep with ear-plugs to get away from a sort of general noisy atmosphere which seems to exist in every conglomeration nowadays, especially in summer when windows are left wide open.

To me, as I continue to play in a few tourna-ments regularly, the most trying thing is a bad starting time — the sort of 12.10 p.m. time, such as I had on the second day in Paris in a recent French Open, is about as bad as I can get. It means eating a hurried lunch at 11.30 a.m., to carry you through the next three hours when you are not the least bit hungry — if it is ready!

I know this seems a lame sort of excuse for poor play, but it means a break from the general routine of life, and I have found no way of getting round the various obvious disadvantages. In America, with a round of golf taking anything up to five hours, I must say they do get the food angle at most country clubs well organized. At the ninth or any suitable hole, there will be a snack-bar complete with tables where can be found hot steak sandwiches or the like and all sorts of

'The Cottons' snapped at Vittel, France, where we do our cure annually, of drinking the waters and resting. I think this sort of yearly rest is essential in everybody's life. Most people's holidays are hectic affairs, more exhausting than otherwise. At Vittel all is designed for rest, even the climate. And do I sleep there! I would hate to disclose how many hours a day, but it sets me up for another busy year. The waters are especially good for gout, kidneys, bladder and uric acid excess and the bottled water is sold throughout France and Europe.

beverages, and so a start can be made at any hour and nourishment taken as required, even if it means letting a few couples through.

I must say the understanding catering staff at the St Germain Golf Club did a great job during the French Open Championship there in 1958, for food was available at almost any hour of the day and with a smile.

When I am asked: 'What would you do with our young golfers to bring them into really top class?' I feel the first point would be to get them into the best possible physical shape and then teach them to keep 'the battery charged', because major tournament golf is a great mental strain, too, and as it is so easy to get run down so I would teach them to eat properly.

To-day in this world of rapid air travel, our leading golf players dash about all over the world collecting substantial sums, without giving a thought to the distances covered and the great physical strain. Who can blame them, because every athlete has the dread of wondering how long will it last? 'Shouldn't I cash in now, while the going is good?' I think, for some, the best advice is: 'Yes, get it all now!' For others, a longer-term view might be better — 'to make the motor last longer', as it were.

If I might bring up my own case again, I have tried to spread things out because I thought my method and swing would stand the test of time, and because I thought I owed it to myself, my friends and my family to go on living.

I see so very few around me really making a big effort to study their own health and enquiring how best to keep 100% fit. They put up with self-inflicted ill-health because of ignorance, and keep going on corrective medicines. One is free to choose how one takes care of 'the battery'. I wish I had been taught more about this part of life at school.

There must be many hotels, I imagine, in really quiet spots throughout the world. Do we use them enough? Or do they expect the clients to suffer their routine or can they just please themselves and laze, relax to the full and allow nature to do the rest?

SHAFTS AND THE MAN

IN this series of photographs the shaft can be seen to be alive. In the photograph of Mr Bruce Coffin, of Maine, U.S.A., the shaft of his No. 4 iron is bending slightly as with his double-handed grip he drags the clubhead away from the ball.

In the photograph of Mr T. N. Danforth, of Piping Rock, Long Island, U.S.A., driving, his True Temper shaft is already whipping to help gain clubhead speed.

Mr E. Bromley Davenport, of London, is seen just prior to impact, and the hit could be a little late, as the shaft seems just to be responding to the hand action. There is no doubt, though, that the hands are now about to let the clubhead pass them.

In the photograph of myself at the after-impact position for a drive, the steps in the shaft can be seen; this shaft has really helped me in this shot.

In the picture of Frank Stranahan (opposite), his right arm is beautifully bent (every good golfer hits the ball on a bent right arm, it straightens only after impact) and is already beginning to 'lever'. So many instructors and golf theorists claim that this is impossible — a club must be swung with the clubhead pulling the golfer through. This works as a beginner idea, but the power players make their own rules. This is not camera distortion. Do not think this is a deception by the camera, it is just what happens when strong hands set out to get the clubhead 'there' on time and are going flat out.

Mr P. A. Vaile, an American theorist of a generation ago, called this 'the Buffer action' and he saw it repeatedly in Bobby Jones's graceful swing of over thirty years ago — the left arm being the

Bruce Coffin   *T. N. Danforth*   *E. Bromley Davenport*

140

Myself, just after impact

Frank Stranahan

buffer against which the right struck.

In the photograph of myself (right) as the club-head overtakes the left arm, the shaft, firmly held at the grip end as in a vice (it must always be so at impact; it can be freely and more loosely held in other parts of the swing, but at impact never otherwise than firm) has just finished its whip forward. This means, in this case, a well-timed shot; the maximum clubhead speed for the effort applied. The helping whip of the shaft can be imagined and the ball can be seen on its way.

George Will, the promising young Scot, seen on the next page, is beginning the 'tug' down from the top and the shaft is already 'experiencing' the change over from up to down. In my swing, seen to the right of George Will, the way the shaft responds to the pull down can be seen clearly, too. Note that hips are already in place.

This bend in the shaft is often seen in a strong swing, so as you look at the other photographs, you can observe that the shaft really does flex helpfully during the swing; it is not a rigid extension of the arms. Note, too, the way the left hand has loosened in George Will's last three fingers, to give life to his action.

In the photograph of myself driving (next page) can be seen the little flashes of light from the steps of my chromium-plated shaft. This is not altogether a camera shutter distortion, but the shaft spring-

Myself, with firm grip at impact

ing the clubhead forward as the power is applied.

Here I am putting all the strain on the hands; they are not funking their task, as I find occurs in the swing of many handicap golfers. My hands have been educated to take the strain, but they need constant training or else they get slack.

141

George Will beginning the tug down

Myself compared with George Will

The rest of the action merits the word classical. Note that this is actually at impact, for there is also the blur of the ball leaving the club-face.

The right shaft will always help the stroke, if the hands are used correctly, but to show how photographs can deceive, the ball seen as a white blur on the right bottom corner of the photograph of Sydney Jacobson ended up over the road seen behind the player — out of bounds. The club-face was slightly closed and the hit was exceptionally inside to out. Both the head and the weight are well behind the ball, but a faster foot action would have saved this shot and got the hips more round. This 'medium' grade shaft has really whipped into the ball. Every player has an ideal steel shaft, because they are made in numerous grades of whip, but few golfers ever bother to experiment.

The stars take lots of trouble to find the right shaft for themselves.

Myself driving

Sydney Jacobson

CLUBHEAD SPEED

Mr William Barnett of Donaghadee, N. Ireland, sent me this poem which is full of sterling advice and sums up the search for clubhead speed. It was originally written for the instruction of his children, Elisabeth and Robert.

GREAT clubhead speed I do aver
Is something which does not occur
By Grace of God or chance remote
But only after careful note
Of certain things which you must do
To make your swing both strong and true.

But right away let me explain
That all advice will be in vain
And each good shot a blatant fluke
Amid a life of slice and hook,
Beyond all hope, beyond the pale,
If on one vital point you fail.

*You cannot play good golf for long
Unless your hands and wrists are strong*
For they alone provide the strength,
The great control, the extra length
Which you require to murder par
And hit a golf ball straight and far.

So start then with a proper grip,
Two well-trained hands which will not slip,
A balanced stance with knees quite bent,
Your head well down, your eyes intent
Upon the ball which, with no doubt,
Must now be struck from inside out.

Commence your swing with firm left hand
And do your best to understand
The clubhead must be taken back
With action smooth, along a track
Close to the ground and so until
Your arms a leisured arc fulfil.

Some further points should not be missed,
So make your fixed right leg resist
The turn of hip, the upward lift
Of braced left arm, the lateral shift
Of weight which if not done with care
Will wreck your swing beyond repair.

Your wrists must flex as you swing back
But never let your grip go slack.
Your shoulder turn should be complete
And once again I will repeat
Your fixed right knee provides the clue
To strength and balance known to few.

With body poised, right elbow in,
The downward swing can now begin;
Try very hard to keep control,
Avoid the plague of shoulder roll
For you must learn there's nothing worse
Than this which is golf's greatest curse.

Just let your shoulders roll about
If you're intent on finding out
Why bluebells grow among the trees
And gorse sways gently in the breeze,
Why fairways are not wide enough
And every course seems choked with rough.

Make no mistake, your hips must lead
And turn away with lightning speed
To build up pace and clear the way
For waiting straight left arm which may
Now strike a really powerful blow
Down past your steady head below.

It has not moved, nor must it yet,
Until your strong left side has met,
Without a break and like a rock,
The forward thrust and fearful shock
Of all the power on which you call
At this late stage to hit the ball.

This latent power, so long contained
But now released and unrestrained,
Explodes from your right hand and wrist
To whip the club without a twist
Straight through the ball and very low
As far as outstretched arms will go.

But pray with all your might and main
That your left wrist will stand the strain
For if it quits and fails you now
May heaven help your shot and HOW!!
*You cannot play good golf for long
Unless your hands and wrists are strong.*

There's nothing more except that you
Can now complete the follow through.
Have all these thoughts at your command
And then I know you'll understand
Why 'length' is yours if you succeed
In building up great clubhead speed.

IS SWINGING EVERYTHING?

WHEN I have travelled around America and played on the many fine courses there, and enjoyed the hospitality of our golfing cousins, it is impossible not to make comparisons and to feel that some of the differences, unfavourable ones, would not exist if our country was in better shape financially — we really are the poor cousins!

There is no place, it seems, on our side of the ocean for the super golf clubhouse with all the services, from barber-shop to grill-room. Golfers at home still consider their clubhouse to be a sports pavilion to change in and get a meal in. Despite all this luxury, the American golfer still has the same golfing problems. In fact I am beginning to form the opinion that once the very top layer of great amateurs and pros. is removed, the mass of golfers do not play, perhaps, as well as our club golfers, despite their regular marking of their scores. They still find it as much a problem to control the golf ball as does the rest of the world.

Now that the top players in America are real power players (and have been for a decade or more) it is only natural that the average golfer copies the stars, and he follows their advice and listens to their explanations of how they do it. He gets the latest golf book and, forgetting that he differs physically from Snead and Hogan, he sets out to copy the double-jointed 'Slamming Sam'

and supple, whip-cord-muscled Ben Hogan. It is for this reason, and because many of the younger teaching pros. admire, quite naturally, their heroes, and try to teach as they play, that Ernest Jones, the veteran English pro. from Chislehurst, in Kent, is doing such a big job in a quiet way in his New York City (Fifth Avenue) school, teaching American golfers to swing the clubhead and to use their hands.

I always call in, when in New York, to see Ernest who, despite the loss of part of a leg in the 1914–18 war, manages to keep moving about all day. He works five days a week from 9 a.m. to 4 p.m. in his small upstairs net where he explains and demonstrates his idea of the golf swing.

I had only a brief chat with him on a recent occasion, as he was booked for months ahead and our gossip came in a pupil's time. He was giving a beginner his first lesson; it was interesting to hear him explain how he sees the golf swing. Ernest still uses his original penknife (a large sort of Boy Scout's knife) with a loop at one end, to which he attaches a silk handkerchief and which he swings to and fro to demonstrate that, if he jerks the hands, it stops the free swing of the pendulum and does not make the end go faster. Then he has a tennis ball on a 4 foot strand of strong elastic cord which he swings backwards and forwards around

LEFT: *Joe Carr, the 1958 edition, with an orthodox grip and swing. He was then Amateur Champion for the second time.*

CENTRE and RIGHT: *Ernest Jones. He makes your golf go with a swing, using his pen-knife and handkerchief and a club all together to show what he means by 'how the clubhead should swing'. Just try to keep these together — you will learn much.*

Macdonald Smith's hands at the top of the back swing. 'Mac', born in Carnoustie, Scotland, lived most of his life in America. He had a smooth swing — it was fairly flat — and his flexible left wrist helped to get the club shaft to the horizontal as can be seen here, but his left arm was never fully extended. Old golfers consider his rhythm, with almost a pause at the top, second to none.

his body, and then, when he twirls it faster, the elastic stretches, to show the centrifugal force. Besides these items he has a small piece of lead and a soft practice golf ball, which he uses to remind golfers of the force of gravity, dropping them at the same moment from the same height. His well-worn slogan 'A golf club cannot be made to travel faster that you can swing it'; some amusing drawings; some photographs; some letters from pupils, and other framed slogans adorn the walls of the small, modest two-room suite on the seventh floor of this old building, whence 'earnest' Ernest has been expounding the gospel of swing, not hit, for many, many years.

There are, of course, pro-Jones and contra-Jones students whom I have come across, and his pro. colleagues at the clinics where he has given demonstrations and lectures are puzzled by the insistence of his use of the words 'swing' and 'hands' in his replies to their questions.

Ernest's playing career was checked by his war amputation, but he has played good golf on one leg (as have, of course, other players), and from a stance on one leg the action of swinging the club can be better felt, and good hand action is essential. I do not think the golfing world in general disagrees with Ernest. They cannot; his idea that the hands are even 90% of the game can be true, but his doctrine ends abruptly, because he does not go the step further and tell his pupils HOW to use their hands better in order to advance in their golf. I find that most of my pupils have a swing. 'No golfer has a perfect swing', said Ernest. 'I have never yet seen the perfect swing', he con-

tinued, but he failed to explain what a perfect swing is. Golfers want to know how to build up their muscles so as to do their swing in the right groove and how to increase their power and so the control by their hands.

It is quite correct to tell a player to 'swing the clubhead', but he still has to deliver the club-face square to the ball at impact, and a driving machine shows that just 2° off the square at impact can make a very big difference in the direction. And so, even given a good swing, a player's fun just begins.

There is one point about a golf-swinging action which is overlooked, and which I did just mention to Ernest in our brief chat; I felt he disagreed. It is fine to sweep the ball off the tee, when it is perched up high, but the same action will not always work for shots from the fairways, especially when the ball is lying tight; the bottom of the arc of the circle has to be flattened out as the hit is made (a descending one also), while Ernest laughs at the thought of the lever or buffer action being present in the swing. I am satisfied it exists, and can be taught to improve the muscles of the hands and arms. It is a first-class muscle-builder and gives a golfer the necessary resistance that all muscles need, if they are to be fortified.

You can go on swinging a club till you are blue in the face and never gain a yard in length unless you work on the 'heart of the swing' — the just-before-and-after-impact section. This cannot be glossed over. I know this is true, because I built up my muscles years ago by this method, and so have many of my pupils, to be able to hit the ball farther and straighter.

THE TEXAS WEDGE

THIS amusing addition to the golfing vocabulary is now in generally accepted use by our golfing cousins in the U.S.A. and refers to a run-up stroke with a putter from off the putting surface. To the real beginner, who never gets his ball to fly properly, this shot seems at first to be distinctly simple; to the improving golfer or the middle range of handicap golfers it is *infra dig.* and cowardly; but to the champion playing for great honour (or a living) it is worth its weight in gold, for an extra chance to get out the putter is never overlooked.

Having played golf for many years regularly on seaside links and others areas of perfect golf turf such as Walton Heath, Ganton, Sunningdale and Wentworth, one finds numerous occasions presenting themselves, when to use a putter from around the green is just plain intelligent — not even being smart.

On some courses, where all the bunkers round the green are bowls with no lips on them,

Alec Hill, ex-Walker Cup Captain, has quickly spotted that he can get a good result with his putter from this hard-bottomed sand trap which has no lip to it to stop a clean run of the ball. The good players always look for this sort of percentage shot — the poor golfers are afraid to play it as they think it 'looks wrong', and risk the difficult shot. (Cannes, 1958.)

bunkered balls can be putted out very safely; and once the drag of the sand is known, the job can be done quite accurately too. This is exceptional, for most bunkers have lips on them, but never overlook a chance to putt out of trouble.

In the Palm Beach tournament, on the Wykagyl Club's course at New Rochelle, N.Y., in 1956, Lloyd Mangrum, playing from the rough, at the drive and a pitch 12th hole, overran the green strongly with the inevitable 'overflyer', which comes from a heavy grass lie, and shot through a little shallow pot bunker, a sort of 'sand splash' which is placed behind the green to punish this very shot. His ball lay beyond the bunker on grass but on a bare hanging lie and the bunker was between him and the hole, some five yards on the green, which sloped away from him, too. He was in a real mess, because the shot he had to play was scarcely 'on' if he took a lofted club from his bag, for he could never stop the ball, and he risked 'thinning' it (or half-topping it, as we say) as well.

He decided to take his aluminium putter — he used this type of club normally — and run the ball into and through the sand. He put the ball just one foot off the cup — a delightful stroke, which qualified as one of the real 'Texas Wedge' variety.

I wondered how many club golfers, or even home professionals, would have 'seen' this shot straight away and then have gauged the sand drag so wonderfully. It was a fluke, if you like, to put it quite dead, but to me, as a victim of this great stroke, it was brilliantly conceived and executed. In his 1953 Ryder Cup single with Dai Rees at Wentworth, Jack Burke, who won, told me later that he owed his win to his use of the 'Texas Wedge' at the 35th green from some 40–50 yards from the pin. From this distance he putted the ball to just two feet from the hole and won a hole he could have lost, for Rees was on the edge of the green and looked like getting a 4. In fact, the success of the 'Texas Wedge' shot shook Rees and he took a 5 to Burke's 4, and the match ended there and then.

There are many occasions in golf when even the large-sized ball does not sit up enough to be safely gripped on the club-face. Then, for the delicate shot to the pin, the putter can be relied upon, when there is no deep hazard between the ball and the hole. There is no technique to learn for this stroke — no right or wrong way to place the ball, to swing, or to grip the club; all that is required is to know what happens in the circumstances, and that means to have played similar shots before.

Yet, how many players even trouble to drop an extra ball during a practice round and see what does happen? Answer: None!

Many players still go on trying to get an academic stroke from a bad lie; often, with the small ball, the back of the ball is very hard to get at, even for the greatest expert with a golden touch, and yet, there in their bag, is the simplest club to use of them all — the putter!

I know there are golfers who think that putting the ball from long distances from the hole ruins their putting touch, but I think this is mostly mental. There is no need to flog the ball; it rarely

Arthur Havers putts from well short of the putting surface. Beyond is Sandy Herd practising his stroke, while waiting his turn to play. Sandy Lodge, 1941.

Tournament Circuit in the U.S.A., where most events are played on inferior courses, where the fairways provide bad lies. And so these hardened tournament players, 'driving for show and putting for dough', as they say, never play a fancy stroke

Dr J. A. Flaherty, of Addington Golf Club, Surrey, uses the 'over 40 finger', as Gene Sarazen calls this extended right index digit, for his approach from off the green. Gene himself often putts this way now.

requires the 'bash' many golfers give it when just on the fringe of the green, for the usually short fringe takes but little off the stroke. I find that I get the best results when I 'comb' up on the ball, 'hit it up and over', and so get it to bound forward, and not nestle down in the longer grass — a half-top, even, will do.

Sometimes even a No. 2 (or No. 4) iron will not get the ball running as nicely as from a putter face. Golfers who think they can do better with a No. 9 or a wedge are recommended to make a test, when out practising, to check on this question. I know what the result will be — the lofted clubs will stay in the bag.

The curious name of 'Texas Wedge' grew to popularity, I gather, from use on the Winter

Would you putt off this slope behind the 17th green at Temple Golf Club, or would you chip it? Most golfers would take a wedge to-day and they would be wrong very often, for they could fluff it, but with a putter I proved it to be a much safer stroke and in half a dozen shots with each club, the putter won. There is no risk with a putter; all I had to do was to get slightly ahead of the ball and play it to run — roll it over as it were. The 'weight' of the semi-rough is easily judged; although to many it will seem dangerous, it can prove to be a stroke saver. Keep it in mind.

LEFT: *Eric Brown plays his putter from the fringe. He attacks the ball very definitely with all his clubs — even his putts are decisive. Walton Heath, 1958.* RIGHT: *Not the 'Texas Wedge'. Bobby Locke — an all-time great around the green — uses his real wedge, not a putter. Note the left wrist action here, club face held down or closed. He has the 'tempo' when playing this stroke of a man with great confidence. Walton Heath, 1958.*

— they play the safe shot all the time.

The big advantage, of course, about taking the putter is that the player does not have to worry about the line; he knows he can aim reasonably straight with this club, anyway, and he cannot really fluff the shot, so there is only the distance to concentrate on.

Results can be obtained, of course, with any type of putter. In fact, I have seen some of the best 'Texas Wedge' shots played by Cyril Tolley with both an aluminium and a wooden-headed putter;

and on courses like St Andrews, when they are dry and bare, the run-up with a putter is on, from as much as 80 yards from the pin. Then, however, it is a bit of a guess for anyone!

A putter has often come to the rescue as a left-handed club, but generally it is just the 'Texas Wedge' for the champions, when not being used to hole out — that legal 'fifteenth' club.

The loftless centre-shafted clubs are not as easy to use as a 'Texas Wedge'; the blade putters seem to be the easiest to employ.

Myself putting from well short of the green. I must have had a bad lie, from the way the ball has jumped, but I took the putter intentionally — for safety. There must have been a danger of fluffing it, which I had recognized. I seem to have given the ball a decided whack, no easy soft stroke here. Cork, Eire, 1953.

148

It is not often the camera catches an actual bal-looned shot. This golfer, Stafford Ingham (the race-horse trainer), hit under the ball, catching it on 'the name' (the mark of shame). From the action, if the ball had been hit in the centre of the face of the club, it is likely the shot would have been satisfac-tory. Often a skied shot comes from leaning into the ball and hitting it steeply. In this case it was simply hitting on too low an arc, or teeing the ball too high.

I would like to see the chin behind the ball and, of course, fewer knuckles, because here can be seen how the left arm and hand are blocked and so no whip of the clubhead is possible. The action of the hands is a push—even the right arm is pushing, not whipping.

HIGHEST TO-DAY!

'HIGHEST to-day!' This very threadbare golf-ing expression is trotted out regularly and almost in harmony by the three other members of any four-ball anywhere as the fourth member goes under his tee shot and balloons the ball when he drives off. Of course, he could have *teed the ball too high*, and this is probably what he mumbles anyhow, by way of excuse, as he waits for his ball to descend at about half its usual distance from the tee — but it could be for other reasons!

The most common cause of this hitting the ball on the name, except for teeing too high, is swaying forward with the down swing, leaning into the shot and attacking the ball on a steep arc.

Some players, of course, genuinely go under the ball, having teed it high up and having expected to hit it cleanly; this can be a miscalculation as to the exact level on which they are swinging, but with the deeper-faced driving clubs of to-day this happens comparatively rarely, which is the main justification for using a deep-faced club — it is possible to have a 'real go' at the ball and swing to slightly different levels and still get a fine result. With the very shallow-faced drivers used by Harry Vardon, for example, the swing had to be exactly on its level to make a centre-of-the-club-face contact. To-day there is quite a big margin for error with the deep-faced driver, but the ball does not go any farther, alas!

For there is still only one sweet spot. I have never used regularly the 'Jumbo-faced' drivers. I have had them, but the test of maximum depth

of driver face for me is to be able to get one up off the fairway if the lie is extra good, and with a very deep driver this is very difficult to do.

A hit down and through, the bottom of the arc coming well after the ball, is ideal for iron club play and, of course, can work for shots with lofted wooden clubs, too, but as these through-the-green clubs are of necessity shallow-faced (they do not work if deep) the arc must not be too steep or else the ball can touch the top edge of the club, and the ball is skied.

A steep back swing can cause a chopping action.

149

Hitting the ball too steeply. This tall veteran golfer, 65 years of age, uses a No. 2 wood from the tee, because he has a tendency to squeeze the ball and he can be seen in a typical pre-impact position. All would be better if the hands were not quite so far ahead of the club at this moment. The impact would then be more that of driving the nail into the post squarely at A in the drawing below — not B as now; but the loft on the club saves the situation. Here is a case where the use of a driver or No. 1 wood would be a handicap.

It is the top edge of the clubhead touching the ball below its centre which sends the ball upwards and can leave quite a noticeable cut in the ball, too!

A steep back swing can cause a chopping action, but very often the player's desire to make sure the club-face is turned in, not out, at impact, causes the arc to become steep on the way down.

Swaying on the ball, when trying to hit late, and weakness of the arms, encourage the player to have a go with what he has got, and so his larger and stronger body and leg muscles cause him to thrust himself through towards the hole, doing work his arms and hands should be doing on the clubhead. The hit becomes too late! Yes, the hit can often be too late if it is too slow. The powerful players, whom golfers like to copy, have such strong hands and arms that they can flash the clubhead through and overtake the instinctive lead of the body; but the poor player never gets the clubhead to catch up.

Before the war at Ashridge Golf Club, when I had classes of players generally in the low handicap range (they were at the time the keenest players around), I found that the big majority hit just a little too late. They were obsessed with the idea of getting into the classical pose at impact, hands in line with the ball (when viewed from the front), club shaft almost horizontal, but they forgot to use their right hands. This meant that the hit was always steep, and the shaft and left arm were never quite in line at impact — they could not be, unless they stopped the arms, so the hit was late and steep and the ball was never hit squarely in the back; it was always slightly squeezed or pinched.

From tee shots, and tee shots only, the ball can be caught on the upward path of the arc, and with advantage because then the ball can be driven forwards and upwards without being squeezed, except from the effect of the few degrees of loft on the club essential, of course, to give back spin. A quite straight-faced driver (no loft) is never workable because it can give no back spin; even a loft below the normal minimum of 7% is of little value either, because it does *not work*. Do not waste time on this experiment; dozens of great players have tried and tried in vain with a putter-faced driver hoping to get more length.

The best tip for those who regularly sky the ball

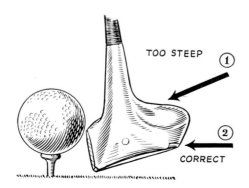

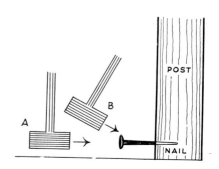

is to have a picture in your minds of staying behind the ball — hitting it from you. Imagine driving a 6 inch nail into the side of the bottom of the tee box with a long-handled hammer — if you leaned into your hammer stroke the nail would be bent; it could not be hit squarely on the head. In my golf schools I always have a long wooden hammer — light to swing — and a suitably placed nail. In practice the nail was not hit hard as it entered too easily into the soft wooden head, but it just supported in a practical way the theory of the stroke of 'the hammer-and-the-nail', and often left a lasting effect on the player: 'Better than a thousand words is the experience.'

A steady head until the ball is hit is still sound advice for non-skying, and I repeat this because I read now and then articles by various people, often of doubtful qualifications, encouraging all golfers to let their heads go with the swing of the club. Now and then, this sort of exhortation can bring results, I know, to those who block their follow through by locking the head. I have given it to myself in sparing doses, when there has been a tendency to freeze out all rhythm and freedom of movement by 'locking the head', but generally the old adage 'keep the head still' is a precious one to follow.

Keeping too much weight on the left foot at the address encourages the body to stay ahead of the ball and prevents width of back swing. A ball actually can be hit 'on the name of the club' if the player hits *too early* on soft turf, but only if he allows his clubhead to slap into the turf behind the ball and so, in fact, lowers his arc level. A 'sclaff' would be a good word, but this would not occur on a tight firm fairway lie.

PLAYING THE BALL AS IT LIES

Anything to save a stroke. Mr Allan Ryan, an American golfing friend, plays one on to the green out of a pond at the 10th hole on the Seminole Golf Club's course in Florida — and the shot came off.

Luckily the ball was just on the water's edge and the water was warm! In one of the larger ponds on this course there was at the time a big crocodile, but I did not see it.

Here is a newspaper report as it appeared with this picture: 'Cotton plays a sucker on the 2nd green: heavy showers made conditions at times very bad, and here Cotton has taken a No. 7 iron to cut the ball up to the 2nd hole. The divot was not sliced right out.'

This incident occurred at Addington in 1936. The latest rules allow for repairing of pitch marks and ball cleaning.

AS A CAPTAIN

I have been a Team Captain a few times in my life. I began young in this job. I suppose my schoolmasters thought I was not afraid to take responsibility. Anyway, here I am in the middle of the front row in the Alleyn's School 'Under 14' Football and Cricket Teams of 1920.

Later I captained Ryder Cup Teams — the 1939 Team which did not travel to America, as the war came, and then in 1947 and 1953.

Here are the teams of those latter years.

1947 Team. BACK ROW. Left to right: Cdr. R. C. T. Roe, James Adams, Max Faulkner, Eric Brown, Charles Ward, Reg. Horne. FRONT ROW: Sam King, Fred Daly, Myself, Dai Rees, Arthur Lees.

1953 Team. BACK ROW. Left to right: Harry Bradshaw, B. J. Hunt, Peter Alliss, Myself, Harry Weetman, James Adams, Eric Brown; FRONT ROW: Max Faulkner, John Panton, Fred Daly, Dai Rees.

GO ON, MOVE YOUR HEAD!

THERE is no doubt that the head does move during the swing of many top golfers, and while this is contradicting my theory and that of thousands of other instructors, the fact remains that the head moves with the swing *to some extent*, in many cases. Art Wall's head (he is a top American pro.) is calculated to move five inches.

I cock my head to the right before beginning the back swing and then on the way through it follows on a little but there is no really free turn until after impact. I really hit past my chin, as can be seen in the picture below.

The timing of the release of the 'head', as it were, is instinctive in the play of good players. The beginners have not got the trick — it has to be acquired.

Just look at these well-known players. Ed. Dudley of Ryder Cup fame has allowed his head to follow the club slightly — compare this with my iron shot swing.

Look at Peter Nelson, the racehorse trainer and a low handicap golfer — he, too, has 'gone with the swing'. There is no hard and fast rule on this, but if your neck is supple you had better look — this is my advice. Even in putting Bobby Jones's head has gone with the club.

Peter Nelson

Ed. Dudley

Myself

Bobby Jones

153

ON WOMEN'S GOLF

Check shorts

Joyce Wethered

Jessie Valentine

I HAVE never understood why lady golfers have given up so readily the golf skirt made to the exact width of their stance, for the doubtful elegance, but possible convenience, of the ski pants or the shorts.

I always felt that if Joyce Wethered was one of the most consistent strikers of a golf ball ever known in her hey-day, it could have been because she always used the same width of stance for her full shots. To help her, her skirt just fitted snugly against her knees during the swing and particularly at the address of the ball, so one variable factor, and an important one, was thereby eliminated — the taking of a different stance each time. I have never tried playing in a skirt, but it does have possibilities!

From the days of the ankle length skirt to the briefest of shorts — which have even caused comments in the nature of a reprimand in recent times in American female tournament golf circles — covers a brief span of sixty years, but the shorts are here to stay and on certain individuals have gallery appeal extending far beyond their nattiness and mere convenience in wear.

I have not had a chance to see all the great players of my time in women's golf, and while I have always the normal appreciation of the play of the 'power types', I have admired more the accurate play of the what might be called the weaker feminine stars.

Mrs Smith, the former 'Bunty' Stephens, or Mrs Jessie Valentine come to mind as petite yet beautiful strikers of the ball; they are also very long indeed 'yard per pound of weight'.

My personal opinion matters little in the question of how women golfers should dress, but I much prefer to see skirts on the golf course rather than

Skirts on the golf course. Left to right: Enid Wilson, Maureen Ruttle (Mrs Garrett), Joan Pemberton (Mrs Cooper).

shorts, tight ski pants or even 'Oxford bags'.

Why I admire the skill of the first-class fragile female is because the weaker the golfer the more accurate needs to be the hit to get decent results; power players can get satisfactory results from blows, say, 80% perfect. I have even broken a course record when continuously striking the ball poorly, mishitting it, but managing to keep out of trouble. A lady champion, with few exceptions, can never do this. The late Mrs Babe Zaharias and Miss Pam Barton could be the possible exceptions.

One of the first points any instructor notices when taking on a new pupil is how long are her finger nails, because the socialite with the 'Chinese' nails starts off with a major problem, how to grip the club firmly without the nails cutting into the pad of the thumb. I ask that my pupils cut their nails, otherwise it is a waste of time trying to play golf. I often lose this point and the pupil!

154

I have found, too, that a double-handed grip both thumbs down the shaft gives a stronger hold of the shaft for most women and cuts down the risk of a 'club turn' during the execution of the stroke. A pair of tight fitting gloves of thin, tacky leather helps those with tender skins to play and practice, but those loose sort of web-fingered, dry feeling, gardening gloves are almost worse than no gloves at all. There is a slip within and a slip without!

Owing to the obvious individual physical difference of women, there is bound to be a big variation in the way a golf swing is made and it is clearly easier for the smaller-bosomed female to do a neat golf swing. One thing is certain — it is unlikely on account of the power factors alone that a woman can swing like a man: size of collar bone and bone and muscle structure alone make the difference.

There is always the tendency to overswing, because smaller collar bones and more flexible joints make a long swing the rule rather than the exception and the long path back of the clubhead to the ball brings in all sorts of problems.

I have often tried to get long swinging pupils to cut down on their back swings, but it is not easy to get the woman who plays for fun to slog away at tightening up the muscles — she prefers to make do as best she can.

In all classes of golf, professionals get asked: 'Why is it that little Mrs B. can hit the ball so far and yet I, so much stronger and bigger, am miles behind off the tee?' The answer: It is the difference in the quality of the muscles which decides everything. I think that if most women golfers would try to build up their hands and strengthen their fingers, without paying any attention to the swing, they could take six strokes off their score right away.

COMING TO THE BALL FROM OUTSIDE

An excessively upright back swing has brought the club slightly on to the outside of the ball as impact approaches (right), and the resultant flight will be a fade. Nothing serious, but a length loser for the handicap golfer.

The raised left heel at this point shows a desire to hold the body steady until after impact.

SWINGING THE CLUBHEAD PERFECTLY

You can never go wrong if you swing the clubhead at the ball and keep the back of the left hand to the hole at impact.

Here Mrs Dolores ('Bob') Hope shows that, for lady golfers, the swing the clubhead theory is sound — it works for all male golfers, too! Note the up on the toes footwork — very common in women's golf. Wearing high heels may be a cause for this spring up on the toes, but I think the earlier hit is more likely to cause it. It is O.K. to copy.

USING THE THUMBS

Mrs Diana Critchley, a former Lady Champion and a really natural golfer, whose temperament has been one of her great assets. Her double-handed grip and use of her thumbs (LEFT) have been two of the reasons for her sound play, with the minimum of practice, over more than twenty years. Here in these photographs can be seen the two 'V's' pointing inside the right shoulder (LEFT). The fully closed club-face (CENTRE) and the correct impact position (RIGHT), with the hallmark of a champion — the bent right arm at impact — are clearly seen. Diana is in her garden at Wentworth, Surrey.

A DOUBLE-JOINTED LEFT WRIST

A wider stance would improve this action right away and cut down the back swing a little, but a double-jointed left wrist causes this overswing, and there is not much anyone can do about tightening up this swing. Half the male golfers would like a little of this freedom.

NO RIGHT HIP

A strong recovery which could have been helped with better foot action, which would have released the right hip. The right foot in at address would have helped. Mme K. Hennessey playing golf at Cannes.

156

PROETTE

I met Marlene Bauer Hagge, one of the top American golfing proettes at Boca Raton, Florida, and asked her to do a swing for me. I did not play a round with her, but our foursome followed the game in which she played and I was impressed with the way she hit the ball.

With a long flowing swing in which she gave the ball 'everything' she sent it a long way. This is a typical costume for golfing in the hot weather in America.

SOUND ENOUGH, BUT...

This is sound enough, but why such a narrow stance? The point I like about this photograph by Pierre Carrivet of St Cloud is that the hands stood up to the task — they held firm. The usual raised left heel, essential to early hitters and very common in women's golf, can be seen, as well as the triangle 'shoulders-arms', which some instructors seek as a key.

HALFWAY TO A CUT

Halfway to a cut ball, the club-face was never brought quite square enough to the impact and so came on to the ball open as well as coming from outside at impact. The ground slopes strongly from the left; therefore, as the aim was bad, this ball never had a chance! The right spot to aim at I have marked 'O'.

YOU ARE WRONG, MR COTTON !

WHEN I get on to controversial topics in my regular articles, correspondence pours in from readers, who obviously enjoy the theory of the game and going that little bit farther on. I wrote in one article that an active golf federation, the committee of which is well known to me, approached me to find out if I had any opinions on the teaching methods of their professionals and the ever increasing number of bad backs occurring among golfers. Could they be related?

This is a dangerous subject to get on to, but I felt that, provided it was considered objectively, I would say my piece, for while I had no wish to criticize colleagues, whose many brilliant pupils testified to their successful teaching, I had an opinion on this point.

For I had noticed for some years — since the war really, and the era of that flood of American golf instruction books from their top stars — that many pros. and amateurs had been teaching and preaching and demonstrating the gospel of the shut club-face, left forearm in line with the left wrist. I have stressed in my lecturing at golf clubs all over the country that the shut-face method is a strong young man's method; it will not always work or suit everyone, and it is the sort of method that is hard to build up.

I was asked repeatedly to give more details of my method than I had given in my earlier golf book *This Game of Golf*, so that brought me to write *My Swing*, not with the idea of offering it as everyone's ideal way to play golf, but as suggesting an easier all-round, 'wristy' way of hitting the ball where the minimum of strain went on to the spine itself.

There is nothing perhaps new in anybody's method when one comes down to it, but as the post-war trend had been to offer books by great champions on how to play golf, and there was a common theme in all of them which showed the body doing tremendous winding and unwinding, I began to be anxious as friends of mine joined the 'slipped disc' brigade and some even got themselves a plaster chassis.

Funnily enough, few victims admit it came from that, but some have confessed and others have given it away following some sly questioning. No one who studies the game will be ignorant enough to say there is only one way to play golf, but it is possible to select for trial a method which can lead to trouble without realizing it.

Every good point in a golf swing can be exaggerated, and one finds that beginners especially are inclined to exaggerate a tip that they have found useful. They need continually bending the other way to strike a mean. It is from the natural

LEFT: *Lloyd Mangrum.* CENTRE: *An old golfer, with a shut-faced action, using his left wrist in line with the forearm and right thumb on the shaft. Note that the ball is right of centre.* RIGHT: *A young professional, J. A. Little, playing in the* News of the World *Match Play Tournament at Walton Heath in 1958, is snapped with a fully shut club face at the top of the back swing. The young man's swing, I call it.*

tendency to exaggerate any successful tip or movement that comes the bad back, for most people do not have a wholly flexible spine and it gets sort of set, in sections, and bends and twists readily only at certain vertebrae, low down the back, so that all the strain — and it is considerable — comes on this limited section.

Why should I tell you to play only when your spine is in condition to twist easily and freely? This will take weeks of regular exercises, and you are playing golf for fun, after all. No; it is simpler to play with the accent on the bits of body you use all the time — the hands, arms, and wrists — and if they are limited in their ability, then all sorts of extra body twisting will only add a small percentage of speed to the clubhead, but a lot of danger.

You must pivot, of course; this does not hurt, if not forced; you must lead with your hips coming down — everyone does this — but you must not expect a whipping action by your spine to supplement your wrist speeding-up, without risk. This is what it comes to, for the shut-face player counts on the body action to hold open the face of the club as impact approaches, and as his wrists are not pronating to the full to increase the snap of the clubhead, he expects the body to add to the push-through of the clubhead as well.

Bernard Hunt, one of our successful young professionals, plays from 'shut to open' using a very short back swing. Here he is with his hips right through but with his shoulders almost square still; this requires a supple body — he has it.

LEFT: *This is a very personal action by professional American golfing star, Claude Harman, a former Master's Champion. Claude is a great golf student. I have not seen him play for a few years, but in his best days he used this method. This requires great strength of arm and great flexibility of body — if you do not believe me just try it and see! Claude interlocks his fingers.* CENTRE: *Tom Haliburton, a neat, stylish golfer of the 'open-shut' class, is seen in action at Turnberry, 1957. His open club-face will snap squarely on to the ball, the hands hardly advancing now while the clubhead continues accelerating.* RIGHT: *Johnny Revolta, an 'over fifty' former American Ryder Cup player, practising at the Augusta National Golf Club. Note the beginning of the back swing. This does not mean that he cannot close the club-face still with his left wrist action, but it is well on the way to be open now.*

159

On reading what I have written several times, it occurs to me that some readers may be confused about the expressions 'shut' and 'open' face. I do not use the expression 'shut face' in a derogatory sense and therefore do not seek to alleviate the imaginary stigma it implies by switching to the expression 'square face', as I have seen recommended, but a shut face, fully shut, is where the club-face faces the sky at the top of its backward path.

I do not like it because I have seen where it finally leads players, as the years go by — to be smotherers of the ball. All good senior players to-day use their wrists to play golf, and play from open to shut. This is evidence in itself.

Players with very young, strong, supple bodies can do well by using much body-work and minimum wrist action to get control, but less flexible players and older ones are advised to play with as much wrist whip as possible.

Once you cut out wrist-rolling you cannot close the face to bring it square to the ball; it must be held closed throughout. There are intermediate stages, admittedly, and these are always the ones to study. The extremes do not really ever pay off so well in golf.

I enjoy teaching spells abroad because pupils arrive from all parts, many fully convinced before they arrive that I teach a one-track method and are often already poisoned against my 'method', and so are surprised to find that golf, as I see it, has the accent on swing, rhythm, relaxation, and this only comes from training of the arms, hands and wrists.

Tension is everybody's undoing. When I see what has happened to many trussed-up golfers, I am happy to feel I can help them, to see the golf swing in its real light.

P.S. I am not wrong, you know!

WITH MY CAMERA

CATCHING THE PHOTOGRAPHER

Douglas Glass from New Zealand is one of the world's top portrait photographers and one day he came to take a study of me, with my 'tools'. Here he is in action studying the best pose. So I got my own back and caught him with my camera. He is not so fierce as he looks.

CATCHING THE ARTIST

Kees Van Dongen, the wonderful Dutch impressionist who lives in Paris, painted 'Toots'. I thought it would be a good idea to get the old maestro at work with my camera. I think my photograph is a bit arty, too!

160

AN OLD GOLFING RIVAL

Captain Horton Smith and I played a charity match in Scotland in 1945. The snap (LEFT) is of Horton Smith in the days of his greatest success, 1929–30. In 1957 Horton had a lung removed and his golfing days looked over, but he still bravely carries on as a successful golf pro. in Detroit.

A GOLFING FIELD-MARSHAL

During the war, Earl Wavell, on leave from active service, came down to Ashridge, Herts., for a game. Our distinguished Field-Marshal, a Scot, always loved a game of golf, and, despite the handicap of one eye, soon got on to his game. This would be about 1940 or 1941. Here he is following a spoon shot. I make sure the camera is in action.

PSYCHOLOGY

Alec Hill, Walker Cup Captain in 1955, and I were responsible for restarting the Pro.-Amateur golf series again, when we took teams to Hoylake in March, 1955. It was almost Walker Cup v Ryder Cup.

    Giving the Amateurs a start of two holes in a 36 holes match, my team won comfortably. I think my two holes up 'psychology' will always be right — the pros. lost badly on level terms three years later at Turnberry. Raymond Oppenheimer had won his point and the match by insisting on playing level. I would not concede this point, but thanks to his four-year training plan the gap between amateurs and pros. has now narrowed considerably.

L

MY FAIR LADY

Rex Harrison and 'My Fair Lady', my wife, 'Toots', at the Sands Point Golf Club, Long Island, U.S.A., where we spent a day golfing with Rex and Stanley Holloway, stars of the great show, which took London by storm, too.

TWO OLD FRIENDS AND RIVALS

Myself and R. A. Whitcombe in 1938. Reggie died in 1957 after a long illness.

A TRAGEDY

Holding my godchild, Rosemary MacKenzie, at her christening outside the Savoy Chapel, London. Bob MacKenzie, a P.G.A. founder member and chairman for many years, was a great friend of mine, and I was deeply grieved when he was obliged to give up his P.G.A. membership on taking up a teaching job in a store. Because he was thought too old to hold a club professional post, he had to earn a living this way. I always feel this blow (being 'thrown out' of the P.G.A.) killed him.

AN AMUSING DAY'S GOLF

An amusing day's golf which began with lunch at my house in Ashridge, provided by John Quaglino and Henri Sartori from the kitchens of their famous London restaurants, Quaglino's and the Coq d'Or, and was followed by a match in which Charles Graves and I played against them.

I do not remember what the match was or what was the result, but we all ate too much.

FROM LEFT TO RIGHT: Sartori, Graves, myself, while Quaglino drives.

AN INTERESTING TABLE

At a News of the World *dinner. The camera caught an interesting mixed bag. I had to make a speech that day. I note I am already working on it. I always prepare them during the meal, rarely before.*

Round the table, left to right: Myself, Sir William Carr, Henry Longhurst, Sir Bracewell Smith, Sir John Hay, Charles Taylor (later Sir Charles), Sir John Nott-Bower, Raymond Oppenheimer, and Joe Davis.

OUR MALIGNED PRESS

It is assumed that our golfing press spend their days in the clubhouse sleeping or drinking, but this is away off the beam in fact. Just look at this team. Left to right: Geoffrey Cousins (London), Charles Scatchard (Yorkshire), Percy Huggins (Scotland), Maurice Hart (London), wearing ear muffs, Bob Ferrier (London), all watching golf in icy conditions at Turnberry.

Henry Longhurst likes to play as well as write.

163

BINGO

'Monty' — otherwise our great Field-Marshal, Viscount Montgomery — was a travelling companion on the 'Queen Elizabeth' coming from the U.S.A. in the spring of 1957. Here we are with Mrs S. L. ('Heddy') Simpson playing Bingo.

'Monty' sent me this charming letter — he is a keen follower of all sport, though not a golfer himself.

ISINGTON MILL.
ALTON.
HANTS.

16 June 1957

My dear Henry

I am delighted that you did so well in the Daks : the first of your tournaments in this country. Now go on and win the Open.

Good luck to you. And my kind regards to your wife.

Yrs. sincerely

Montgomery of Alamein

WITH M. FRANÇOIS ANDRÉ

Myself correcting M. François André's grip of his famous umbrella outside the Casino at Deauville. M. André, besides being a 'Casino King', has three golf courses in his companies — at Mougins, near Cannes, La Baule and Deauville.

LIFE AT RYE

Life at Rye Golf Club when I was a seventeen-year-old assistant, lodging with the pro. and his wife, Mr and Mrs Alec Simpson, in a house right on the first tee. In those days the radio was almost the latest thing. I took this photograph. My set of earphones are perched on the back of the settee while I worked the camera. Scene in the winter of 1924. I must admit this rather dates me. I refer to Alec Simpson's use of his hands on the next page.

164

A SECTION ON HANDS AND FINGERS

IN this section on the hands which I have tried to break down into useful chapters, there is much repetition, I fear, but while bringing out various points, I found I inevitably wandered back to 'finger tension control'. I attach so much importance to this part of the golf swing that maybe in this, I hope, pardonable repetition, the reader will become more impressed by its value. Golf is 85% hands.

HANDS ARE THE KEY TO GOOD GOLF

IT is true — and always has been — that a golfer is as good as his hands. I remember how, by just building up the wrists and hands of a pupil, I reduced his handicap, in just a few weeks, from 15 to 6.

As a boy assistant to the late Alec Simpson at Rye, Sussex, I was always very impressed with the way he used his hands. He was really a one-legged golfer, for a war wound, which left him with no hip-joint on his right side, caused him to play off his sound leg only. He could play very well.

Alec Simpson used to chalk a white dot, the size of a golf ball, on the cork linoleum of the professional's shop, then obliterate it by skidding the sole of his pitching club on the floor. He was so accurate that he could scrub out the chalk circle in six strokes, or even fewer.

This particular accuracy was seen in his ability to cut the legs from under the ball and send it almost vertically into the air from the hard, close-cropped fairways at Rye. A dangerous shot if it misfired. The scuffling of the club on the linoleum is very good practice. Aiming at the chalk spot is a check on your accuracy, for you can see exactly where the bottom of the swing comes each time. As an indoor check-up on how precise is your swing, it is without equal.

With the arrival of the weighted head cover to fit on to an ordinary clubhead and make it a 20-ounce club or more, the short heavy club seems to have lost favour. But for keeping the wrists strong and flexible in confined spaces, it is still worth having, so is the leaded-up Indian club with a golf grip on it.

THAT GOLF TENSION

MANY golfers have asked me about this question of acquiring the control of individual finger tension. Most follow eagerly any tips on the question of their grip, but they have never really set out to achieve method in this vital part of the game; they just acquire a form of gripping the club and try to repeat it.

Tommy Armour says: 'Hold tightly with the last three fingers of the left hand.' But he will be assuming that the rest of the fingers of the left hand and all those on the right will be playing the correct complementary part. Vardon stressed the importance of a firm index finger and thumb hold with both hands, obviously presuming that the rest of the fingers did what was correct, anyhow.

What is your professional getting at when he advises you to hold firmly with the left hand and loosely with the right hand? He is merely trying to find out if this adjustment of the tension of the fingers regulates the timing and can keep the right hand from 'freezing' on the grip during the shot.

Players are just beginning to realize that, while

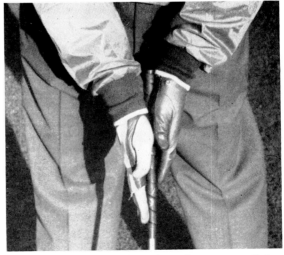

My own grip showing how the palms are parallel on the shaft. I am wearing a right hand mitt as well as my usual left hand glove. I just grip the club now, without altering the angle of the hands on the shaft.

165

THE LOOSE THROW UP

A shot I have always found easy to execute, I think because of my exceptionally loose wrists.

Here I have played from a good lie a shot to the high plateau green of the 5th hole of the King's Course at Gleneagles from below the green on the right. Do not ask me what I am doing there — it looks like a foursome!

This shot is possible only from a good lie and the best way to play it is to make your arc a 'U' — that is, not to spread out too wide in the back swing nor in the follow-through. This stroke has a soft blow, a sort of throwing up of the ball as if it were done by hand, going slowly through the ball at impact.

slicing comes from outside-to-in-hitting, it can also be caused by too much tension in the RIGHT hand. Note *right* hand.

Hooking comes from inside-to-out hitting and is inspired by the *left* hand. That is why so many players wear a glove on that hand. The tackiness of the glove (it should be new) means that a non-slip hold on the club-shaft can be obtained. So any required degree of individual finger tension is a greater possibility.

How many players have ever tried a *pair* of thin skin golf gloves? I do not advocate this as a permanent procedure for all — although in cool weather it makes a big difference to my own game to wear a fingerless right-hand mitt as well as my left-hand glove. The non-slip security in the fingers of the right hand changes completely the tension during the swing and I find breeds confidence.

Just pick up a club, shuffle your fingers into position and waggle it. Right away you see how you can alter the feel of your action by pressing tight and then loose with various fingers in turn. You can move the clubhead backwards and forwards quite violently without moving your wrists — just by throwing the club about in the hands, by tightening and loosening the fingers in turn.

Most golfers of medium ability well know that if they want to try a high-flying shot from a good lie they can flick the ball with a loose finger grip and get very good results.

This does not mean that I recommend the opening and closing of the hands as the open road to success. Every golfer has a different problem, so it is no use setting out to imitate other players indiscriminately, without being sure that you have a muscular resemblance. But please realize that with strong well trained fingers you can play all the shots and so have more fun.

FINGERS MAKE OR MAR YOUR GOLF

MANY British golfers who have never had the chance to play in America are inclined to forget that, while America is the land of great champions, it is also the land of 'dubs', as the high-handicap players are called. We would call them 'rabbits', and there are millions of them.

'Dubs' eagerly follow all the latest tips, and I even noticed many of them trying out the flat swing recommended by Ben Hogan. However, some of those I have talked to said they were disillusioned because the 'medicine' did not suit them.

When golf stars write about their style of play,

they invariably assume that the readers who will be attempting to follow their advice possess strong, educated golf hands. It is not always appreciated that the 'dub's' biggest problem is how to hold on to the club and swing it.

This holding on — the control of the tension of the fingers — is, as I have repeatedly stated, the secret of golf. You can have all your tips on stance and swing, but finally it is all in the hands, the tension in the fingers, in fact, which makes or mars the shots.

The secret is to have the correct tension as

impact approaches, so as not to slow up the club-head by gripping too tightly, nor to grip too loosely and so permit the club-shaft to turn round.

Some famous players, possessing strong hands and flexible wrists, consider they can ignore possible variation in grip tension. They merely swing the arms and club as one unit. But such cases are rare, and I am sure that even with this fortunate few there arises the need to study grip tension.

Of course, it is not easy to achieve this, but many top-class players have used and still do use the loose-grip-at-address, tight-at-impact and loose-after technique. In other words, 'loose-tight-loose' is their slogan.

So many golfers try this in their own way, and spoil shots by not relaxing again *after impact*. They just tighten in the impact area and freeze on the shot, holding on to the bitter end.

A Walker Cup captain, A. A. Duncan, has a short back swing. A beautiful left hand position, but here can be seen how he uses his right hand — there is clearly a finger throw here. He is still a very accurate golfer — so this is another lesson in the use of the right hand. It must be so used that it does not interfere with the arc of the left arm.

LIGHT GRIPPING

I HAVE often stressed the importance of the tension of each of the fingers, and expressed my opinion that the club should be held only just tightly enough to stop it turning in the hands during a full stroke. If this is to be achieved satisfactorily, the finger tension must not only be varied but carefully controlled during the course of the swing.

Some golfers need to relax the grip of one or both hands during the swing in order to get a smooth-flowing swing and rhythmic change-over from up to down, with a 'nice ringing of the bell' action at the top of the swing. While I do not begin by encouraging a new pupil to let go, to open the hands at any time during the swing, I have long since realized that to many short-fingered, stiff-wristed players such licence must be granted, and the advantages of cheating in this way outweigh the disadvantages. To many the slogan 'Loose-Tight-Loose' — tight at impact only — is a good one. It is the 'loose *after* impact' part which is the secret, as it were, of the light grippers.

There is one point which I feel is essential in order to get the maximum advantage from the swing: the palms of the hands must be parallel. They can be so placed that the 'V's' point right up and down the top of the shaft, pointing to the nose, or they can under certain conditions point to the right shoulder, but they must be parallel.

When the 'V's' point to the nose, the wrists are in the ideal maximum hingeing position, as everyone's wrists flap, shall we say, to and fro or sideways only, and this is the to-and-fro action.

Harold Hilton demonstrated years ago that a moderately strong player, who would perhaps be called short by to-day's standard, could more than hold his own if his finger control was good —i.e., the tension of his grip was under perfect control. He used a definite 'closing of the hands action' to add snap to his shots and to put effect on the ball. Players who specialize in trick shots only succeed in doing the big variety of shots they demonstrate because they use the opening and closing of their fingers to help them. They have live hands. Not

Harold Hilton

167

Norman Sutton uses a double-handed grip and continues to play fine golf for an over-fifty — and when he and Gene Sarazen played off for the World's Professional Senior Title in 1958, it was interesting to note that both players had 'personal' grips with the left thumb off the shaft.

for them is the iron, vice-like grip of some of the champions of to-day, but a superb light touch of the club with their fingers.

Do not get the idea that I am advocating a sloppy grip; far from it. But I am sure that if the hands are strong, a very big variation in the range of tension in the individual fingers is available, not only to play special strokes, but to make corrections for directional errors and to compensate for climatic conditions. Just look at Norman Sutton's grip at the top of the back swing.

After all, the top players of the day go on to the practice tee prior to playing a round only to get their hands into condition, to feel the club. They know their swings have not changed from the previous day, but the hands may have done. They vary according to the temperature and the health of the player; they can feel thick or thin, strong or weak, and it takes very little to upset this sensitive part of the anatomy. I was always intrigued, as a youth, when I travelled to exhibition matches with the Old Masters, to find they did not carry a heavy suitcase on the day they were to play, as the arm unused to carry abnormal weights got tired, trembled even, and the previous touch was lost subsequently for many hours. I proved this to my own satisfaction many times; and driving a heavy car destroyed the fine touch, too.

As the object of the game is to deliver a square blow to the ball with every club, regulated only in speed, once the fingers are educated to their task, it is surprising how instinctive it is to bring up the club face square enough for a decent result, by all sorts of means — rolling the face from open to shut and bringing it through the impact area squarely, or endeavouring, as some do, to hold it square all the time from the beginning to the end. There is no distinct advantage to be seen in either method, because despite the latest idea that the 'square all the time' is, in theory, obviously the best, in practice it has not proved to be so, and certainly it is not the average golfer's method. When you flick a ping-pong ball to your opponent at the other end of the table you do not think about square; your instinct guides your bat. Give this instinct a chance on the golf course!

As I see it, the stronger the hands the bigger the range of variations in tension and so the firmer the grip of the club can be without freezing. If I say I grip more with certain fingers, at certain times, to get certain effects, I do not think it does anything but confuse, because I have no means of conveying how strong is the grip of each finger anyway, before I start; but I have proved that practice with each hand separately teaches much and readily shows up which hand is letting a golfer down, in his aim to improve. Extensive normal (overlapping grip) two-handed practice often leaves the actual balance of power between right and left as it was, and so little real progress is ever made.

Myself practising

168

THE FINGER SECRET

THE secret of the golf game is the control of the tension of the fingers during the stroke. You can look anywhere else you like, and people always do, but the fact remains that golf is a game of hands, touch, control, or whatever else you like to call it; and in the end it is the gripping of the club which gives every golfer his category, sorting the wheat from the chaff.

I have long realized that golf would be an easier game if the hands were 'level' on the shaft, that if the right hand was not below the left on the club there would be many fewer problems. To some extent the little finger of the right hand over the index finger of the left hand has the effect of making the hands work together, and does lift the right hand up the shaft and so alters slightly the body action. Even overlapping two fingers lifts the right side that bit more, and helps to eliminate often any hasty punch in the stroke, but such a change needs study.

I have pupils playing improved golf using all types of grips of the club, many even a double-handed grip, which of course lowers the right hand on the shaft and thus alters the body action as well as the finger and hand action, because all the digits of the hands are touching the shaft. It does not matter what sort of a swing a golfer has, how it loops or how long it is, for the club face must after all be brought square to the ball at impact, if a successful shot is to be played.

As the human being is not a machine, it rests finally on the fingers to guide the club-face squarely to the ball at impact. An alteration in the final gripping pressure can make the hand action different and make an alteration in the club face impact position, besides affecting the timing. The difficult part of the golf swing lies in the fact that the left-arm blow is back-handed, while the right-hand blow is fore-handed, and so whatever the type of grip employed, the arms must be built up to enable the hands to deliver the blow when working together to the best advantage.

How many people are there playing golf to-day who place their hands so badly on the shaft that if the hands were used separately — one-at-a-time I mean — they could not deliver a decent whack at any ball? Millions, one can say.

Believe me, if your hands, used independently, cannot send a golf ball somewhere towards the target (a ball teed well up is allowed for this exercise and test) you are going to find it tough going to use them together when placed in the same position on the shaft as they are on their individual tests.

This is 'let go' exaggeration, but the ball can be sent a very long way from this top of the swing position. I call this the piccolo grip for obvious reasons. It is a bit like Harold Hilton's grip on page 167.

It is the actual shape of the hands themselves which guides golfers into the type of grip of the club they use best, and all the stuff written on where to grip, with which fingers and where the shaft should lie in the hands, is just particular golfers writing really on 'How I do It'; though often, to give their efforts more importance, they are much more dogmatic and say that *this* is the only way to succeed.

Now grip the club as if you were about to shake hands, as tightly only as you grip your knife and fork, not much tighter with the left than with the right. Grip firmly with the index finger and thumb of both hands; grip with the last two fingers of the left hand or with the middle two fingers of the right hand. 'Use a long thumb' — i.e., a thumb extended down the shaft as far as possible — was a recent sort of 'holy quote', but all such tips, valuable as they can be for certain people, may aid only temporarily, but the basic need for control of the tension by individual fingers of both hands still exists for all golfers.

Grip thickness plays a considerable part in this 'tension story', yet few golfers to-day ever experiment; they buy a set of clubs and mould their game around the clubs, being satisfied with whatever thickness the maker has fitted. It is obvious that with thinner grips the club shaft lies more in the fingers and this encourages wrist action and a looser breed of stroke, while the thicker grip, as can readily be noticed if a tennis racket is gripped as if it were a golf shaft, 'chokes' the hands and seems to tighten the wrists.

The wrist joint's main function is hingeing. This control of the tension means for so many, not freezing on to the shaft, like a drowning man clinging to a rope or a raft, a matter of life or death, but being able to work up to the correct tension, so as not to tire the grip itself during the swing and so let go at impact; or, alternatively, to grip too tightly and slow up the whole wrist action.

I am not one of those who thinks the only way to play golf is to close the fingers of both hands firmly on the shaft so that the shaft and arms are all one and must remain so throughout the swing. I agree it must be ideal, if the wrists are flexible enough and the body supple enough, for the clubhead speed not to be affected in the least, but to so

many golfers, with such tension, good golf is out of the question.

I am with the school which claims that the club must only be held tightly enough to stop it turning in the hands during a full stroke, and that if the strength of the fingers is built up, then up to five consecutive full shots can be played without having to adjust the fingers on the shaft. (Hogan told me he could do twenty.) This I put as a sort of passing-out test to an average scratch golfer. There is quite a big gap between a piccolo-player, one who opens one or both hands very much during the swing, and a solid, vice-like gripper throughout the swing.

Just how relaxed the grip can afford to be depends on the wrists and hands of each individual player.

THE REHEARSAL

I HAVE always considered the correct grip of the golf club as being most important. It enables you to deliver a square-faced blow at the ball, with the club held firmly enough not to twist at impact. These are the conditions every golfer is asked to fulfil.

Though the grip will not be the same for every

The elbows must be held close together.

golfer — so many personal physical details make a difference — it is the one which enables you to do a free, fast and accurate swing which is correct. Flexibility of the wrists, size and strength of the hands and the shape of the left thumb all count in seeking the ideal grip.

I am sure that Ernest Jones, who, as I have mentioned earlier, is now established in New York as one of the greatest teachers, has been following the soundest of all themes with 'swing the clubhead' as his chief slogan and 'a club cannot be made to move faster than you can swing it' as his second string.

I have never disagreed with this part of his doctrine. I hope, in fact, I have added to it by trying to get more strength into essential parts of the action by specific exercises. The clubhead cannot swing itself; the golfer must create the power.

Swinging a club strongly backwards and forwards as a practice movement, with the elbows held together, is far more valuable to most than just one 'rehearsal' swing alongside the ball.

How many of your friends insist on this aimless 'rehearsal' practice and swing before each shot? Dozens! I have never quite understood why, for in nearly every case this swing, the free, elegant 'daisy-cutter', is smooth and fast, while the actual swing, cramped by the anticipated resistance of the ball, is altogether another thing.

It is far better to do a couple of strong to and fro swings before each full shot, to warm up the muscles and strengthen the hands, and furthermore, the head stays down better.

When doing a fast swing, most golfers find that

their hands are not strong enough to hold on to the club (without freezing on the grip) and they have difficulty in guiding the centre of the head to the centre of the back of the ball. The centrifugal force creates and governs balance, but you need enough strength in the hands to steer the club and resist its outward swinging tendency. Hitting many golf balls is the accepted way to acquire precision,

but supervised practice is best.

With the slower pace of play in general, golfers feel the cold more and I am sure that the extra clothing one wears for protection against the elements causes swings to become faster and shorter. This is always my own personal winter problem; that is why I try to get to the warmer climes in winter.

YOU CAN GRASP THIS GOLF ANGLE

WHATEVER is written about golf, you can never get away from the fact that the grip has the most important rôle in your golf action. By just altering the angle of the hands and adjusting the fingers on the grip, your whole movement can change and so needs all sorts of compensations to be effective. But even without changing the position of the hands, any variation in grip tension — either intentionally or accidentally — has the greatest effect on all of your shots.

When I go out on a playing lesson with a golfer who has just gone off his average form, it is more than likely his grip is letting him down. This means that his hand position will have moved. Most likely it would seem to be the same as usual, but during the address and the swing his grip tension will have varied.

Inconsistent golf — one shot high, one low; one shot left, one right — usually comes from a 'club slip' in the fingers; do not look any further. An old shiny grip; dry hands; an old dry left-hand glove and, of course, weak fingers, these all cause inconsistency. So these points must be checked.

You fit a new grip, you smear an adhesive on your hands, buy a new glove and still all is not

well. What next? We have arrived at the real crisis. It is no use simply saying: 'I must hang on at all costs.' To many people that would mean freezing the whole hand action, and it is more than likely the hands would be tired by the time the club is brought to strike the ball from the address, and the fingers will slacken their hold rather than be firm at the moment of impact.

I have found that players who are primarily wristy golfers have a looser grip than the body players, and count on getting that violent snap or whip into their shots by being free of tension in their fingers, till they actually hit the ball.

In this action photograph of myself playing a No. 7 iron shot, the student can see that everything is more or less classical. But what he wants to know to get the full picture is how tight is my grip at this point. This is hard to put into words because one man's tightness is another man's looseness! But the shaft is still held firmly at this point — I relax the hands later.

I feel it is best to experiment to find your own tension, for no one can say, except yourself, when you are overdoing or underdoing the gripping of the club.

LEFT: *The angle of my hands.* CENTRE: *Myself playing No. 7 iron shot.* RIGHT: *I relax the hands after an iron shot.*

THE HARRY VARDON GRIP

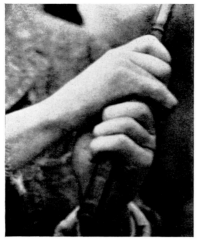

Here can be seen the Old Maestro's grip as it would appear when you asked him to show how he overlapped. LEFT: *Notice how his long little finger fits round the left index finger, overlapping it completely. Note too the 'trigger' bend in the right index finger.* CENTRE: *His particularly fleshy hands give an impression of a three-knuckle grip, but really only two knuckles are showing.* RIGHT: *At the finish of an iron shot, the relaxed hands can be seen as well as his perfect balance.*

A WEAK GRIP

IN these two cases both players — single figure handicap golfers (by reason of experience and a good short game) — make it difficult for themselves by addressing the ball with the two 'V's' opposing one another. The 'V's' must be parallel always.

It is against the 'rules' to hold the hands in this way, as the ball tends to be pushed not whipped — it makes a good putting grip for this reason, because the hands are high.

As the right hand goes under the shaft, so the tendency increases to lift the hands even more on striking the ball. When the right hand is forced over the shaft there is a tendency to hold the hands more down at impact — this gives more clubhead speed.

These players may have tried all other ways and settled for this type of grip, but if they have not they still have another world of golf to explore. I think the fact that they are both thick-chested types makes the hands fall more easily on the shaft — with the elbows spread and the hands, 'V's' outwards.

THE FINGERS AGAIN

Gloves can make a big difference

MY golf secret, for which, alas, I did not get 10,000 dollars, is the control of the individual tension in the fingers, which decides how good a player is going to be.

I have often met club golfers who were never fully conscious of the part their fingers could play in grooving their swings and applying the power until they heard of my idea of tension control, and the majority claim to have improved their play since they began experimenting with the shifting about of the tension from one finger to another, and from one type of grip of the fingers to another. This is, anyhow, possible only within the range of flexibility and actual gripping value they possess in each finger; but by exercises and practice, by concentrating on these members, much more control can be acquired.

Players handling clubs all day, which most professionals and good amateurs would do, find they unconsciously have acquired this control of individual finger tension, which I consider the secret. And artisans, who do work in which their fingers especially are used, can play good golf with the minimum of practice. One finds this everywhere in Scotland; artisans can hold their form year in and year out with the minimum of practice — just a few practice swings to loosen up are often enough, before they set out to play a fine game. Most office workers would settle willingly for the standard of play reached by many artisans.

Harry Vardon, whose grip is shown opposite, had an exceptionally well-developed pincer action with his index finger and thumb, and having thick, fleshy hands, he could hold the club firmly without freezing on it. He offered the grip of the club with the finger and thumb as the key, but it would have been interesting to have asked him what pressure he had with the other fingers at different times. There is no way of measuring this in pounds per square inch, for example, but these statistics would be interesting if they were available.

Naturally, there will be a slight variation in the tension of the individual fingers on the shaft almost daily; it will just happen. The 'feel of the club', which one talks about, means that the balancing of the finger pressures is satisfactorily achieved. Through the waggling of the club at the address, players seek the 'tension for the day'.

I do not think the hands tire more quickly than other parts of the body when practising hard, but the skin, of course, becomes tender if long spells of hitting balls are indulged in. All the same, I have

The tight-fitting left-hand glove. Many golfers go only halfway to using this valuable golfing accessory to the full. They continue to use old, dry, ill-fitting gloves. It is not an economy to buy a cheap glove — your hands are the key to good golf. Get the best quality tacky leather designed by those who use them; and in hot weather use two a round — they last longer and will give better results.

found it necessary to do contra hand-stretching exercises in the past to counteract the incessant gripping or closing of the hand in intensive practice, as sometimes my hands want to stay almost closed up.

Exercises to spread the fingers out, such as press-ups made on the hands or on the finger-tips even, and pressing the finger-tips together, have their value. Looking back on my golf career I have made mistakes in the practice and preparation fields of the game, because I did not appreciate, in time, the value of contra exercises to avoid the muscles working all the same way all the time, as well as the need to combat mental staleness.

The left hand does less guiding in most swings than it should. It is the first link between the shaft and the body, and its main function is to form the swing, and yet at the right moment it resists the hit of the powerful right hand. A thin skin glove on the left hand is almost universal in these days, and because of the centrifugal pull of the club, the better the grip of the surface in contact with the handle, the freer and faster can be the hit, because

LEFT: *The tacky paste (my own prescription) that I put on my hands and gloves before playing just supplies that extra bit of necessary adhesion. I cannot afford the slightest club slip — nor can any other golfer!* RIGHT: *Hogan waggling the club.*

there is less need to clutch at the handle like the devil. The tacky surface offered by gloves can vary a little, too, and an old dry glove offers less help.

So long as the club does not turn during the shot, the grip is tight enough. This is your guide.

I do not know any way of measuring individual finger tension during a swing, but I have found that by squeezing with different fingers deliberately all sorts of possibilities are opened up. The hands need educating to be able to experiment to the full.

Since I have been discussing this matter with pupils and professionals, I find the expression, 'Why did we not think of it before?' cropping up. It is just one of those points that everyone knew about in a vague sort of way, but which needed spot-lighting. Everybody's hands are different in size and power, so this finger tension requires much study. I am sure the very fact of concentrating on different sections of the hands when gripping the club will help the play of all golfers. Dai Rees had a successful golfing year in 1959, the first year he had ever used a left-hand glove.

SWITCHING THE GRIP

ONE of the everlasting clubhouse discussions is how to get a bit more distance from the tee. Everyone is interested from the rabbit amateur to the tiger professional. And there are theories galore. One September I played a round at Gleneagles with that studious Scottish professional, Jack McLean, and we discussed this problem.

Jack was a successful amateur in his day and was almost unbeatable because of his relentless accuracy. He was never a long player, but even nowadays his iron shots to the pin remind me of his greatest amateur days.

I suggested, having found many pupils of mine gain yards by switching to a double-handed grip instead of sticking to the classical overlapping type, that it might be worth an experiment, especially as he had never tried it. Straightaway he began to hit the ball farther. Even from off the fairway the ball flew higher and straighter and his tendency to hook disappeared.

As I had been ill during the middle part of that particular summer and had been obliged to stop playing for a few weeks, I thought I had better try some of my own medicine. There and then I experimented seriously with the double-handed grip. I had hit odd shots at times with it when demonstrating to pupils, but had never studied it so as to be able to quote from personal experience.

So I played with it regularly for the next three months, even in tournaments, and I can say I could not blame it for any failures. Apart from changing the action of the hands in the swing, it added flexibility to the wrist work.

I am sure players with weak hands or short fingers cannot afford to 'give away' the little finger of the right hand. There are champions using it all over the world to-day — so do not think you are going to be out of date.

You will find that the outside of the little finger of the right hand will get sore where it runs against the index finger of the left hand at first, but this is quite normal.

Myself using the double-handed grip. Club held in the fingers, left thumb inside.

174

ARE YOU MISSING THE BOAT?

HARRISON Johnston, one of America's top amateurs of a generation ago, successfully used a double-handed grip with the left thumb outside the hands, all his life. Here, in the photographs above, his hands can be seen at the top of the back swing and at the finish of the follow-through.

This grip is not a popular one with instructors as there is a certain looseness in the left hand, because the squeeze, between the left thumb and forefinger, such an important part of the Vardon grip and even the ordinary double-handed grip, is missing. It is, however, an ideal grip for anybody with a damaged left thumb or any sort of stiffness in this part of the left hand, as it allows a great degree of freedom in the back swing and relieves the left thumb of any shock at impact. That first-grade golf can be played with such a grip has been shown by Alex ('Sandy') Herd and Harrison Johnston, just two great names which come to mind.

I record this because I feel that so many golfers have never explored every chance that exists to improve their golf. They often flog a dead horse by conservatively sticking to an unsuitable grip of the club. Perhaps you are missing the boat!

LEFT: *'Sandy' Herd, showing his grip and his stance for a mashie when in his seventieth year. Note his grip; his short, thick fingers made his grip a palm grip.*

RIGHT: *A good enough grip to win the Amateur Championship in the U.S.A. in the days of Bobby Jones. I show the double-handed palm grip.*

HANDS AGAIN

AVERAGE golfers are the backbone of the game and they love watching, playing and learning about it. I do not, however, suppose for one minute that I have put the preceding interests in their correct order! But one and all they are apt to take for granted the part their own *hands* play in the swinging of the golf club.

Great players and teachers often treat the hands as just another part of the body, and only occasionally do some put accent on them, often under the simple heading of 'The Grip'. 'The value of the left thumb on the shaft', explained Seymour Dunn in 1925, 'is that the more sensitive nerves are in the finger ends, and especially in the thumb and forefinger. We want the most acute sense of feeling possible in the clubhead. With the club handle held between the tip of the thumb and the forefinger it is possible to get that feeling in the clubhead, so that it almost seems as if there were prolonged nerves which run down from the thumb and forefinger down the shaft into the clubhead itself.' This is real common sense; and then Dunn goes on to explain the 'the Vardon grip is for strong hands only, weaker players will do better with the double-handed grip'. Sound advice this, which I endorse, and advise many of my pupils to try out.

Jumping forward thirty-odd years we find Jack

Hogan in sand

Burke, named golfer of the year in 1956 in the U.S.A. because of his wins in the 'Masters' and P.G.A. events, pointing out, in a chapter in his book on 'How to Hold the Club', that you hold the club no tighter than you do when taking it from your caddie; all the squeezing necessary in hitting a golf ball comes instinctively, as your hands enter the hitting area. To squeeze the club shaft beforehand prevents the clubhead from gaining maximum speed. Burke continues: 'I have seen good golfers with a bad hand position, but I have never seen a bad golfer with a good hand position. Hold your hands properly. After all, they are the only parts of the body attached to the club.' Alas, I can question the part about a bad golfer and good hand position. It would be just too easy; it is not quite a guarantee.

Burke comments on the statement that the 'V's' formed by index fingers and thumbs of the hands should point toward the right shoulder. They should point right up the shaft, I always say. But he later adds: 'Between the head and the shoulder is O.K. without fixing any exact spot.' This I will accept as sound, for it is within an acceptable range anyway.

I mention these interesting observations by other leading golfers, as they more or less coincide with my own views, and they get down to confirming the vital part the hands play; they are the link between the clubhead and the body, and their importance cannot be too highly stressed.

Tension — here in this word is the golf secret; control of the tension; domination of the tension of the individual fingers is the secret of the great players! They are able to regulate this, which is why so many use left-hand gloves to try and get the tension more constant, because of a standard adhesion between hand and club, independent of the temperature. I use a right-hand mitt, too, when I feel my right hand is not in 'gripping shape'.

Here Hogan has even counted on the left hand alone to see a successful climax in this recovery shot he has played. He has realized that a firm grip of the right hand after impact in this situation would probably have pulled the clubhead off its path to the pin, as his normal body action is restricted by the situation, so he has let the right hand go, once it has made up the necessary clubhead speed. Here his 'long' thumb can be seen. Whereas the thumb lies nearly always hidden inside the right hand, here it is on show, and the way the hand is extended down the shaft is clear. This is very personal and few can copy it.

SOME USEFUL TIPS

THE RIGHT HAND AGAIN

IT is quite surprising how many golfers, who think they use their right hands too much, cannot in fact hit a decent shot at all with this hand alone on the club. I have tested this out with dozens of golfers and although, of course, it no longer astounds me, it does surprise the golfer put to the test. He usually thinks his right hand is responsible for doing too much work in the swing and, therefore, causes all the poor shots. I have for many years now studied this question of the part played by the two hands, ever trying to establish a sort of power ratio.

I cannot say that I have succeeded in this exactly, but I have acquired a lot of knowledge of hand action and hand training; in fact, I consider myself somewhat of a specialist in this matter, for I have handled all grades of players from champions to novices.

So many golfers think it is sufficient to perform an action which looks like the ideal golf swing, but so few could ever hit a second ball without a shuffling of the fingers to regain the original hand position, before being able to attempt a second stroke. Four times out of five it is the so-called *strong, active right hand* which has slipped.

When a golfer is made to hit balls with his right hand only, he is quickly made aware of the weakness of this part of the body, 'golfingly speaking'. I am convinced that it cannot be satisfactorily trained or built up if it goes along, all the time, with a dominating left arm. It needs individual treatment, and the vast majority of players will not be bothered. It does not mean that ordinary golf practice, as one might term hitting out balls regularly, will not contribute to the aim to play better, but I have found that it rarely alters the ratio of power. If the right hand does not respond to the command from the brain to play a different rôle when it is asked, then it simply means it needs educating. It is as simple as that.

I have come across many golfers who find that after a full shot the right hand has slipped more over the club; just a tiny bit, but enough to say it is not in the same position; and I find they can 'cure' this as a start by beginning the swing with the hand in the newly-acquired position, so at least it cannot move to the usual position, for it is already there. Any compensations required to true up the position of the club-face at impact can be made at the address.

Many, many golfers provide themselves with a good tight-fitting left-hand glove, which helps

This hand has slipped. The clubhead struck the ground well behind the ball (see dust) but skidded on to make a contact.

this hand to play its rôle well, but then they allow the right hand to slip — it can slip either over or under the shaft as the power is applied. I construe these slips as meaning that the hand was not so much 'not-holding-tightly-enough-at-impact', but 'incorrectly placed at the address'.

If I get a pupil making this error regularly, I just see what happens when he begins with the hand in the place in which it finishes. Best cure: hitting balls right hand only to train this hand to take the hit.

Right hand practice. This particular shot was topped, but this low single figure handicap player, Mr Ignacio Urquijo, soon began to get his right arm muscles toned up and then later, with both hands together on the club, all went better.

177

THE START BACK

ONE hears very little in these days of the forward press and the drag back of the clubhead with the hands, but here I have caught with my camera a top-grade week-end golfer, Mr E. Bromley-Davenport, with his shaft definitely bent, proving that he has started to drag the hands away first. This action has value to all golfers, as it is part of the smooth take away of the clubhead from the ball, necessary in everybody's swing. I suppose in the days of the hickory shaft, with its torsion and usually greater whip (though some steel shafts can be found which are very whippy, but they seem to be less fashionable), this drag back could be seen more easily, but it still does exist in many successful swings, and most golfers could benefit from 'a dose of it'. I still feel that the instinctive kick forward of the right knee, and the slight push forward of hands towards the hole prior to the drag back is still part of the ideal golf swing.

Some golfers push the club from the left shoulder in one stiff piece, as they begin the back swing, almost giving the effect of lifting it away rather than swinging it back from the ball, but this action seems to have the effect of minimizing the fluidity of the wrist whip. There is something of the old 'flail' action, which was so often written about in the period between the wars, in this drag away with the hands. Having been primarily what is called a 'hand player' all my life I can see nothing but good in this smooth drag away of the clubhead from the ball. Even on long approach putts this particular action seems to give the player more leisure to 'time the ball'. It can be overdone, of course, but first of all see that it is part of your swing.

If you know a slip is inevitable because your hands, anticipating a slip, are weak, then you could, of course, compensate as this lady golfer has done. It is difficult to gauge this sort of slip, but as fair results will occur, the end justifies the means.

Mr E. Bromley-Davenport dragging the clubhead back with his steel-shafted driver.

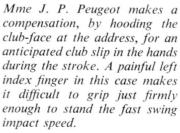

J. H. Taylor in his best days dragging his hickory-shafted club away from the ball. Note the give in the shaft.

Mme J. P. Peugeot makes a compensation, by hooding the club-face at the address, for an anticipated club slip in the hands during the stroke. A painful left index finger in this case makes it difficult to grip just firmly enough to stand the fast swing impact speed.

CRUEL FLAMES DID THIS

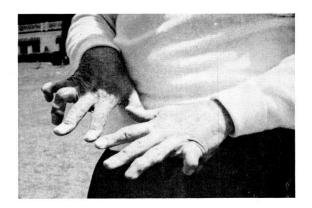

Gifted U.S. Ryder Cup golfer, 'Skip' Alexander, shows his crippled hands which were terribly burned in an aeroplane crash some five years ago. He is lucky to be alive and luckier still to be able to play golf. The bent fingers seen here are permanently bent — yet he can grip the club well, using an interlocking grip. He is not quite in the top class to-day, but plays par golf and enjoys his life as a club professional in Florida.

MY HANDS

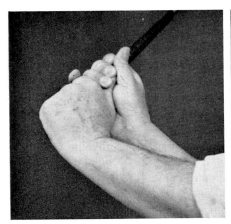 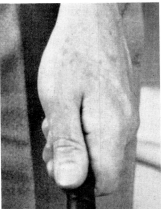 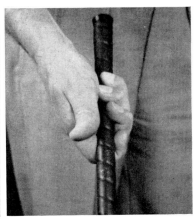

Three photographs giving an idea of how my hands fit on to the club. I usually overlap with my little finger of the right hand on the top of the index finger exactly — not always lying between the index and second finger, as Hogan recommends, though I can play either way. How the fingers fit *depends on the shape of the hands entirely*, while the thickness of the grip also plays a part.

The way the shaft lies in the fingers of my right hand can be seen. The shaft lies across the left hand, the club shaft fits under 'the muscular pad of the inside heel of this hand', but my left hand does not fold over the shaft, because I use a thickish grip. With a thin grip my left hand tends to get more on top of the shaft and show more knuckles. If your left hand shows many knuckles, check not only where the shaft lies, but the grip thickness.

The size of the hand is important. I do not pretend that it is an extraordinary feat to hold five balls in one hand, but it gives you an idea of the size and shape of my hand. This picture might give you an idea of how big my hands are when making a comparison with your own. I cannot tear telephone books nor hold a driver between my first and second fingers, holding it at the top of the grip at arms length, but I have trained my fingers to hang on.

179

I DISLIKE THESE GRIPS

Hands low: if this player raised his hands at the address then it is possible they would fit on the shaft like mine. It is a good idea to bend your back, but the hands must not drop like this.

In the photograph below the 'V's' point almost outside the right shoulder. With this grip a smothered shot can result when an attempt is made to whip the ball; the left arm collapses. If the left elbow is locked and a lofted club is used, as seen here, to drive with, then if the movement is a 'pusher' one, fair results can be obtained. This

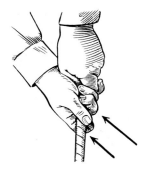

grip is regularly taught to players to get them along quickly and it does give encouraging results at first, I have noticed, but it is the sort of grip which *leads nowhere* — that is why I dislike it. If the hands are lifted they would lie on the shaft more like mine, but then golf muscles would be needed to hold the left arm straight instead of the locked elbow joint.

My hands.

The four-knuckle grip.

PICARD'S LEFT THUMB

As I have already mentioned on a previous page, a successful grip of the club can be made with the left thumb outside the hands and for a damaged thumb this is a great idea. Henry Picard, a top professional in pre-war days, had the grip of the club as seen in the photograph (BELOW). His right hand was then under a little more than usual perhaps, but his left thumb *was* on the shaft. He damaged his thumb and could not play without great pain, so he took a new grip. I discussed his new grip, which was inspired by talks with Alex. Morrison, who went nap on this grip in the 1930's and made a fortune 'selling it' to pupils. Henry had to find a grip where his left thumb had no strain on it. Here he is using his 'interlocking-left-thumb-outside' grip.

He posed for these photographs for me at the Seminole Golf Club, Florida, where he is professional. Note left-hand glove and rough rubber grip. His stance is narrow for big a man, although he is using only a No. 6 iron. Henry still plays very well despite having reached the veteran stage.

This is the grip which works only with a lofted club from the tee (unless the body action is exceptionally fast and the hit fast, too). It is often taught to beginners to get them off the mark quickly and to keep the left arm straight, so as to form a swing readily. It works up to a point and players using it frequently reach their ceiling early in their golfing life and then stick!

BELOW : *Picard in action with a No. 6 iron.*

181

BELIEVE IT OR NOT!

You can hit a golf ball well with your left hand as far under the shaft as this — one knuckle showing — because the right hand instinctively forces the back of the left hand to the hole, when the power is applied. Many golfers hardly believe their eyes, even when I demonstrate to them, but although it feels a weak position, it is an ideal one to use to educate *the right hand* to work correctly — not necessarily for playing for evermore.

A GREAT FINGER GRIP GOLFER

Roger Wethered was always an exciting golfer to watch in his best days, but was often erratic, I think because he was purely a 'finger grip golfer'. He allowed the shaft the maximum of play in his hands during the swing and if he was not judging the tension correctly, considerable error could creep in, as he hit so hard. Here he is cutting up a spoon shot and there is no doubt in my mind, as I look at the photograph, that he is cutting the ball; it is stamped there by his finish.

ABE MITCHELL'S GRIP

Now this was Abe Mitchell's grip: a sort of reverse overlap where the index finger of the left hand rode the little finger of the right hand — left thumb going outside. This is a lovely grip to use, I find, but I cannot bear the pain of squeezing the finger nail of my little finger. If I *had* to use this grip I should need a plastic protector of some sort for the nail; then I could play with it.

I find it excellent for short shots and have often used it for half No. 9 iron and shots downwards, but even on little shots I hurt my nail and am inclined to let go — and this means a poor result.

Mitchell seemed to keep his little finger nail clear at the address somehow. There was always a lot of slackness in this Mitchell grip. Even the right fore-finger was loose — it remained loose all the time

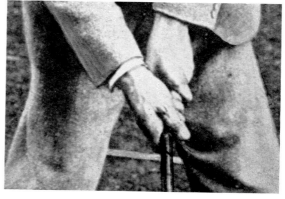

and at the top of the backswing it could be seen sticking up in the air, yet he was a beautifully consistent striker of the ball and with hickory shafts, too! He knew his hand tension, and could re-grip perfectly as impact approached.

ALL HANDS ARE DIFFERENT

I AM absolutely satisfied that many golfers spoil the back swing which they would like to do, and could do, because they insist on freezing on to the club handle throughout their whole action.

Just to clutch on to the handle firmly, if the wrists and arms are not shaped for golf, will cause the club to come off its best arc; few golfers realize this.

In this section on the hands I trust I have offered enough evidence to show that there is not one grip for everyone. Each player must be prepared to hold the club in the best way suited to his muscle and bone structure.

My friend Vernon Sangster, getting towards sixty years of age (RIGHT), could improve his whole action — the left elbow position points too much forward and the club-face position is too shut — if he could learn to relax his hands at the top of the back swing. He hangs on too firmly for a man of his years — flexible youngsters have different problems altogether.

So swing the clubhead freely and make *your hands fit in the picture*; do not let your grip spoil your action.

ON PRECISION

To read photographs one really should know where the ball went and then often no comment is possible on a particular swing because just half an inch error in the point of contact, club-to-ball, can ruin any good swing. Who can tell that this shot of Mr W. F. E. Carr (LEFT) was a half hit? Or that this down swing (RIGHT) produced a shot off at an angle of 30° and a mere 50 yards when one of 170 was hoped for?

CLUBHEAD SPEED DEMONSTRATED

JAMES BRAID

R. A. WHITCOMBE

MYSELF DRIVING

BALL

Here I am seen driving in the famous 72 holes match at Walton Heath in 1938, which Reg Whitcombe and I just won against Locke and Brews of South Africa. There is no doubt about 'head down', but I pick out as an important point the way the clubhead speed has carried my arms on after the ball, on the line to the hole.

THE PIVOT

Even for a short iron shot, the top of the body must turn. *This gives time to make a correctly timed stroke and avoids hurrying down to the ball. Sam Snead is an outstanding example of the full-pivot-wait-for-it action.*

Here I am caught by the camera just prior to beginning to move down towards the ball. Note full shoulder pivot, but lesser hip turn — ball near the centre.

A WRIST EXERCISE

Spring grips of varying powers according to choice — strong, medium, weak — are excellent for building up the arms, wrists and hands, but the 'trick' is not just to squeeze them and let them go, but to hold as tightly as possible and then to waggle the wrists. Here I am using a pair of strong grips and working my wrists to and fro. This is harder than it looks and is a great way to loosen-up the forearms while maintaining a strong grip.

184

TRY ANOTHER GOLF GRIP

Do you use the Harry Vardon overlapping grip only because you think you should? This classic style of the great golfing master is now considered the main orthodox type, but have you tried others?

Because they were shown this form of placing the hands when they took up golf, many people think they cannot play any other way. They are wrong!

While I teach the orthodox overlapping grip as part of a basic attack on the game, I am ready to help a pupil to experiment. His progress may be held up because his fingers are too short or, perhaps, the right hand does not play a sufficiently important rôle.

The overlapping grip helps the hands to work together, but it *does* take some power away from the right hand — a loss which can be very serious. If the wrists are stiff, such a grip denies any extra flexibility which a separate hand-grip allows, thus reducing the right-hand force available.

We have great players — Dai Rees, for example, and Harrison Johnston, former U.S. Amateur Champion — who not only use a double-handed grip, but allow the shaft to slide in the right hand as they swing. This gives a sort of hand-snatch action which is clearly necessary for Dai's game, and though a dangerous-looking motion, the danger is almost eliminated if the left hand is firmly on the club shaft throughout.

The Duke of Sutherland, a week-end golfing veteran, has a very definite right-hand palm grip, even under the shaft as well, palm uppermost. As his left hand stays firm, it all works out well and he gives the ball a most natural, healthy, consistent whack. No teacher would be wise to suggest a change for him. Necessity has invented his grip.

This is not to advocate a general switch from the Vardon grip — which is the best, in my opinion — but just to remind golfers there are others to study.

Another grip which works is below right — the overlapping of two fingers of the right hand over the left. This sells the feel of swinging the clubhead better than any other tip I know. It stops 'slugging' at the ball and obliges the player to 'swing at it'. I find I lose no length playing all my shots this way and for fairway shots it seems to eliminate digging, if there is a tendency to do this.

The Duke of Sutherland shows his grip, which I find very interesting and which works! An infrequent player, the Duke still gets a big kick out of his golf. Alfred Perry won the Open Championship in 1935 with a grip as original as this — left thumb on the shaft though! Have you tried it?

I try out the right-hand palm grip, but hold my left thumb hard on the shaft.

This is another grip.

185

THE BIGGEST HALF OF THE GAME

Go to any golf club where there is a place to practise and you will, more often than not, find more golfers practising their long shots than their putting — yet they all know that putting is as much as half the game for many of them. Why is this? Not because they do not recognize its value, but because they get a much bigger kick out of sending a golf ball a long way than rolling it along the ground on a specially prepared surface. All the same, while I am on this rolling of the ball along the ground topic, very few people in the world consistently roll the ball along the ground both in the correct direction and the correct distance; the vast majority hit very few putts perfectly in an entire round.

All successful golfers are good putters. Some rely on their putting; others only 'get by' and have a better long game, but when you read that so-and-so had a 72 and had 'so many' three-putt greens, discount this a little, as you can be assured he holed a number of good ones.

Putting for me has always been guessing. There has been no way that I have discovered of getting it mechanized, and when I have seen putting machines at work I have become satisfied that it requires not only skill but luck as well to hole many putts. I tried for years to evolve an action which I thought reduced the margin of error, but even having acquired a more or less repeatable stroke, I found I could still guess wrong just as the putting machine does the first time; it has to be adjusted by trial and error.

A blade kept square to the line 'ball to hole' most carefully gave, I found, no more assurance that all would be well than the casual rolling open to shut action when it came to holing out for the prizes. It was not until I began to try to putt as I drove, without measuring up everything so much, that I began to enjoy putting; and as the years have gone by I have putted generally better, because I have so long given up the search for 'the method'.

Putting anyway is more a question of nerve and touch than method and few of the great putters (do not think I consider them just lucky) ever seem to bother about method — they usually carry out a certain casual 'rite' about their address and dispatch of the ball and then hey presto! the ball is rolled up to the hole side from all over the place.

I do think that the weight of the putter is most important. I think that it is more important even than the model of head. It used to be called balance and maybe that is the right term, but each

In his later playing years, when his putting went, Walter Hagen improved his long game by practising, a thing he had rarely done in his life. But better stroke production could not make up for his weak putting. At this particular period, 1937, his play through the green was better than it had ever been. But he could not score, for his magic touch had gone — for ever! Ben Hogan has also had putting troubles in recent years.

individual has an ideal weight for his touch, and I feel sure that it would be right to have different weights of putter for different speeds of green.

I think that lie of club and length of shaft are important, too, because they have a direct influence on the lining up of the putt and for aiming the stroke. The eyes, I think, come into this, whether the sizing up of the shot is easiest from 'up there' or 'down there'.

I have never satisfied myself whether stiff-wristed putters are better than flowing wristy strikers of the ball. I think it all boils down to the state of the nerves in the hands and fingers. Once the nerves become frayed badly, there is no way to guarantee that a little jerk or twitch will not appear, and I have seen them all with it at times, from Vardon to Snead and Hogan. Some can cure it by building up their general health, but often the morale has been destroyed and then it sticks. Walter Hagen, of the iron constitution, finally lost his ability to win when his nerve failed on the greens and he began to miss the putts he usually could hole under pressure.

IN PUTTING IT'S THE NERVE THAT COUNTS

THE golfing world was stirred in 1957 when it was announced that Ben Hogan had discovered he could putt better, using a double-handed grip, with a gap of at least one inch between the hands. Earlier that year, Ben was not happy about his putting; he was missing too many short ones. But the double-handed grip, he said, made all the difference, for he found he could use his right hand more freely. It was all written up as something almost new in golf, yet in every old book on the game one finds golfers demonstrating how to putt, using this style of grip, and I presume it worked well for many players. Hogan did not stick to it for long; he still missed the little ones.

I used this sort of grip — no gap between the hands — successfully for a time just before the war and again in 1953, when I even tried it for all my clubs. David Snell beat Harry Weetman in the final of the *News of the World* Match Play Championship in 1959 using this very grip for putting.

It is true that the right hand does work freely on its own, and the value I place on this grip for all golfers is that after you use it for a time it becomes a wonderful point from which to go back to the usual overlapping grip; your right hand seems more alive and willing to respond to any command. Many of my pupils, to whom I recommend a trial using all the fingers of both hands on the club shaft, stick to it for good, as they find they hold and control the club better.

In the end, however, putting is not a question of method but of nerve. I know that by practising a certain way continually you can build up confidence and the stroke can be mechanized. But to use the stroke to the best advantage, that mysterious thing called 'touch' is required, and that goes with nerve.

The great putters, it is true, play each putt with the same routine of stance, address, and stroke, never hurrying and never playing the shot carelessly. But all this needs discipline and coolness, qualities which hours of back-aching practice will not capture.

From what I have learned about putters and putting, it seems to me that *we must practise a lot or not at all*. The half-hearted, infrequent, casual practice spells just before a tournament usually serve only to confuse a player, by awakening him to the fact that he can hit the ball in dozens of different ways and still miss them.

To most enthusiasts, putting is still half the game, and that in figures means a lot of hits at the ball. I can remember only once getting fewer than 25 putts for a round, and for me that's a sign I've missed the green too many times. If you hit many greens with your seconds, then often more putts are required than if you miss the cut part of the green and chip up.

It has been suggested that to make putting a smaller proportion of the game holes should be made larger. With all the heartbreaks I've experienced on the green, I would not like to see this change, and in case you do not realize it, big greens make low scoring more difficult.

THE PUTTING MACHINE

A simple type of putting machine which is used to check on the trueness of putting surfaces. Yet outside say twelve feet on a perfect green it is not very certain that all putts will be holed even when the machine is well set. Of course the balls eventually wear a groove in the grass and that helps to steer the balls into the hole as they run down a track. This makes the magical putting of certain players seem all the more remarkable, for they only have one chance and have to get everything right first time.

PUTTING BY NON-GOLFERS

Bobby Locke continues to use an old favourite.

WHEN it comes to putting poorly, people finally resolve themselves into two categories — those who believe it is their own fault when they putt poorly, sticking obstinately to one club and saying to themselves 'only poor workmen complain of their tools', and those who are ready to put the blame on to the club and try others, on the ground that 'it can't be *me*, it *must* be the club'. Let me say that I understand perfectly the two categories.

It is a terrific test of fidelity to remain loyal to one putter through thick and thin times, on fast, on rough, on slow greens, and when playing very frequently. I know from experience that a temporary change, often using something 'worse' for a time, restores one's love of the old favourite. Some players, to whom rolling the silly little white ball along the surface of the ground has never been a problem, just take any club and use it, hardly bothering to note if the grip is thin or the lie is flat. They do not bother to practise either, which is also exasperating — they have a natural gift to perform this tantalizing part of the game with skill and confidence.

In France, at most holiday resorts and in the parks of the big towns, I have come across these miniature golf courses — 'Tom Thumb' putting courses, we used to call them — where the ball is rolled up slopes, under tunnels and through old motor tyres serving as hazards, with crowds queueing up to play. At Deauville, in Calvados in France, some competitions attracted up to 150 entrants and the winning score was usually 43 or 44, which was about par for 18 holes — some holes, played in sections, had, quite rightly, 3 as a par.

I do not think that more than half a dozen entrants had ever played golf before, yet they were able to negotiate these hazards, rolling the ball on a fast red earth surface with considerable skill and, curiously enough, many arrived at an almost normal sort of golf putting stance and grip.

I had a good look at these non-golfers in action, just to see if there was any 'doing-what-comes-naturally' action about them; but after beginning often with the hands reversed (as children do when they take up a club at first) and placed wide apart, they usually ended up by copying the more successful players, and used a standard sort of grip.

I have noted also with classes of young golfers, some take to putting almost like a duck to water; they do not give the impression they are putting with boxing gloves on; they seem to have the idea from the very start. Others need to be shown a method and coaxed into rolling the ball gently along the ground, and must be stopped from hitting the ball to and fro past the hole endlessly.

The ability to putt very well was a 'forte' of

The Miniature Golf game still flourishes on the Continent. This lady has her ideas on how to grip and she will probably do well until someone shows her 'how to putt', then her troubles may begin. Obviously, no one has told her anything so far!

Gene Sarazen in his younger days, for no golfer ever putted more confidently. His skill has diminished somewhat with the years, and often with his right index finger pointed down the side of the shaft (his 'over-forty finger', he calls it), the little wizard cries out for a six inch hole, as it were, to end the agony. But although I have had my putting crises, I would not change the old 'four-and-a-bit inch hole', because it is almost the only thing left in the game which prevents it from being a completely 'power game' to-day — it levels up the skill *v.* power fight, somewhat.

The main thing missing from the game to-day is to make every tee shot a target shot as it used to be, and not just a thoughtless slug into a field as it often is now, with enough rough to make the next shot a non-precision effort.

Quite a number of clubs have smaller holes, $2\frac{1}{2}$ inches in diameter, cut in their practice putting greens, to make putting into the normal hole seem like putting into a bucket. This is a good idea, but most good putters admit to a regular spell on the carpet at home as a sound way to built-up touch and to cultivate a smooth stroke. All the great players, Hogan among them, always have a golf club or two in their own living-room or in their hotel bedroom. When you see John Panton going home at any time from the golf course you will see that he usually has his trusty putter under his arm.

Once you have tested a method or methods — for few are the players who do not have slight variations or compensations to make for daily muscular changes — then it all becomes a question of nerves. And for far too many to-day the medicine-chest plays a vital rôle. There are all sorts of pep pills (and dulling drugs for those who are too anxious), but when I came in it was a triple Kümmel or a double port which were known as putter's medicines, and I have known even a stiff brandy to be swallowed hurriedly by some players before teeing off.

When I see prominent players begin to slide

Myself using a stiff-wristed action, ball on the left toe. This action means the ball is pushed and is, I have found, any good only on a true green. I do not do well with this stroke on greens with nap or which have coarse grass.

down the prize list too regularly, it can be guaranteed that it is their putting which lets them down, and it is not a faulty method but their nerves which have become frayed, with the wear and tear of dozens of successive tournaments. I do not think the human frame can stand up to the pounding it gets from tournament golf, despite the assistance from vitamins, etc., and there is often regular air travel, too, just to add to the strain.

Ben Hogan, as I have already mentioned, one of those great players who made himself strong in every department of the game, has now begun to have doubts in his putting; the short putts are torture, and so the need to put every long putt on the edge of the hole is becoming a great strain. And with him it is definitely not lack of practice!

A PUTTING TIP

Dr Garfield Evans, from Cardiff, Wales, a student of putting theory if ever there was one, writes: 'I move the right forearm in a pure arc with its centre the point of the elbow held close to the right side, above the right hip. If the putter is held firmly in the right hand the putter will also move in a pure arc. When the face of the putter in the address is placed square to the ball and the line of the putt, it is quite correct to say that the putter face is always square, when the putter is moved in a pure arc, without any intrinsic rotation of the forearm, while moving in its pure arc. With the intrinsic rotation of the forearm, namely supination or pronation, the forearm does not move in space; it simply rotates on its own long axis.' This is not a new idea, but it might ring a bell for someone who is too lazy to find his own method.

A COMMON AMERICAN SYSTEM

'*Dick, show me how you are putting these days.*' *I asked 1957 U.S. Open Champion, Dick Mayer, to demonstrate his putting action to me. Dick has the reputation of being a fine pressure putter. Using a wry-necked, long-shafted, aluminium-headed club with a hard metal face insert, Dick, showing all the fingers of his left hand to the front and with his right thumb on the top of the shaft, uses a reverse overlapping grip and '*hinges*' the club back from the left elbow.*

Actually he works from the left elbow and 'in his mind' moves the left thumb back. From the very shut club-face position at the top of the back stroke, the clubhead is lifted well clear of the ground. Dick proceeds to hold the face square as the impact point approaches. The ball is very near the left toe and very close in; this goes with this particular method.

The head is held almost desperately steady and after impact, as the left thumb moves towards the hole, the face of the club is forced under, as it were, so that it still is square to the line of 'ball-to-hole'.

Dick won his place as golfer of the year and leading money winner of 1957 with this action. It is a popular one, yet I have never been able to do much good with it. Why, I do not know, but it must be something to do with my vision, as I do not seem to see the line when 'crowding over the ball'.

EYES AND PUTTING

IT has long been a theory of mine that such great putters as Bobby Jones, Walter Hagen, Bobby Locke and Peter Thomson have the natural ability to see the lines on a golf green better than most of us. Now I read that there is an optic law concerning putting.

I do not know Frank J. Douglass, the authority for the statements on this subject, but he says that the optic law, which has no big importance in everyday life, demands that the eyes must be on a horizontal plane before they can transmit an exact image of a flat surface or a lateral line in the field of vision.

When taking the line of a putt, most golfers squat or bend forward to observe the surface of the green from as near as possible. This means that the head is not vertical; the eyes are 'displaced'. So the player gets an incorrect picture.

It is easy to check if a line is traced on a slope from left to right. Look at it from low down. If the head is turned towards the right, the line seems horizontal; turned to the left, the slope is accentuated. This optical illusion can explain many missed putts.

Stand upright in a relaxed position behind the ball. You will avoid the illusion and see the real line the ball should take.

I must admit that I have never found I could see the lines better by getting down to them. I have always done this — just to make sure, as I thought, yet often, I guess, to complicate matters.

Come to think of it, we all putt well when we do not study the shots so much. Maybe Mr Douglass

Tony Coop bends down to look at his putt.

has something! So take a look standing up from now on and see if it works out better.

While on this subject of seeing the line in golf I must say that I have found some improvement in this direction since taking to glasses for reading. My eyes are more rested, and I not only see the lines on the greens better, but I can look at the ball longer when I play through the green. This is a great advantage because I do not have the feeling that I must hurry to hit the ball before the sharpness goes, which was what was happening before.

I am experimenting with slightly coloured non-magnifying lenses in spectacles for all my golf, which my oculist thinks will cut out certain rays and will act as a 'windscreen' against the winds, which tire the eyes.

Few golfers go to this extreme to study a line on the green, but some swear by it as the last word in picking the line. This is Alan ('Tiger') Poulton, a good putter, too, getting a worm's eye view of the lie of the land.

YOU NEED A GOOD CLICK WHEN YOU PUTT

The Earl of Carnarvon putting at Deauville; he putts well with this style.

I THINK that putting clubs which have a good click when the ball is struck give the best results and sell best. There is no actual rule of thumb regarding their model; it is a question of feel and maybe taste.

The putter face becomes in the end an extension of your fingers — I think all good putters do have their eyes over the ball, no matter how they stand. The old maestro, Ted Ray, claimed that bouncing the ball up and down on his putter face taught him to feel the ball and to judge the bounce off the club-face as he sent the ball different heights, before letting it come finally to rest on the club. He could do this as he walked along; I have seen quite a number of other players do this. I have never done it very well, but have never practised it, I admit.

A centre-shafted mallet is seen used successfully by a veteran golfer. Note stance and grip — with any head-up the eyes are still on the line of the putt. This club gives a good click.

A TOP TAP PUTTER

DOUG. Ford is the 'stage' name of this famous player — his real name is Fortunato — and since becoming a professional soon after the war he has climbed slowly to the top in America, principally due to his play from '80 yards in' and to his brave putting. Ford at the time this photograph was taken was in his middle thirties. He is one of the few players I have known who, in professional parlance, *charges* the hole. It does not mean he always run four feet past, but he holes more of those putts, which hit the back of the hole and jump up in the air and then drop, than almost all the other players together.

Ford has a normal sort of stance, right foot drawn back slightly, and uses a reverse overlap combined with an interlock. He strikes the ball generally in the heel of the club and is a 'tap putter' — not a loose follow-through swinger of the club. He is one of those who works at putting daily, spending hours on the putting green, and unlike many modern pros., wastes no time in getting on with the job; he is possibly the only player about whom complaints have been made for going *too fast*. Note the way his right thumb lies on the shaft and his reverse interlocking grip.

MISSED IT!

HINGEING

Putting at the Royal Golf Club in Madrid. On my visit to Spain, I putted extra well with a new style for me — steel-shafted, shallow-bladed putter — and somehow got a long back-swing going and a hinge. I changed back later. Note here the six Spanish workwomen removing weeds from the green. A rare sight these days when most Clubs have labour troubles.

N

ONE-HANDED PUTTING

Joe Turnesa, eldest of the fine family of Italian–American golfing brothers, was always a good swinger of the golf club and in his younger days was a fine putter. But a 'twitch' came into his game and the only way he beat it was to putt with his right hand only; and he became the first top ranking golfer, to my knowledge, to win a major event using this method. He is seen here ready to strike the ball.

We all have tried this out occasionally and it nearly always works, so I am surprised that really more golfers do not use it regularly. When I play with a golfer who putts with one hand only — it is usually the right hand, too — I always have a feeling that he is going to 'hole the lot'. Have you tried it?

LEFT: *Joe Turnesa putting.*

RIGHT: *Joe Turnesa before his putting left him.*

A PRIME MINISTER PUTTS

Lord Brookeborough, Prime Minister of Northern Ireland, uses the elbow spreading method. One sees less of this style now—at one time I seemed to see many players using it. With an aluminium-headed club he gets the ball rolling very well. Some golfers have this gift, it seems, though I have met successful putters who stab or chop the ball, almost taking a divot. This method of a stab is good for the timid putter, as he has no time to change his mind before the ball has gone.

ALAS, ILLEGAL!

Henry Longhurst tries out the best type of putter in the game, better than the through-the-legs mallet — a hammer head with a thin, long tail, but alas, illegal! The hitting area is smaller than the ball, but how easy it is to swing it truly. (The Rules of Golf say: 'The length of a clubhead from the back of the heel to the toe shall be greater than the breadth from the face to the back of the head at the broadest point.')

I had this putter sent to me and the first time out I took only 29 putts for the round. It helped to get me tapping the ball instead of swinging too freely and it did not wobble in the back swing.

THE ONE-PIECE STROKE

This is the 'no wrist action' stroke. The arms, elbows outward thrust, and the wrists are locked and the whole framework is moved to and fro slowly. The length of the back swing dictates the distance the ball has to travel. This suits nervous putters and many golfers get surprisingly good results this way. I have used forms of it, but have felt it work only on good true greens for short and middle distance putts. The shoulders play a big rôle in this action.

195

TWO YOUNG CHAMPIONS PUTTING

Gary Player, the young South African, owes much to his temperament and his putting. This was the method he used to win the British Open Championship at Muirfield in 1959. He has learned to be a great pressure putter. Note elbows against the body and head right over the ball.

Peter Thomson, a sound golfer in all departments, is an exceptional putter. This putt on the 7th green on the Burma Road at Wentworth went in for a 4 after his second had gone over the green. Note economy of movement — a tap. Thomson uses a shallow-headed blade putter.

CLIPPING THE BALL

Christy O'Connor, from Dublin, Eire, who began to make a name for himself in the 'fifties, is a natural sort of golfer, very strong and slashing. His whole action is casual, almost careless, and he uses a loose type of grip, as in his swing and even in his putting there is a sort of closing and opening of the hands, as if to add crispness to the shot.

His putting varies; he is one of the inspired sort of golfers, and in the putting stroke, just finished here, he has already stopped the clubhead on a putt of some eight yards.

He seems to 'clip' the ball, to 'snap' it, to hit it smartly, and on his day, and I suppose on certan sorts of putting green surfaces, especially of the keen type, he can be very good. It is not a method instructors would set out to teach people, but those with 'live hands' could acquire it; it is a finger action.

GREAT PUTTERS

THE STYLES OF GREAT PUTTERS

Walter Hagen in his great days was a master putter. He used a wide stance with the ball well forward and, with a reverse overlapping grip, putted with great confidence and slightly opening and closing blade on his moderately deep-faced blade putter. He had the weight well forward on his left foot, and was not afraid to swing the putter well back. He said he imagined he was lofting the ball into the hole as he struck it.

Richard Burton, in the immediate pre-war years, wielded his blade putter with a long, flowing, hingeing, wristy action. It always looked the ideal casual way to putt, but to those who did not have the touch or the nerve it spelt disaster. Dick, all the same, putted magnificently this way. It is a method which many abandoned, for rather like Hagen's, it seemed not to be so efficient as the years passed, though Dick, I must admit, still putts well with it.

Alfred Padgham was another of those wristy putters. Standing a long way from the ball, Padgham putted as he drove, with a sort of nonchalance, with the arms well off the body, but this method seemed to fail on the short putts, especially as the years passed.

ALWAYS LOCKE!

Bobby Locke, as a very young slim man, was a great putter, almost in the class he was later to become as he matured. He kept his putter blade closed on the way through, as he did later. So he seemed thereby to get the ball hugging the turf from the start. He claims that he holds the blade down going back, never opening it.

His forearms were always close to the body and the ball well forward; his putting skill has stayed with him although now, of course, his forearms rest on his massive torso.

Bobby Locke (1958) stands very closed for all his shots, even on the green, his right foot well behind the left. Note (LEFT) short follow-on after the ball, as the club stops in the follow-through on this 4 yards putt.

Great care is taken even on the shortest of putts to hit the ball truly. The ball is struck in the heel of the club on this short putt (RIGHT).

THE MAN WITH THE PAUSE

MACDONALD Smith, one of the famous Carnoustie golfing brothers, was one of those great players who never won a major championship. Mac was always a lovely swinger of the club, and while it could not be said he lacked competitive courage, he seemed just to miss the big ones, being runner-up many times.

His putting was lovely to watch; he generally used a long-shafted aluminium-headed club and developed a distinct pause at the top of his backswing. He claimed that his pause, made at varying lengths according to the distance to be putted, enabled him to gauge his distance better. His grip is unusual, because he uses his two thumbs down the top of the grip and presses on the shaft with the tip of his right thumb. His blade opens slightly, there is no deliberate attempt made to hold it square to the ball.

His dress is typical of what the best dressed golfer wore in the 20's. Not that he actually played in a coat, but the rest of the outfit, the plus twos (fours?), the striped shirt and bow tie, were of his generation — very 'chic', too. In those days there were no laundry problems and so the tie-less sports shirts of to-day were of no advantage and would have been considered slovenly. I must say, although I favour them, they do not look as neat as a silk shirt and a tie.

LINING UP

EVERY golfer is sometimes baffled by the line of a putt. On a strange course even the most experienced professional can take the wrong borrow. Here is an 'infallible' (?) way of telling if it comes in from the right or left; here I am demonstrating it. Stand about three yards behind the ball, hold the putter lightly at the end of the grip in the thumb and forefinger and in front of your head.

Use your right eye, and shut the other. Cover the hole with the shaft.

If you do not see the ball, the putt is straight. If the ball appears on the left of the shaft, the borrow is from the left. If the ball is on the right, the borrow is from the right.

I first saw this method used by Allen Geiberger, junior American ace. He finds it handy on his undulating seaside links in California. Gerald Micklem said it was a great help at Porthcawl during the internationals there. It has not caught on here, but it had a brief vogue in America. I am not satisfied that it is worth the trouble.

PUTTING UNDER DIFFICULTIES

On board ship — 'Angel Golf', as it is called. The ball has to go through the discs, beginning at nine different starting points from left to right of the board. This is a very tantalizing game even when there is no roll of the ship to gauge, but on the Royal Mail Line ships across the South Atlantic there is always a putting competition between Lisbon and Rio do Janeiro. 'Toots' is judging the roll of the ship. The ship rolls so evenly that by watching the shadows it is possible to strike the ball when the board is just horizontal.

It is hard enough to putt without your two dogs walking about on the green and throwing shadows on the line of your putt, but this golfer does not seem to notice the additional problems. Scene is the San Remo Golf Club, Italian Riviera.

WHAT DO YOU UNDERSTAND BY FOLLOW-THROUGH?

Here I have been snapped after playing a No. 8 iron shot. I have followed through well. The club-head can be said to have been thrown through on the line to the hole. This is only one way to finish this type of shot and, curiously enough, I find I can over-do it and many shots of mine which finish, say, flag-high left of the pin, come from following through too much. Many good golfers break their left arms long before this.

SOME GOLFING COMMON-SENSE

HERE on this page are tips — logic really or just plain golfing common-sense; nothing new, but something that does not do any golfer, however good, any harm to see in black and white once in a while. Most golfers could write this themselves, but there is probably one point they would have missed and maybe this is the very point that is holding up their fun:

The most important shot in golf is the one you are about to make.

Keep your head still on all shots; look at the ball but do not stare.

Do all your thinking and make all your decisions as to what you are going to do *before addressing the ball*.

Players with a pleasant disposition play better golf. Most things in golf are simple and easy when you learn to do them right.

Arms, hands and wrists will get you out of the trouble they put you in, if you do not tighten up.

Trying too hard, hitting too late, gripping too tight and looking up, these are the most common golfing faults.

Relax mentally and physically. You can't relax if you are worried, if you are angry, if you hurry and rush.

Have confidence in your clubs and in your ability to do the shot; as *you* are attempting the shot and only have yourself to beat, the odds are on *you*.

The shorter shots demand a narrower stance, the club held shorter and the hands near the body.

High shots will stop better than low ones.

For a low drive some even tee the ball high and hit it with plenty of roll of the wrist or endeavour to hit the ball thinly — that is, on the lower half of the club-face.

Cut out fancy strokes such as cuts and hooks wherever possible.

For a high ball, play the ball off the left foot from a high tee and hold the weight back, helping the ball to rise with extra wrist flick. Hit earlier in effect.

Do not play clever shots. The good players don't; they play safe ones all the time.

Never get careless, but do not concentrate too hard.

If your mind is relaxed, your muscles will follow their usual groove.

If you are really scared and much hangs on the shot, do an exhibition swing: don't 'steer the ball'.

Keeping your eye on the ball means, too, that you must think what you are doing.

Never think of the hazards after you have decided which shot to play; just try to play that shot.

Golf is as easy or as hard as you make it.

Play the game, not your opponent. You can only win back one hole at a time.

Many bad breaks are usually the result of bad play.

Trouble presents itself on a golf course; don't go looking for it.

Don't get into the habit of picking up. Finish out the holes to see how really good you are.

Don't offer advice to other players; wait until they almost beg for help and then wait till you have won! I have learned this lesson the hard way.

Don't blame others for a bad shot.

If you are going to play golf, be a good golfer.

If you feel stiff and clumsy, try swinging two or three clubs at once, to loosen up.

Don't do several fast practice swings before every shot; it tires you.

Whistling relaxes and helps to avoid tension. Exhale before hitting the ball — never fill the lungs first before swinging at the ball.

Keep the palm of the right hand facing the hole for putting — going back and going through.

From a bad lie use a spoon if you need length, but play it as an iron shot, hit down and through; turn face in because bend in shaft tends to spring face open.

Weight on left heel at finish of swing often means ball has been cut.

Open stance shortens back-swing and lengthens follow-through.

Closed or shut stance lengthens back-swing, but shortens follow-through.

Run up shots: play with stiff wrists and use straight-faced iron clubs such as Nos. 3, 4 or 5.

Pitch shots: cock wrists evenly and go back as far as you go through.

Buried ball in sand comes out (if you dig behind the ball, too) with forward run always.

Right thumbnail pressed into putter grip is popular with top putters.

Many players hit short putts in the heel.

A slice with a No. 3 iron goes about as far as a hook with a No. 5 iron.

Aim at the back of the ball, not just at a 'white blurr'— the ball.

Yes, I know, you could think of lots more. I suppose I could, too; but I am sure that some points will get home to every golfer.

A CHAMPION PITCHES

Julius Boros, one of America's top tournament players, who is considered a great 'pressure player', plays a short pitch. Note how forward the ball is — the soft spongy fairways are responsible for this position. Note club-face held down to the ball in the photograph on the left.

DO YOU HOLD THE FACE SQUARE?

LEFT: *Holding the face square by Harry Weetman — many golfers lay the club-face out and do not know they are doing it.* RIGHT: *I show what an open face looks like from the front.*

THE WALTER HAGEN STORY

ABOUT the time I was in Rochester, New York, in 1956, Walter Hagen's book came out and it was fun talking to him about it there.

Ever since I met 'The Haig' in his home town that June, I have been wanting to comment on his book. Walter, then sixty-four years of age, and a real heavyweight now, suffers from arthritis. If he does not try to play golf all is well, but when he gets tempted to hit at a ball, he suffers afterwards from acute pains in his wrists, so he simply does not play. He fishes instead from the porch of his log cabin on a lake in Michigan.

A tree was planted that summer at the Oak Hill County Club, Rochester, N.Y., during the U.S. Open Championship there, to honour their native son, for Walter was born in this northern part of New York State of German parents. His father, William, was a blacksmith and, as Walter says, 'the family got along fine on eighteen dollars a week, which was good pay in the early part of this century'.

Walter began caddying to make the extras, because there was not much left over after plenty of good plain food had been eaten by mother and father and four healthy children.

Walter points out that at any game he played he was always relaxed — and whether it was pool, marbles, baseball, shooting or golf, 'I played to win'. He went in Andrew Christy's pro.'s shop at the age of fourteen, and there learned to make clubs, and until 1920 he gained all his successes with a 'collection of odds and ends' making up his set of clubs, and his record to that date included two American Opens. How different from the equipment available to *every* golfer to-day!

There are pages of interesting description of his many matches, for in his day the challenge match had not become a thing of the past, as it has done to-day. The top players of the day were not afraid to see who was 'top-dog' in hand-to-hand battle, and 'The Haig' played them all and almost invariably won.

Perhaps his greatest match was against Bobby Jones in 1926 — the 'immortal Bobby' who was later to win the four major titles in one year, 'The Impregnable Quadrilateral', as it was aptly called. Here a 'pro. *versus* amateur' match was staged and Hagen won by 12 and 11 over 72 holes, and he won 7,600 dollars, the biggest fee ever paid to a golfer for an exhibition or challenge match. He gave Bobby a present of a pair of diamond and platinum cuff-links and kept 6,800 dollars himself. To-day this would certainly be equal to 20,000 dollars.

'I always used a lot of strategy and psychology', writes Hagen, 'and it often paid off; I used it on

A photograph not in his book. 'The Haig' and I shake hands at Muirfield in 1929, the year he won his last Open Championship. I was to win my last Open there nineteen years later. Ernest Hargreaves, the bright lad carrying Walter's bag, is on the left of the photograph. Hargreaves later became my caddie, then my caddie-valet, then my butler. Now he is steward at Temple Golf Club, Berkshire, after working three years as a manager on the Trust House Hotels Circuit.

Hargreaves took his holiday at Muirfield to see me win in 1948. Note the small-sized golf bags of the day and 'The Haig's' clubs without covers on the wooden clubs.

them all. . . . I set up the shots the way a movie director sets up his scenes, to pull all the suspense possible from every move. I strutted and I smiled.' There is the real Hagen the British learned to love and follow.

I often feel that golfers forget that, in Hagen's day, to come to Europe meant a seven-day sea voyage, and often a lay-off from golf for at least ten days and right in the middle of the tournament season, too. I know an effort was sometimes made to drive balls into the sea from the ship for practice but that, I have found, did more harm than good. To-day no top player in his senses would think of a ten-day lay-off before beginning a championship.

Referring to his clubs, Hagen writes: 'Curiously enough, also, the type and the limited number of clubs we carried then contributed to the greater skill we acquired in the varied types of shots we were compelled to make with them. We had no wedge, the most popular club among golfers to-day. As late as 1921, we were playing wedge shots with a niblick, or the equivalent of an 8 iron or with any club having sufficient loft to pitch cleanly out of a trap and over projecting heights.'

'I got quite a kick out of collecting medals and getting my name on every trophy. Some of the toughest competitors didn't get their names on many trophies or get listed as champions, but they were great golfers. I'm thinking of fellows like Tommy McNamara, Tommy Kerrigan, Harry Cooper, Bobby Cruickshank, Macdonald Smith, and many more.'

A world tour with Hagen, which took in big-game hunting and fishing, was 'something' in the good old days between the wars, when things were done on a big scale. Walter Hagen is possessed of tolerance and often exasperating patience and a sound German stubbornness. His keen sense of humour makes him a great tease and a joker. His attention to detail remains as constantly fastidious as when he selected his first cashmere sweaters and his famed fleecy coats and beautifully mono-grammed shirts, Paisley ascots, hand-crafted shoes, custom-tailored suits in the same browns, greys or blues . . . the Walter Hagen of yesterday and to-day.

'A wonderful and hospitable host, "The Haig", who likes to dine shortly before midnight on a thick steak and Chef salad.' Well, that is part of one of the final pages of the book, called 'An afterword' by the collaborator with Walter Hagen in *The Walter Hagen Story*, which I recommend to all would-be golf champions. Margaret Seaton Heck, who had difficulty in getting 'The Haig' to

A back view of Walter Hagen in 1933 when his tournament career was nearly over. This is a typical Hagen finish. Note how the club has 'slid' into the palm of the right hand and the length of the follow-through. A photograph by Frank E. Beresford, the famous artist who loves photography.

concentrate on supplying material for this book, studied newspaper articles and clippings for two and a half years on the 'fabulous Hagen' before she could get organized to give us this story of his life. It is not quite what I had expected, somehow, but I know golfers will enjoy reading it. It records some intimate side-lights of one who did so much for golf, and professional golf in particular.

When Hagen first came to Britain, he and all other professionals competing in our events did not use the clubhouses; they changed in tents or pro.'s shops, as had been customary. Long before he retired, we were considered 'gentlemen' and I for one appreciated his efforts to break this barrier. I do not think the young professionals to-day ever think of his contribution to their present status.

LOOKING AT THE BALL

I HAVE always been satisfied that I play better when looking at the ball, trying to see the clubhead hit the ball. This, however, is physically impossible for full shots, as the clubhead travels too fast, but it is possible for putts, and I know it helps even to try. Just at the moment, I notice quite an amount of support for the idea that there is no need to hold the head steady or to look at the ball even; it is reckoned just a fetish. I differ entirely.

In every decent round played, I suppose that one badly executed shot at least can be attributed to plain 'head-up'. Under this title can come 'eye off the ball', because for the little pitches and the shorter shots, the head would move little, as the movement is an arm one, the body action being very limited.

When teaching, I have repeatedly noticed that once you have convinced your pupil that he does not see the ball when he hits it, he often glues his head down so much that he does no swing at all, because he cramps his entire movement. It is from this overdoing of things that this 'anti-head-down' line springs.

This head down, chin back business is a very noticeable feature of all good players, regardless of style or build, but I am convinced that, in order to imitate some of our leading players, many middle-aged golfers would need new necks and

Myself in 1953 when practising, keeping my chin behind the ball.

some of the heavily-built ones longer ones, as there is a certain flexibility and strength of muscles in the neck required to hold the head steady without cramping the swing.

Just see if you can turn your head easily and smartly to the side without turning your shoulders. You will need to do this if you want to hit past your head. (You seniors will hear crackles and feel stabs, I bet, like a knife thrust — uric acid, old boy!)

There are hundreds — one could say truthfully thousands and thousands — of golfers who play quite well and yet they never look at the ball. They just have a good eye, judge the distance from the ball well and have, as we instructors say, a good memory. These are the very players who play poorly at first when told to keep their heads steady and their eye on the ball, and so they willingly become crusading members of the 'not-looking-at-the-ball' brigade. The natural games player type often has a perpetual head-up, but his natural ability gets him by. I am sure that players who do not look at the ball well will always be limited in their ultimate success. The fact of looking at the ball steadies the head and trues up the swing, by fixing the centre of gravity, for the head is a very heavy part of the anatomy, and when it starts waving about it destroys the balance. One famous teacher even suggests throwing the head back

'He often glues his head down so much that he does no swing at all.'

205

Al Besselink, watched by the 1958 U.S. Open Champion, Tommy Bolt, keeps his eye on the ball. 'Bessie', as the pros. call this handsome athlete, has a fine swing, with a more than average 'look at the ball' part in it. Few golfers can play well and look at the ball this much, without getting cramped.

slightly against the hit through, as a sort of counterweight effect, and he reads this action into every great swing.

It is essential to decide right away, when teaching, whether a player can hit past his head physically or not. Heavily-built, short players with broad shoulders and short necks knock up their heads with their shoulders as they get near impact. I have found that such players do better when not restricting their pivot and making the swing as much of an arm swing as possible, but their heads have to go with the shoulders and very few become champions.

Players who hit the ball with all their might and main generally are erratic because they put in the maximum effort they can with their bodies, trying to step up the maximum speed their hands can create, and then it can be seen that the head weaves about. These are not my pattern to copy. I keep my head well back of the ball generally and I look at the ball with my left eye on the way back as I cock my head to the side.

This cocking of the head to the side I developed, as it gave my head quite a wide arc to turn through before it was up in the impact area, and so I could look at the ball throughout this period. This is the big advantage over the two-eyed stance. The advisability of adopting it will lie as much with the eyes themselves as with the neck

muscles. Many people could be completely disorganized if asked to look at the ball with one eye for a few instants during the swing. The nose obstructs the view of the right eye when the head is fully cocked to the side.

A very sound way to check up on how much you look at the ball is to pitch to a flag without seeing the results of your shots, getting a friend to guide you only by telling you where the shots have finished. In this way you can acquire touch and control, and even good players are completely lost at first when cutting out that peek at the flag which takes place as the shot is being hit.

In the short game it is the last-minute glance at the flag which often alters the power being applied and causes a hesitation and a resultant fluff. If a player has the courage to say: 'I am going to hit this ball — this much — bang! and I will take a chance on having stood correctly to the hole', then the result will nearly always be satisfactory.

I remember playing on one occasion with a golfer who never hits past his chin; he went out in 34, but I always felt it was much above his form. Then coming back, after one mishit, he mishit a dozen more shots and came home in 42 strokes (on a short course S.S.S. 67). His last nine holes contained the shots he will always do when he particularly wants to play well and tries to take more careful aim, because then he looks up more quickly than ever. One of the great slogans of golf is 'swing under your head' — i.e., not *with* your head *turning* as you swing. Try looking at the ball for a change; it will steady your head and true up your swing.

I look at the ball with my left eye.

206

LOOKING AT DIFFERENT ANGLES

Charley Penna, brother of Tony, who designs golf clubs for the famous MacGregor Company in the U.S.A., is a successful golf pro., despite a neck injury which causes his head to turn in a curious way as he does his back-swing. Compare this action (LEFT) with Ben Hogan's back swing (RIGHT). Charley hits the ball a long way and very solidly, too, because his grip of the club, as can be seen, is 100% sound.

CLASSIC HEAD-UPS

It is interesting how they all run to type; the body knocks the head up in most cases. The poor foot action and weakness of the hands have meant that the golfers seen here have had to use their right shoulders to move the ball.

207

THE ANXIOUS LOOK UP

These three photographs are of the 'curiosity' type of head-up — anxiety to see the result. Such strokes have no solidity about them and rarely hit the target. Again the feet have not contributed to the stroke. Yet if you got these golfers to listen to your explanation about poor foot action, I doubt if they would practice 'foot drill'.

PLEASE COPY!

Please do not practise like my friend, the Marquis Luis de Bolarque in Madrid (LEFT). Here he is getting plenty of exercise hitting out balls on the wonderful practice-ground of the Royal Golf Club at Puerto del Hierro, but he would do better golfingly if he copied my action in the photograph (RIGHT), taken using the same club, by hitting past his chin.

HOW MUCH SHOULD THE HEAD STAY DOWN?

FROM my own experience I am perfectly sure that I play my best golf from tee to hole when I look at the ball, holding my head steady for drives and putts alike. In putting I, alas, have rarely been able to say: 'I 'its and 'arks', for I find myself peeking incurably. But I am satisfied, all the same, that I hit the ball more truly with a better impact when I 'see the ball hit'.

For the full shots, there is no question that the ball is more correctly struck, in my own case, when I look at the ball, and in general I am a 'good-looker-at-it', as photographs taken at all sorts of odd moments without my knowledge prove. I am sure, too, that my pupils succeed in their efforts to hit the ball repeatedly on the centre of the club-face when they, too, look at the ball.

I am not a subscriber to the theory that it is unnecessary to look at the ball, and that it is old-fashioned. I have seen good players swing casually through, hitting the ball 'from memory', and I have been beaten by them at times, but they have not stayed the course because, maybe, 'their memories have failed'!

To say 'Do not keep your head down' is good advice in catering to a public weakness, pandering to a common golfing vice, and if the 'head-up champion' of the club gleefully says: 'There you are, Jackie Burke said it', it does not, I bet, improve his game, nor that of others, just to see it in print. The old adage, 'keep your head down', trotted out by thousands of golf pros. daily throughout the world, is just as important for success to-day as when it was first used in 1318 by the executioner in the Tower of London!

Your head down is not only the key to keeping your eye on the ball, but it gives you a chance to swing your shoulders under your head and to hit late, to hit on a bent right arm, and to keep your clubhead on the correct arc. When the head goes with the stroke and is not, therefore, steady, the right shoulder comes up, too, and then it becomes essential in order to reach the ball to straighten the right arm too soon, and this very often will throw the clubhead off the correct arc. Apart also from taking the eye off the spot where contact is to be made — i.e., the back centre of the ball — the 'head-up golfer' often straightens his back and hits the ball off the point of the club, or if his right arm straightens violently he hits the ball in 'the neck'.

'I simply cannot keep my head down', says many a pupil. On the shorter strokes around the green it may be sheer curiosity, anxiety even, to

LEFT: *Gary Player — a good looker at the ball.* RIGHT: *Exaggerating the action of looking at the ball expressly. There is no point in locking the head this much.*

see the result, but in a large number of cases in the full shots the head can be knocked off the ball by faulty body action.

Many golfers have a feeling that if they allow their feet to move — 'left heel up, right heel up' — in turn as the club is swung, there is a danger that the clubhead will get off its true arc more readily, but the opposite is the case. Fixing the feet on the ground can dull the hip action and so get the shoulders doing too much.

The right idea to have is that, as the clubhead swings to and fro, the body does nothing but ease this action. It does not act as a brake at any time, but the swing must go under the head.

Just take a look at these handicap golfers in action on the next page.

1. This lady knew I was there with my camera and so made a special head-down effort, cramping the right side and blocking the follow-through and, in fact, hit a little behind the ball — a sort of half-fluff. Her natural and normal action would have included a bit more thrust through with the right knee and the right shoulder, but this photograph is typical of the 'I must, at all costs, look at the ball' action — but the clubhead has not gone on naturally.

2. This golfer sees the ball well enough, but his head is turning slightly with the swing. There is no

o

1. *2.* *3.*

hit-past-the-chin here. A square blow is being delivered, left leg is well braced, right arm is bent, and for a handicap golfer it is more than a sound action. I doubt, in his case, if he would do as well by locking his head in place a little longer: only looser neck muscles would help him in this objective.

3. This is a good way to get any golfer to experience the feel of hitting the ball with his head steady, to swing under the head. I am in no danger of being hit by the club and I have found that if a player's head is held still in this way, he quickly learns to use his feet properly.

4. Here we have the usual result of an attempt to look at the ball at all costs. Right side completely blocked and, although there is a hit under the head, the arms cannot follow through properly and so the left arm collapses. The next step for-

ward from this position is to loosen up the right side, to 'kick' the right knee in towards the ball. Now compare illustrations 5 and 6.

5. Here you will see a high-handicap golfer, of the sturdy, short-necked build, allowing his own head to go with the clubhead, and he really hits the ball from memory. He could be taught to hold his head still at impact, but it would not come easily. All the same, it would help his game very much.

6. This is myself playing a No. 2 iron shot and, as can be seen, the arms have really done all the work. There is no fast rule outlining exactly the point at which the head can come up during the swing: physical differences govern this alone, but I can say very confidently that 'far too many golfers look at the ball too little; they would be better off if they gave it that little extra bit of attention'.

4. *5.* *6.*

GOLFING DRESS

OF course when golfers compare scores of pre-1914 with scores of to-day, a big difference is noticed and a conclusion is readily drawn that the old heroes were never as good as the hot scoring machines of to-day.

The older generations usually defend their era, by pointing out how much the equipment has improved, how the indestructible fast-whipping steel shaft, the matched set, and the high compression ball which fairly darts off the club face have made all the difference. Then they offer the preparation of courses to-day, the facilities for practice, and the way the rough has disappeared, and how the artificial watering makes for standardizing the play; add to this distance markers on the fairways, standard 10-foot high flag sticks, elimination of blind holes, levelling of fairways to get rid of awkward stances and luck, not forgetting the extra millions now playing the game, as further reasons for the generally lower scores, of anything up to five strokes a round.

But usually the freedom enjoyed in dressing more suitably for the game to-day is completely overlooked.

I came in at the end of the golf jacket, starched collar and tie, plus fours, and thick woollen stockings era; and my clothes for comfort, sweaters and sports shirts, were from Jack Izod, that dapper leader of the west end of London men's sporting fashions between the wars. Jack died in 1950.

I first developed the very wide, no pull sweater sleeve with him, which now is generally accepted as the best exterior wear model of woollen golf

I don't want to be a millionaire — as Walter Hagen used to say — just to live like one! Here I am on the steps of the Château de Haar, in Holland, where I stayed for a few days in the late summer of 1959. Just off to play golf in comfortable modern clothes — open-neck sports shirt, silk neck-scarf fixed with a special ring, loose-fitting wool cardigan and grey flannel slacks.

Tom Williamson against the tree.

In wide-sleeved pullover.

garment, but in those days I wore a shirt and tie with it. I was not uncomfortable by any means, but by comparison with the rather casual, almost untidy tie-less sporting era of to-day, I looked almost overdressed.

Abe Mitchell wore a rather tight jacket to stop him feeling too loose. In fact, he wore a very well-made single-breasted coat, part of a plus four suit, and looked like the country squire ready to take a walk in the country and not a golf champion going to the first tee. This reminds me I have never yet tried a tight-fitting coat on a lady golfer as a cure for over-swinging — it should work.

I wonder how much better Braid, Vardon and Taylor in their day, for example, would have played in to-day's wearing apparel. The plus four era has almost gone, simply because, in hot weather, linen (now replaced by some synthetic non-creasing fibre-base cloth) slacks are cooler and the costly long stockings are a nuisance to wash, while waterproof over-trousers have become an essential part of all golfers' equipment, for wet and cold spells. All the same, well-made plus fours of the best woollen cloth are great for golf — they do not flop in the wind and squatting down to look at the lines on the greens seems easier.

What the well-dressed golfer wore around 1895: Tom Williamson, a professional golfer who never deserted his club job enough to become the great player he should have been (seen on the previous page aged twenty-four). His note on the back of

Old Tom Morris with beard.

the photograph says: 'Just recovering from an attack of tonsilitis', which would no doubt explain the scarf around his neck, because at this time, with his suit and waistcoat, would go a shallow starched collar and tie. This photograph is interesting as it shows the type of driver used to propel the gutty ball. The medal was no doubt won at golf — to-day I have seen them dangling

Bobby Jones and his crowd. Note dress of the period. Frank E. Beresford, the artist, took this picture.

from the waist-band of slacks attached to a watch snugly fitted in a special watch pocket. Note, too, the laced boots which would have hob nails in them; how different from the super long nylon spiked golf shoes of to-day. The only item in his wardrobe which would be accepted to-day would be his cloth cap, which he wears at a jaunty angle.

The even earlier photograph, of old Tom Morris of St Andrews putting, shows him in his jacket. Note the double-handed grip and the long-headed wooden putter. I do not know if a nice bushy beard is a handicap to golfers. I have never heard of a champion growing one, but if the head moves it would certainly brush on the coat and make a noise.

The photograph of Bobby Jones driving in 1930 shows a popular golf costume of the 20's — tweed plus fours, belt and shirt with sleeves and a tie. Spectators, too, seem to be favouring plus fours. I often wonder if plus fours will not return again to popularity.

Alfred Perry, Open Champion of 1935, is seen sporting a wide and extra long style of plus fours with his cloth windcheater jacket — almost plus eights!

Mr H. M. Bray is seen wearing the tighter, shorter model of plus fours, which were favoured by thin golfers in immediate pre-war days. I often wore striped plus fours of the narrow style, but unlike Abe Mitchell I did not favour a crease in mine, but in America at this period it was considered well dressed to have a nice crease in one's plus fours.

Then after the war came the casual, almost sloppy vogue in American male golfing fashion — the outside, often startling coloured shirt, linen slacks, long-peaked linen cap and the inevitable towel hanging from the belt. It is comfortable and cool, but far from elegant.

The American male is very fashion conscious, but on a golf course, except for an odd golfer who perhaps over-dresses for the colour and style, most are untidily dressed for golf. I must say that it is very easy to get into the habit of being too casual in one's golfing attire, when one is inclined to dress for comfort only.

Tommy Bolt, seen below as a study in white, looks very smart indeed — white buckskin shoes, off-white slacks, cap and cardigan to match.

The most comfortable clothes I can find — cotton sports shirt, open-neck, loose alpaca cardigan and light-weight slacks. There is a picture of myself in 1957 on the next page.

I think that expensive laundry service, the need to travel light because of air travel, and the general trend of more practical clothing have brought about this change in golf wear. It is for the better, too, there is no question.

STYLES OF THE DAY

LEFT: *Alfred Perry (Open Champion of 1935) seen at Moor Park in April, 1938.* CENTRE: *Mr H. M. Bray. Neat golfing attire — check cap, narrow plus fours, shirt and tie and two pullovers. January, at Rye, 1938.* RIGHT: *A Symphony in White. Tommy Bolt at Greenbrier, North Carolina, 1956.*

LEFT: *Cotton sports shirt and alpaca cardigan, 1957.* CENTRE: *An American in the summer. Shirt worn outside trousers — usual, sensible long-peaked cap and inevitable towel to dry perspiring hands.* RIGHT: *My first plus four suit, aged fifteen.*

LEFT: *Harold Henning, the young South African professional, is discreetly and smartly dressed while practising at Hoylake. Note left hand and arm position for his No. 6 iron.*

BELOW LEFT: *Bobby Locke (with inevitable white shoes), one of the last of the old plus four brigade — looking at the line of a putt. Walton Heath, 1958.*

BELOW: *U.S. Vice-President Richard Nixon and myself at White Sulphur Springs. Mr Nixon began golf when he got in with the Eisenhower Administration — caught the bug from the President. Here he is sporting a typical American open-neck, short-sleeved shirt.*

A SLICE COMING UP!

PART 1

This very swing produced a slice (I saw it) and it always will, for this golfer was on the way to getting outside the ball, because his shoulder unwind has been too rapid for his arm action. This upright back-swing is not wrong, provided the clubhead loops backwards, as in most successful actions; and the back-swing action of Alec Fox, seen right, could serve as a model. Left wrist more in line with forearm at the top of the back-swing; club-face more closed.

PART 2

Here my friend George Elliott could have used this excellent back-swing of his (LEFT) to strike a ball without the fade he dreads, if he could train his clubhead to fall to the position marked A (RIGHT).

It means that the clubhead must fall behind the player; it must not advance towards the ball. When it advances, as seen here, the clubhead crosses the line I have dotted.

A SLICE NOT COMING UP!

PART 3

Dick Mayer, former U.S. Open Champion, shows the way to stay on the inside. Note similar foot action to George Elliott's in photograph 2, Part 2 of 'A Slice Coming Up!', but what a difference in the hand action and the position of the clubhead.

SHORT AND STOUT

I DO not think a short, stout golfer can go under and through, in the accepted classical way, and give the ball its biggest thrashing. From observation, I have noted he tends to lock his action, because of the absence of that essential fast hip unwind.

In the two photographs I show here, I think that the big difference in the results of these shots is because in the photograph (LEFT), the right shoulder has gone further under and the clubhead has been forced to the right (the ball never started on the line) and so the ball started pushed out (face being open) and never recovered. In the photograph (RIGHT), the right shoulder has come up sooner and the clubhead has been at one moment directly on the line to the hole; it has not been forced to the right, the ball began straight for the hole. This particular shot was very good, only a strong cross-wind moved the ball to the right of the flag. This golfer could not have done better.

These photographs, I feel, help average golfers to see their own problems better — endless photographs of the champions only confuse. It must be remembered that 'they, the short and stout, also play golf' — and are very numerous.

Heavyweights — As a suggestion, try a closed stance — it often helps, as it gives the clubhead a chance to get back on the inside and helps the pivot, but the club-face must be very square at impact, even shut.

ANXIETY

A common sort of head-up action; anxiety to see where the ball has gone. This particular shot ended in the trees on the right. The top of the body was ahead of the stroke, because the hips did not make the initial movement down — which keeps the shoulders behind the ball. Hitting and swishing the clubhead back directly after impact will give better results and guarantee a head down, till you can look at the ball; it also builds up impact firmness.

THE POWER-FADE

GOLFERS often ask me what is meant by 'the power-fade'. It is nothing really new. Ben Hogan and I discussed this action away back in 1948, when he was trying to get away from a treacherous hook.

Hogan had a natural inside-to-outside action at this period, producing a definite hooked ball for all shots. At times, his shots got sadly out of control; so, with his usual thoroughness, he set out to see if he could do better by coming on to the ball *slightly* from the outside for his strokes and 'power-fading' the ball.

To perfect this change required as much practice for him as is needed for a slicer to learn to hit from the inside. Thus came this power-fade period of his — which is really a slice — the minimum of slice, if you like, or a small pulled slice, for the ball begins left of centre and ends up straight on the target.

Yet few of the present generation knew that Harry Vardon recommended more than fifty years ago a 'controlled cut' as the safest shot in golf.

To most golfers a shot which slices at all savours of the unhealthy. But Antonio Cerda, the Argentine professional, told me at one time that he had finished with the hook. For him the fade was the thing in the future. To make sure that he pulled his arms across the ball — on an outside-to-in line — he addressed the ball right on the shaft, on the neck of the club, so he had to pull his arms in or shank the ball. I must say that it looks frightening to see the socket of the iron clubs aimed deliberately at the ball. Cerda admitted that he did not hit the ball as far as he had done before and enjoys taking his No. 3 iron, when previously he would have used a No. 5 iron and hit the ball with a swinging hook.

In his early days Hogan was always a dangerously big hooker, but having power to spare in those days, he could afford to cut across the ball slightly and still be long enough to master all courses. He had most of his great wins as a 'power-fader'.

However, I would like to disillusion those golfers who think the power-fade method is the one and only way to play successfully. It is just one more way to play. Of golfers with limited power I definitely say that they cannot afford to cut across the ball at any time — for them the inside-out method is the best to strive for. I am sure it must amuse born slicers (and they are in the majority) to think that some unfortunate fellow golfers are practising like mad to do what comes naturally

Here I was working on the power-fade, to see what results it would give me. I moved the ball well forward on to the left foot and got a driver with the face lying off slightly, and then made sure that my shoulders were unwinding faster than usual, which tended to throw the clubhead forward, to bring it on to the ball slightly from the outside. I did not find it any advantage in my own game, but to consistent hookers of the ball who go out of control at times, it does help to have this shot in their repertoire.

to them, to come across the ball. They would readily sell a bit of their fade.

Already I can see the pendulum swinging back and the controlled hook being the fashion, for there has been an exaggeration of this outside-to-in theory. It all boils down to the fact that, if a controlled shot is essential in golf, what is wrong with trying to hit the ball straight? The very latest news — Hogan and Cerda found they needed the length as the years have slipped by, and now both are working from inside-to-out again!

As a young professional I played all my shots with a three-quarter swing and a slice and was very accurate, but short in length. Then I went to America in 1928 where the fashion was to have a hooking flight and I returned with a hook.

I always remember Harry Vardon calling the uncontrolled hook the worst shot in the game.

HITTING THE BALL FROM MEMORY

This golfer, so keen to do a full back-swing, has allowed his eye to come off the ball during the action and so has a 'blind spot'. This overswing is dangerous as the body has too far to go to get back to the ball. The address position has been wrong, because the player has stood too straight and so has not twisted his trunk under his head. Myself (RIGHT) addressing the ball for a drive.

YOU MIGHT TRY THIS TRICK

Here you have Horton Smith in his prime in 1937, playing with his left heel well clear of the ground — and has he looked at the ball, too! Horton was a hooker of the ball, by the way! In dozens of photographs of crack golfers, men and women, the left heel is raised at impact. They are not lifting the heel by accident — they need to do so.

A HOGAN COPY

Gardiner Dickinson, an American professional who has modelled his play on Ben Hogan. He does not quite get near his idol in results, though he does win an open tournament now and then. Here he is practising at Rochester in 1956 prior to the U.S. Open. I do not think that he has quite enough power to copy Hogan, as he is a little too frail. I think he could have been a better player still if he had worked out his own game.

This position is classical, and being slim he can do this full free swing with his left heel almost on the ground. He is the sort of enthusiastic golfer who conceivably could wear himself out, because he practises so much.

218

ARE YOU AN ELBOW SPREADER?

Here (LEFT) *I show that with the elbows held together at the address by a harness strap — as recommended by teachers universally — it makes no difference to my finish* (CENTRE). *If your action is sound you will not feel you have the harness on.* RIGHT: *This golfer has failed to keep his elbows together. Has hit too early and has not used his wrists at all. His body action — pulling in the arms, wrong use of his weight — has prevented the club from having a rhythmic swing.*

YOU CAN PLAY THIS WAY

ONCE again comes the problem of the average golfer — he knows what to do, but cannot do it. A golfer wrote to me as follows: 'I work on your statement that golf is 85% arms and wrists, letting my body follow. Am I right?' Yes, keep these approximate figures in mind. I say approximate, because there is no way to measure such things and they will vary for each person.

He continues: 'I find, however, that I cannot hit from inside-to-out as I want to. Once I let the club swing freely the head gets "outside" and along comes the "banana" slice. The clubhead is well on the inside-going-up, but on the way down it seems to get outside. As I invariably hit a high ball with all clubs my down arc is narrow. I can use my driver off the fairway, and get the ball up, but, alas, with a slice on it. Efforts to flatten my downswing still further have met with little success.'

I have been dealing with this problem ever since I began to play and teach golf, so I can claim to know something about it. A golfer must train his left arm so that it can begin the down-swing without the shoulders turning too soon, thus pulling the clubhead forward. *I say this, because most hooking in the good player class comes from the left arm, not the right.* Please note. But unless the

golfer is prepared to train his arm, it means using a trick to check the body so that the arms can catch up and pass the body once it has arrived square to the ball and so make a square impact.

The main trick — and I have not found a better one — is quite simple even if it sounds and feels awkward. It is to try putting an empty golf ball box under your left heel. I suggest this sort of box only because it is just about the right height for most people and is available at most pro.'s shops. A piece of wood would do, of course.

Such forcing-up of the left heel checks the unwinding of the body, so the clubhead can overtake the body and the hands. The fact that the follow-through feels restricted matters little. Hands and arms will be playing their part in the right proportions, because the body will not be in a hurry to finish the swing. See Horton Smith's photograph in 'You Might Try This Trick' on previous page.

Once the body check has been acquired the feeling will be of the arms and wrists doing their job, the heel can then he held up just long enough on its own, without a support and then nearly dropped after impact. Best friends will not even notice such a trick — I guarantee that.

A STYLE STUDY

Son of a professional, later a top money-winning professional, ex-Amateur Champion Arnold Palmer practising No. 9 iron shots at Augusta, Georgia, prior to the 1957 Masters. LEFT: *He shows the grip (note caddie's uniform). Palmer, a very powerful golfer, has enormously strong hands and for these shots did all he could to keep his wrists firm; he used a great deal of body action for this shot.* CENTRE: *He stands very close to the ball — most golfers using a lot of body do — and had the ball right of centre, with the blade definitely laid open. Note knees pushed together to brace body movement.* RIGHT: *The shoulders and arms take the club away from the ball as the body moves under the head.*

LEFT: *Here we have that left forearm and back of hand in line position again; left heel has not moved.* CENTRE: *No head up here, footwork kept to a minimum and right arm now straight. The figure in white is not Arnold's caddie; his 'target' is near the trees on the right.* RIGHT: *The right side has now come through and the whole body has lifted. This lifting up at the end is just as important as staying down at impact; it is part of the proper golf swing. Arnold's left elbow is forced away from the body as he fights to keep the club-face open on the ball.*

I always feel that Arnold Palmer with his great power and fine temperament can be an even better player still one day. He won the Masters in 1958 and was top money-winner of the year.

IRON SHOTS AND SWINGING

'I AM completely unaware of making any attempt to swing one club differently than another.' These are Byron Nelson's words, and here we have a great golfer, with an uncomplicated style, stating a fact which continues to escape many golfers.

When setting out to write on the various clubs — long irons, medium irons and short irons — it is only to be expected that the reader wants complete information on all the clubs, and if the matter were dismissed entirely with the above words, he would feel he had been almost neglected, even insulted. But the fact remains that the swing is the same basically. *The angle of the hit is altered.* The shortness of the various clubs and their differing lies necessitate this, anyhow; these very club differences take care of this point.

It is not to be denied, however, that when playing golf on courses when the ball lies closely, often really tightly, a plain, simple, free swing, such as one does, say, from a peg tee, will not work, because the back of the ball has to be reached on a steeper arc; and to do this some adjustments must be made in the action, so as not to dig the club too deeply into the earth.

It is these problems which interest high-handicap golfers. To be able to play all the shots, they somehow take for granted the fact that a ball can be swung from a tee with an iron club and often resent using a peg tee at a short hole. My advice is always use a peg tee.

What is always a problem with iron clubs is to hit the ball firmly, punch it with the wrists tightening, in an effort to prevent the turf turning the blade of club, and yet not get the swing out of true.

I have repeatedly noticed that golfers brought up on seaside courses, where uneven stances, blustering winds, firm greens and close lies are the rule rather than the exception, do not count on doing one swing for all their shots through the green, because an exceptional amount of originality and inventiveness is required in every round to master the conditions, and the one-track swing needs some adapting to bring results.

I am also sure that from the point of view of learning to play golf and to acquire a good swing, seaside golf can be very trying, and it is on the usual standard inland layout that golfers can expect common playing conditions, which ask nothing more than standard strokes.

The American way of seeing the golf game has, in fact, contributed much to the development of the playing technique of the game. For it has made level fairways and soft, easy sloped greens — things that are considered over there as strictly fair to all — the essential parts of a good golf course, and has taught a generation of golfers to consider anything other than this as freakish. I have perhaps clung too much to my heritage, because I like to think of a game of golf as an exciting adventure, a competition against the course and the elements. I know that in many countries long dry spells of weather often make inland courses play the same way every day, and if these are the conditions, then the best and simplest swing can be counted on to give the best results always, and that justifies the 'one swing' swing.

Swinging under my head with an iron club. This angle shows my hand action and how the nose of the club will be pointing to the hole at this moment of the follow-through.

I like to think that iron shots, in general, are firmer blows, verging towards a sharp hit. I think that all the successful iron club players do punch at the ball, but the additional firmness they put into the stroke comes from leverage, the right hand past the left. This can do no harm in any swing if it is left to the impact area.

A punched iron shot where the left arm checks, and so the follow-through is restricted, is a very safe type of shot, especially in the lofted shot to the flag. J. H. Taylor, a hero of my schoolboy days, I still always picture as the ideal model of crisp iron play, but this sort of observation must not be allowed to distract from the basic fact that the clubhead must swing, the hit must find its way into the path of the clubhead without causing a deviation in its path.

Byron Nelson is obviously right in maintaining that he makes no attempt to vary his swing for different strokes; his action from the thousands of swings he has made will be mechanical and automatic, and his instinct will bring the centre of the back of the club-face to the centre of the back of the ball naturally. His problem exists only in sizing up the shot correctly and of not allowing his concentration to weaken, and so to hit the shot in two minds or hesitatingly. He had the minimum of seaside links lie problems.

So to sum it up, it can, I feel, be fairly stated that the swing can be the same for all clubs, but swinging the clubhead for all iron shots must not imply sloppiness, as it very easily can be seen to do, especially when this one-swing-for-all technique is carried through to the shorter iron clubs.

Horton Smith, a contemporary of mine, as a young man was the best one-swing-for-all-shots golfer I ever saw. He could really be said to be wound up and set off on the round. Over here on our courses, and with the smaller ball, he did not succeed quite as well, as I imagined. Ben Hogan, an all-time 'great', confessed to having to adapt his iron play to our conditions, and this he did, as his win at Carnoustie in the 1953 Open Championship showed, because his swing-everything-freely method was not foolproof on the closely-knitted turf of this championship seaside links. His shots needed more firmness. He soon found the answer.

I offer Fred Daly and Sam King at their best as two of the crispest iron players in the game — as well as two with the shortest examples of follow-through.

LEFT: *The U.S. Open Champion of 1957, Dick Mayer, practising No. 6 iron shots at Lindrick, Yorkshire, prior to the Ryder Cup match. Mayer, a slim golfer with a full swing for all his shots, would not be my choice as a rough weather player, but when mechanical golf is required he can play along with the best.*

This back-swing is unquestionably a full one and his 'driver back-swing' goes no further. He can be said to be a real swinger of iron shots and like all top-grade American players to-day is great from 100 yards in. Note left hand and forearm in line — right elbow down and the straight right leg. There is no question either about the left shoulder not pointing at the ball — he is pivoting to the maximum.

CENTRE: *Tommy Bolt, the U.S. Open Champion in 1958. He is seen practising at Lindrick in 1957 for the Ryder Cup match in which Eric Brown beat him handsomely.*

Tommy is a very strong player with huge hands and he has a fine smooth action. His iron play is first class and he has a very compact swing. Using a stiffish-looking back-swing, the club is lifted or pushed back more than just swung.

He has a full pivot and on this particular morning the caddie did very little more than move a pace or two to the right or left to pick up the balls from his full No. 5 iron shots. Note left heel flat on the ground.

RIGHT: *Here he is, the backbone of the game, the high handicap amateur taking his No. 6 iron. He has limited strength but wants to play like the pros., and he has more than fifty birthdays on the slate. He looks the same as many of the heroes seen in this book, even in dress, but he cannot genuinely imitate them.*

From here he should produce a good stroke, but his hands are not quite strong enough and cannot stand the speed he generates, so this ball can go anywhere, if the club turns in the hands or the left arm collapses.

Sam Snead could get down from here perfectly. This worthy always has a problem, like the millions of others, because he has very limited power in his hands.

222

LEFT: *Charles Jackson, an American Walker Cup class golfer, has definitely pulled away the top of his body from the ball. Charles maybe is not quite in the top class of golfers, but millions would settle for his game and, as can be seen, he does move his head to the right going back.*
CENTRE: *Jack Burke.* RIGHT: *Cary Middlecoff.*

THE TOP OF THE SWING

Just take the classical advice on the correct positioning. There should be two-thirds of the weight of the body on the right leg. The shoulders should make a full 90% turn so that the left shoulder points to the ball and the head should not have moved.

We all know that, strictly, there is no actual top-of-the-swing position because, even as the club reaches the usual horizontal position, the hips have already started down. But let us forget that and just call the top of the back-swing the position when the club is just horizontal or nearly so. While studying a number of the top-of-the-swing positions by power golfers, I am sure that quite a number allow the shoulders and the head to move away from the ball with the club. They do not, of course, roll the shoulders. The left shoulder goes under the head and the hips stay steady — they pivot, of course — but there is a distinct pull away of the top of the body to the right going up. It does not show very much to the naked eye, maybe, but now and then the camera catches it.

I have tried this out at odd times in the past and find that it does help to keep the top of the body behind the ball and encourages the 'hip slide' so many golfers talk about. I think that in the case of

Ben Hogan, much of his power comes from this very pronounced hip slide into the ball, but it is a hip slide from underneath and not a lean into the ball with the shoulders getting ahead — they are always behind the ball. Even in Hogan's first book, *Power Golf*, when he had a different method from his latest one, this slight top-of-the-body pull-away was there.

In the two actual top-of-the-swing positions of professionals Jack Burke and Cary Middlecoff, there is clear evidence that there has been this slight pull-away. Despite what the book says, there has been a head movement to the right, too.

Keeping the head steady is always sound advice, but the tigers are allowed some licence, and many who really hit the ball a long way give the ball everything — and that means really moving into it.

As most golfers in the top class have very fast hip-and-foot-work when they really go out to give the ball everything, this slight move-away must be an extra insurance against swaying the top of the body that little extra bit coming down, and maybe getting ahead of the shot, as the power is applied.

I think there is a powerful look about these top-of-the-swing positions.

I notice than in setting the head and the body to the right of centre at the address, this pull-away

223

My head is exactly over the ball.

The picture of myself half-way back for a big iron shot shows the usual wide arc and the shoulder turn under the head, but I have deliberately pulled away from the ball on this occasion. I mention this pull-away of the top of the body because it will be an interesting point for students to watch when they visit their next major golf tournaments. I can hit the ball further, I feel, but it is dangerous.

John Ball, a golfing giant of the past, has also moved away slightly, but has the ball well off the right foot. This will be because he intends to drive the ball down. His grip is interesting — the palm grip with the right hand was common in his day and is still used to-day by some top golfers, even if they begin at the address with a classical finger grip position.

That old master, Ted Ray, never a consistent driver, but a really long hitter in his day, believed that he got extra length by swaying away from the ball in his up swing. 'I bring into play a fresh and additional force and a very important one, too, seeing that I have behind it the whole of my somewhat considerable avoirdupois.' This is a quote from Ted's interesting book, *Inland Golf*, but Ted certainly never used such long words in his conversation!

Ted admitted that swivelling on his left toe, allowing the toe to point finally to the hole, helped his long game — it does make the finishing of the swing easier for many, I have noticed. This is another argument for shorter spikes in golf shoes — you cannot swivel with long spikes. So the vertebrae suffer. Discs can go! And do!

is little noticed. Years ago a pronounced drag-away with the hands was used to shift the weight.

In the photograph of my own full driver swing I have kept my head exactly over the ball. It has not moved in the slightest going back, and this is favoured still by many players and teachers. Top golfers, have the habit of making their own rules as they go along. Art Wall, a U.S. Masters Champion, has a five-inch lateral shift of the head.

Half-way back for an iron shot.

John Ball

Ted Ray.

THE SAGA OF SAGAN

'SAGA, an old heroic Scandinavian tale' — so says my dictionary. I am sure when you hear the story of the Sagan Golf Club you will excuse the liberty I have taken in using this word — though it nearly fits exactly if, perhaps, another word was substituted for Scandinavia.

Ex-P.O.W. Flight-Lieutenant P. A. Ward Thomas called on me in June, 1945, with the story of this golf course made in the prisoner of war camp at Sagan near the old Polish frontier, 100 miles south-east of Berlin.

Thomas wanted to become a golf journalist. He had always loved golf and nearly five years in German hands had not weakened that resolve — in fact, it had strengthened it. He had lived for the day when he could devote his attention to writing of events of more national importance than the competitions played week in, week out, on the 9 holes laid out in a small compound, 350 yards by 150 yards and running between and around the barrack huts. He is now golf correspondent of *The Guardian* and of *Country Life*.

These competitions were enjoyed by the players and followed by enthusiastic galleries, and for many months were carried through with only one golf club between them all, and that a hickory-shafted ladies' mashie! This treasure was cared for by the senior officer in the camp, Group Captain Kellett, C.B.E., D.F.C., A.F.C.

One can scarcely imagine a whole competition being carried through where players put up with the inconvenience of sharing just one club which must be used for every stroke — and such a precious club, too, that it could not be thrown from player to player to save those few yards walking between the balls to be played.

I cannot do better than quote from Ward Thomas's story of the Sagan Golf Club, excellently

Pat Ward Thomas, who writes on golf brilliantly for The Guardian *and* Country Life, *at work, while Henry Longhurst, who writes for the* Sunday Times, *and having no edition to catch, fits in 'forty winks' after an extra good golf Club lunch, in the new St Germain Country Club lounge, near Paris.*

written on some twenty pages, in which he describes the growth of the interest in the game from the time when only a handful of keen golfers played, to the day when over half the camp — some 300 men — competed, and of the exciting matches which were followed by most of the camp.

The making of the golf balls from odd materials is a unique story itself and when I handled one of the shiny black leather-covered balls (black because the course was on white sand), I was deeply impressed by the skilled craftsmanship shown in their making. To help newcomers to make golf balls to the best advantage, the 'recipe' was printed, and here it is:

INGREDIENTS

Small metal ball, solder or lead, approximately 4 mm. in diameter.
Soft rubber 15 mm. cube.
Old gym shoe or inner tube.
Leather, minimum quantity 11 cm. by 6·5 cm.
Cotton, 50 feet of No. 40.

TOOLS

Sharp knife.
Razor blade.
Punch — broken needle in a handle.
Wax or German boot polish.
Scissors.
Tin patterns, various sizes.

Chip the solid rubber core to a sphere and bisect it. Hollow out the two sections enough to hold

A green of sand within a ridge.

A match in progress.

the metal centre. White lead is, of course, ideal for the centre, but is unfortunately unobtainable now. (One ball was made using it and was most successful.) Cut the rubber into strips, using scissors. To avoid 'nicks' and to bring it to the necessary thinness, pull the strips through a razor blade fixed firmly into the edge of the table. Place the metal core into the soft rubber sections and commence the winding. Experience alone will prove the correct tension. Tight winding produces a 'wooden' ball which has poor carrying qualities, and the rubber, being too taut, is liable to snap if hit badly, almost always resulting in a cut case. Slack winding will result in a 'pudding' ball. Continue winding to the size of the ball required, usually that of a real ball — i.e., 12·5 cm.

Allow for the stretch of the leather, usually 5 mm. for thick leather. Pin the pattern to the leather and trace with a needle, mark in the stitch holes, the most popular number varies around the 80 mark. Remove the pattern and prick the stitch holes. Cut out the leather, using a sharp knife. Bevel the inside edge of the leather 'eight' to ensure a flat seam.

Divide the cotton into three equal lengths. Thread these through the needle which is fixed into the wall and anchor each end, keeping strands separate. Tighten the twist of each strand separately to a shrinkage of about one foot. Hold the six strands together and untwist. This should make a soft thread. Wax finished thread, which should be about eight feet in length. Knot the end and remove the needle, which is obviously built into the six ply.

Commence stitching the pattern 'eights' loosely, and when halfway slip the ball in, continuing to stitch with the same gap allowances. When the entire stitching is done, repeat the first stitch, knot the end, having cut off the needle, and tighten in reverse in a similar way to lacing a football case. Always sew outwards-inwards and tighten inwards-outwards. Do not let the thread or the stitch hole take the pressure when tightening, but work the leather together; this will save breakages.

Roll the finished ball under a flat board and polish.

This ball, after twelve months of development, is accurate, strong and has no vices; it gives a distance of about 150 yards, with a 5 iron.

That is how you make a golf ball.

'For the benefit of those who have never had the misfortune to visit a prison camp', Ward Thomas continues, 'it is necessary to explain that inside the main barbed wire fence is a strip of ground running fully round the perimeter, varying in width from six to ten yards. This is bordered by a low rail known as the warning barrier or trip wire. Inside this no-man's land the prisoners may not go unless they wish to be shot. With golf and football being played all day it was inevitable that balls should frequently go over the trip wire. To wait for a German to fetch the ball often meant a considerable delay, and so they finally agreed to give us two white coats so that anyone could don one of these, the wearing of which was in effect a parole that one would not attempt to escape, hop over the wire and retrieve the ball. If the ball went over the main fence or out of the camp there was, of course, no alternative but to wait for someone passing to throw it back.

The crowd lining the hole.

'As the summer wore on the Germans became used to seeing golf balls sail over the wire; they were very helpful, and it was not an uncommon sight to see a guard (from his look-out) using his field glasses to guide some erring golfer to his ball. The Germans, altogether, were very reasonable about golf, despite many windows being smashed and the frequent use of white coats. In the early days we had some difficulties in getting permission to use spades for building of bunkers and banks which was regarded with some suspicion until they realized there was nothing ulterior in our motive!'

There were challenge matches, medal scores, inter-hut competitions, in fact every type of event. I cannot mention all the players by name, but the leading players gave lessons all day and taught the others, and as Ward Thomas says: 'Golf clubs were being swung everywhere.' This was, of course, at a later period, when other clubs had arrived.

So, in this small compound, far from the green fields of England, dozens of men met golf for the first time. They certainly learned it the hard way.

Note: I was able to get some golf clubs sent out to the prisoners *via* the Red Cross, following an appeal to me to try to do something.

PROGRESS — OR IS IT?

WHENEVER golf's Boswell writes on his pet subject — he can write on anything, as his fourth leaders in *The Times* have so often testified in years past — it should be read. The first customers should not just be his contemporaries, eager to flip over the pages of their overlapping pasts, but the younger generation of golfers and especially the young professionals.

One is never too old to learn, and it does me good to see a game like golf again unfolded from a long scroll of the past dating back over fifty years and presented through the eyes of a real golfing observer, for 'Bernardo', as his friends call him, has been blessed with that capacity to see what almost is not there, as well as the obvious.

A journalist and an author is, of course, permitted licence, but when telling of a game like golf, such licence can make the subject frivolous — *vide* some daily paper reports on golf — or it can become more dignified and glorious. So for years past, I forget how many, it was: 'What does *The Times* say'? For under the modest title of 'Our Golfing Correspondent' appeared poetic words on golf matches from a master pen.

Bernard Darwin has found time to write many golf books and one of them bears the simple title *Golf*. This is because it is part of a series of books in a 'Pleasures of Life Series', but it perhaps could be better entitled *Looking at Golf in My Lifetime*, for it takes the reader along from the 'nineties to the present day.

On this occasion 'Bernardo' has filled up many pages with quotes, delving into books from his shelves and selecting stories which fit into his life and which complement his own anecdotes. Big slices of chapters from authors, often themselves competitors and therefore objects of his own articles, tell of championship battles from the inside, when he viewed them from outside, and so a complete picture is presented.

The book will appeal to golfers of all ages, because it truly presents a picture of the golf game — not just dry as history, but as alive as to-day's news.

Just take a paragraph in the middle of a quote from a book by Garden G. Smith, written in 1898 — the gutty ball days. It runs: 'A long driver when he hits the ball clean will carry some 150 to 170 yards and a less powerful player some 130 to 150 yards. From 100–130 yards, then, there should be another hazard of some sort to catch balls which, though good enough to escape the primal punishment for topped balls, have been hit with considerable inaccuracy.'

Bernard Darwin's comment on this paragraph goes like this: 'Mr Garden Smith was "wery" fierce, essentially a member of what to-day would be the "penal" school. He was surely a little hard on the poor topper, and this ferocity is the more notable because, at the date when he wrote, topping was a commoner and easier crime than to-day and, moreover, brought its own punishment with it to a far greater extent than it does now.'

There is a chapter entitled 'Architecture', which is just as full of interest and information as other chapters with more exciting titles such as 'Some Great Matches' or 'Temperament'. To go on finding interesting bits in this book is easy, but I hope I have given my readers a glimpse into the past as seen through the eyes of the one and only Bernard Darwin.

Just think of a long drive being 150–170 yards! Golf must have been a different game from the game we have learned to play. A round of golf on a long course meant a walk of three miles — to-day it can go well over four miles just on the card. Progress — or is it ?

LEFT: *Myself, Bernard Darwin and Charles Macfarlane at an Open Championship.* RIGHT: *Bernard Darwin putts. I wonder how he would describe this style of putting — no chance to sway here.*

BERNARD DARWIN

BERNARD Darwin, now over eighty-three years of age and finding it more and more difficult to take his aching bones about, still finds it the simplest of matters to take his agile pen over the pages as he tells of a long lifetime of personal experiences dating from his earliest years up to to-day. No writer in the English language can put down so well his everyday thoughts and describe age-old incidents with such ease.

His autobiography *The World that Fred Made*, which is what his very latest book really is, starts off by intriguing the reader with its original title, but this is quickly explained in the first chapter, which is as beautiful a chapter as we could ever wish to read, for it paints a picture of a world which went with the passing of the last century. Fred was the gardener of the family who in the eyes of little boys could make anything.

There is an old school tie atmosphere about this book, which is inevitable, as the author was Prep. School, Eton and Cambridge, and then with such an inborn gift of self-expression it was but a step to M.A., solicitor and then barrister; and when he began writing regular articles in 1908, first for the old *Evening Standard*, his natural talents were seen to good advantage especially as it was about his real love, golf, that he began to write.

This book is not at all a golf book. It is of boyhood days in an unusual arena of father, aunts, uncles and grandparents — for his beautiful (the photograph of her is lovely) mother died when he was born. Of uncles and aunts living in the generally comfortable and affluent circumstances of the upper class of that period, with country houses and faithful happy family retainers, of Wales, of

travelling to golfing week-ends by train with regular companions, almost unheard of in these days of the commonplace motor-car.

Our author sold his wig and took to writing in 1908 and he tells of life as a golfing journalist — 'Our Golfing Correspondent' of *The Times* until five years ago and of *Country Life*, to which magazine he contributed a regular weekly article non-stop for nearly fifty years. I like his common-sense admission and advice to golf writers that as he could not be in two places at once, he set out to try to write well about one particular match he saw and not to compose a story about

What Bernard Darwin's swing looked like in his Walker Cup Team days, for he played in this match in the 'twenties.

228

all the matches gleaned from bar-room talk; but then only a person with a great knowledge of the game can do this.

In his early days there were fewer events to visit and a golf journalist's life was different — exciting hand-to-hand encounters in exhibition and challenge matches between the great players and just a few match play events and the Open Championship (the run of dreary 72 holes of medal play events had not come) of 'Golf's Golden Age', as one chapter is titled.

It is not essential to be a golfer to enjoy this book, but it will add to the pleasure of reading it if one does know golf as so many golfing heroes' names appear. It is Oxford and Cambridge Golfing Society, Rye, Aberdovey, the Royal and Ancient Club of St Andrews, Walker Cup in America in the 20's, the Law, the Darwin family, peeps of memory. Our author has such a gift for writing that one is naturally envious of the facile way the most trifling incidents become tales worth telling and reading about. Incidents which in what I call ordinary English one could not swallow, but from such an essayist are delightful tit-bits readily enjoyed.

I spoke of this book to a friend of my own age before beginning to write these words, and he said: 'Exactly the book for Uncle for Christmas.' I had not thought of it in this way, but it will certainly give much pleasure to many parents whose lives overlap the periods I have mentioned and younger people will enjoy 'living' with an immortal.

'STOP THAT SLICE'

THIS is the inviting title of a golf book which was published in America some years ago. It is intriguing, for the biggest percentage of average golfers are slicers and will turn to anything which will rid their balls of that 'shortening banana flight to the right'. It is also rather curious to read that the basic point in the cure offered is a two-knuckle grip with the left hand. This is in strict contrast — in fact, in direct opposition — to the not-so-long-ago-recommended four-knuckle grip then offered as *the* cure for slicers.

This is a sort of discovery coming from America, but *I must gleefully point out that I have preached this and written about it all my adult golfing life.* I made no discovery either, for I had seen Vardon and Taylor using a two-knuckle grip as a boy. One of the biggest handicaps to consistent golf I have always considered to be the four-knuckle grip and the body and arm method which goes with it — as, of course, it is gradually being acknowledged that successful golfers must stick to their category, whatever their grip. But I have always been satisfied that four-knuckle grippers fight a dangerous quick hook (a smother really) all the time, if they use their wrists freely, or a slice, if they hold the left wrist firm at impact.

The idea of combining the two-knuckle grip with the left hand in line with the back of the left arm as a way of holding the face more square (or more shut is my normal phraseology) is not new either. It has been a method I have always used when wishing to flight the ball lower — play a push shot, that is — or hold it up to the left. The book is dedicated to the inventor of the 'square-faced system'. This is a nice compliment to the father of one of the joint authors, but I personally should hesitate to claim that any one person invented it; it has always been so. Even photographs in George Beldam's book published

Here is a shut face action of fifty years ago — a classical action not with an overlapping grip but with the club-face held fully shut. This golfer, Humphrey Ellis, was a hooker of the ball.

229

LEFT: *An iron shot to the 4th hole at Pine Valley, U.S.A. From this open club-face position I get myself safely on an in-to-out path coming down, by manoeuvring the hips and the hands.* CENTRE: *The attack must come from the inside now.* RIGHT: *Nearing impact, the right arm still glued to the side and the hands bringing in the club-face square and supplying the clubhead speed.*

in 1902 show champions of the day using the 'square face', as the latest modern parlance seems to prefer (the normal term is 'shut face', and I like this better), and a two-knuckle grip on the left hand.

The whole secret of not hitting the ball with a slice is to hit it from inside-to-out with the face square or shut at impact, and that the face of the club at impact *should have some loft on it; this is very important.* This is an unalterable fact, and so how the body itself works matters little *so long as the path of the club is not interfered with on its course to travel across the line ball-to-hole from inside-to-out.*

I am always suspicious of the instructions which insist on the right hand being bent back at the top of the swing so that the palm faces the sky, because I know that few golfers have such flexibility of wrist and also the necessary flexibility of body to hold this wrist position until the hitting area is reached.

When I was lecturing in Belfast in 1958 — where, by the way, I found one of the keenest golfing communities I know — one questioner tried to pin me down as to what exactly is the first movement in the down swing, for golfers like to feel they have something very positive to work on. To such questions there is really no one answer. There is no such thing as 'if you do this series of movements there is a guaranteed result', because it is possible you are already doing them; in whole or

in part you would then exaggerate, for some need to throw the clubhead out almost from the top to hit earlier.

If you say 'pull down with the left arm', this advice might be useless as possibly your left arm will be doing too much and you will hit too late. If, as the authors of *Stop That Slice* (Jim Dante and Len Elliot) say, 'The first move from the top is a turn of the hips, forward and around, to the left with the right shoulder going down, not around. Let the turn of the hips and body pull the hands down. Don't try to turn the shoulders. Make sure that you keep your right shoulder back as the shoulders are pulled round with the hips. The right shoulder must go down and through rather than round', they are not far away from the general plan which I endorse.

This is, of course, all very sound, and you can see it works in practice for my swing, but I work my club-face from more open to more shut than the American authors recommend.

That golfers fail to do what I do, for example, is not always that they do not understand, alas, but because they do not have their muscles trained. It is worth while, I have found with pupils, to have a try at making *your body* do a swing from inside-to-out — swing away until you can do it. Some of these positions I show are not easy for everybody to do, but you must hit from inside-to-out to stop that slice and remember the club-face must be square or shut to impart hook-spin on the ball.

A 'LOCAL' PRESS CUTTING

'HENRY COTTON'S BIRTHPLACE GETS DEATH SENTENCE'

'IT was the best-built house in Holmes Chapel, Cheshire, say some of the old inhabitants. Now the solid old building is being demolished to make way for further extension at the Crown Wallpaper Co's works in Macclesfield Road.

'Nearly fifty years ago, the famous golfer, Henry Cotton, romped in its high-ceilinged rooms and in the garden adjoining his father's iron foundry. Mr Alfred Platt, seventy-eight-year-old former employee of Mr George Cotton at the foundry, remembers when young Henry was born in the house. He recalls nursing him, watching him grow into a sturdy little boy, before his father closed down the business and the premises became a wallpaper manufacturing concern.

'Only once since then has Mr Platt (Tinker was his nickname) seen a member of the Cotton family. That was when Henry Cotton's half-brother, Sidney, called to see him with an invitation to spend a holiday at his home.

'Alfred has the clearest recollection of the works in the old Mr Cotton's day. "He was a wonderful boss", he says. "I could come and go in the house as I pleased, and I was always welcome to join the family at a meal."

'Now Alfred spends all his days in his garden, despite the after-effects of a fractured spine last August. He has few wants, but would dearly like to see some member of his old employer's family once again.'

THE OLD GOLF CHAMPION CRACKS UP....

(Quote from a leading daily paper)

'COTTON 163. IT LOOKS LIKE HIS FINALE'   YEAR, 1954

'FORMER Open Champion Henry Cotton gave his admirers their saddest day when he finished at the tail end of the field after the first two rounds of the Dunlop Masters Tournament at Sandwich to-day. Cotton had a first round 84 — 42 out, 42 home, seven 5's and three 6's on the 6,864 yards Prince's course.

'There was no joy watching Cotton, weary, drawn and looking all his forty-seven years, willing in a 3-foot putt on the 18th green to avoid a second round of 80. He again took 42 shots to the turn. This is not the way one wants to see once majestic Cotton end his career.

'Said Cotton: "I have never played so well for such a high score, but the ball did not run for me. An 84 is my all-time high. At lunch-time I felt like tearing up."

'If Cotton says he played well he is fooling nobody but himself. He played tired golf, and it showed most in his putting. Said Cotton: "I had to drive 500 miles in a day to get here from St Andrews. I could do that twenty years ago, but it is a bit too much now, I guess!"'

End of story.

My comment

This is the sort of treatment you get when you return a poor card — there are no extenuating circumstances. You must play well when you have a reputation — or else.

Now the U.S.P.G.A. is fining its members 100 dollars for tearing up their cards. What a life! Many of the younger generation of professionals to-day think nothing of tearing up their cards if it will mean a high score on the board. Perhaps they are right to avoid this slamming, but I was brought up differently.

After this I did get in the first few places nearly every time I competed, so my press friend has gallantly eaten his words.

PICTURE-FRAME FINISH

I HAVE found, when teaching golf, that many players can get extra zip into their approach strokes if they aim at throwing the clubhead forward at the end of the swing, as if bringing the clubhead back over the ball.

This makes the club go through the ball and under the body, as distinct from around the body.

Many of my older pupils will recall their days in Brussels in 1935–6 when they visited me at the Waterloo Golf Club to work with me on solving some of the game's mysteries and how we christened this finish 'The Picture-Frame'.

231

A slim young lady golfer makes a picture-frame finish.

Myself 'picture-framing'.

Many good players achieved this finish unconsciously, for it comes as a result of correct hand action at the bottom of the swing. It helps the timing because it stops an exaggerated follow-through after the ball, and a lurch forward with the top of the body — the cause of so much mishitting.

This finish is a sound method with all clubs, but

I feel that it has most value when used on shots to the flag with medium and short irons.

So, if you feel you are not achieving that snap in your shots to the pin, see if you can get into a 'Picture-Frame Finish', and help your timing.

The champions do it. I have seen players bring their shaft so far forward that it lies at right angles to ball-to-hole line and in front of the face.

GETTING DOWN TO IT

A golfing friend of mine in the U.S.A., showing me his putting stance and grip of the club. This is quite serious, though on slimy ground he risks doing himself grave damage if his feet slide!

He actually putted well and said he kept his head down better — at least he could not lift it up readily, but there was always a danger of pinching his finger between the club and the ball! If you have not tried this style you have not tried everything. Don't practise too long like this — you may never get up again. Compare this style with that of Bernard Darwin on page 228.

CISSY! SAID HENRY LONGHURST

'I FIND myself in the dilemma of wishing at one and the same time to administer a pat on the back and precisely the opposite, whatever that may be, to my illustrious namesake, Henry Cotton. It is he who is responsible for the fixture at Hoylake, over the last week-end in March, between the Walker Cup team of amateurs and what is in effect, if not playing as such, the Ryder Cup team of professionals.

In some games I believe an amateur is held to be tainted if he is seen so much as talking to a professional, but here golf is one of the more fortunate pastimes. Nothing happier exists than the relationship between the paid and the unpaid, and the only pity is that they do not play with or against each other more often.

I look forward tremendously to this match at Hoylake — 36 holes of foursomes on the Saturday and singles on the Sunday. It will sharpen up the Walker Cup team for their match in May, which they obviously have some sort of chance of winning, and it will also, although for reasons of "face" they give a two-up start, give a jerk to the professionals, most of whom get no chance of playing a 36-hole match between one Ryder Cup and the next.

The professionals, from the playing point of view, are in a poor way. Entirely their own fault, of course, for running for so long the ludicrous closed shop which prevented the entry of new talent except the sons of professionals, but they have now opened the door and in ten years' time may be seeing the fruits of their enlightenment. In the meantime they look desperately for a "star" to replace Cotton who has drawn the crowds and inspired the publicity almost single-handed for twenty years.

Cotton himself is the complete realist, thinking never less than five years ahead of the rest. They have no genuine star? Very well then, manufacture an ersatz one. If they cannot win the Open against Locke, Thompson and such Americans as may be present, let us invent a tournament they *can* win — in other words a British closed championship. Then, even if he is only one of the old gang, at least we have so and so "The British Champion".

These professional tournaments are only entertainment — or "promotion" as the Americans call it — and if you are in the entertainment business it is your job to entertain. To this extent I am in sympathy with Cotton's realistic attitude, though I give notice that I shall never regard the "British Professional Champion" as anything in particular, but he goes a step further and here we part company irrevocably and for ever.

At the risk of again giving offence on the other side of the Atlantic, where none is intended, I confess that I regard any golfing development imported from America with automatic suspicion — and the one which Cotton wishes to import is quite one of the worst. For reasons of publicity, promoters of certain tournaments in the United States will do anything to secure low scores. One man the other day did a 60 — a "world record" — but nobody bothered to report on what sort of course he did it.

The fact is that many of these courses are pure "pushovers". What is more, the flag is put in the easiest parts of the green and they play from the ladies' tees. In the year immediately following the war they even used to tee-up on the fairway. It is this sort of thing which Cotton wishes to import for the "British Championship", at any rate for the first two rounds.

Easy course, ladies' tees, sensational improvement in professional golf — and if you don't believe it, just look at the scores.

This is something, to quote the time-honoured phrase, up with which I will not put. I will do my best to stomach the British Champion, but not as a dubious-sexed creature like this. If they want to play from the ladies' tees, their path is clear. Amalgamate with the Ladies' Golf Union.'

COTTON COMMENT

When I suggested a P.G.A. National Championship for home players, my friend Henry Longhurst handed this out in his *Sunday Times* column.

All the same it has proved a success. The amateur–pro. match which I resurrected is now an annual fixture, and when the professionals ceased to start the amateurs '2 up', they took an awful hiding at Turnberry in 1958 on level terms. I know I did not say play from the ladies' tees in the Close Championship, but my friendly namesake, who by the way writes my signature brilliantly when surrounded with hordes of small boys with autograph books on the grounds that they like 'yours better', is a great kidder, but I did prove to be right in my pro.–amateur match handicapping — psychologically, it must work. Since this series began, as I have already mentioned, amateur golf in Britain has really improved.

MY OLD PUTTER

I was very pleased to present to Golf House (in New York City, home of the U.S.G.A.) for their museum, the putter I used in the Open Championship, which I won in 1934 at Sandwich. This old aluminium-headed putter, stamped Claude Gray, Beckenham, had a very bent shaft — curved, as was the fashion, to give a sort of centre line to the face. It was light in weight, flat of lie, and I putted best 'off the nose' of it.

Joe C. Dey, the executive director of the U.S.G.A., is with me outside Golf House.

INTERESTING FACTS

AN error of 1° in the squaring-up of the angle of the club-face at impact for a driver means, at 225 yards, an error of 30–40 feet.

The speed of the clubhead at impact for a drive by a top grade professional is around 140 miles per hour.

The left hand and arm takes the hit. This is a photograph by Pierre Conivet, from St Cloud, Paris, snapped at 1/2500 of a second. An error of 1° in this No. 2 iron shot 'impact squaring up' means that the ball will be 20–30 feet off line.

It is considered by some that a slight bulge on a driver face helps to penetrate the ball better and so compress it more, thus correcting the error in direction when a ball is not struck on the dead centre of the club-face — helping a ball off the heel not to slice, or a ball off the nose not to hook.

The ideal height for a drive is between 70–80 feet; that is, producing maximum carry for a given blow, again always in the top professional range.

The best loft for a driver is from 7% to 10%. With less loft than this a club is difficult to handle, for it is hard to get a grip on the ball and to drive many successively good shots.

Average driver length 43–43½ inches. Weight of my own driver is 14¾ ounces, which is considered heavy. I prefer a leather grip slightly thicker than standard, because my hands are large (size 8½ gloves), with long fingers.

I play best when my fingers feel thin.

In winter time or in very hot weather I have found that a right-hand mitt, no fingers, helps my play very much.

I can stretch finger tip to finger tip 4 inches more than my height. Can you? You should stretch your height, it is said.

234

AGE AND THE FLAT SWING

I HAD an interesting chat at Deauville, during a summer holiday there, with Sir Dallas Brooks, Governor-General of Victoria, Australia, and I learned from this keen golfer that this State has some 360 golf courses in it. Champion golfer Peter Thomson is from Victoria.

Sir Dallas, a fit, lean, sixty-year-old golfer, possessor of a 5 handicap, admits that his gradual loss of length is his main golfing problem, though he has found out for himself that by swinging flatter and encouraging a hooking flight on his longer shots, he 'gets by'.

His main query was whether he should persevere with this round-the-body back-swing, which he found easier to do, or to try to swing on a more upright arc and so get a longer back-swing; he found the latter was very difficult. He had noticed, he told me, not only in his own game but in that of his contemporaries, that with the passing years the back-swing had got appreciably shorter and flatter. This made him keen to watch me play again to see how my back-swing had remained throughout the years.

I have long noticed among my pupils that as the muscles age they lose the ability to swing the club high in the back-swing. I think that the golf-club, being light, is not able to stretch the arms enough; it is not quite a strong enough exercise in itself just to swing to and fro, even with a weighted club. My own swing, due to my joint and muscle construction, has never been very long; but it has been long enough, I consider, because if the hands are head-high or shoulder-high, there is enough height from which to deliver a fast attack.

I am sure that Sir Dallas's swing will get shorter and shorter unless he 'tears' the muscles, stretches them by such an exercise as hanging from a bar, which I have found to be the best of all, because the whole weight of the body stretches the arms above the head, and this makes it an easier matter for the club to go well up in the back-swing.

One finds in the golfing world that many people have by chance an ideal construction of muscles for the golf swing, while others struggle to make a set of golfing muscles. Of one thing I am certain; it is not enough to copy a certain style of play, even if one can do so exactly; there must be a similarity of muscle flexibility and power. I know that many golfers — the majority, in fact — have not the desire or the energy to make golf a burden, and so to recommend any long-term programme of training is really a waste of time.

When one plays a lot of holiday rounds with

How my club starts back.

golfers of varying handicaps, usually in the senior golfer class, I am often called upon to get a player 'going' when things are going wrong, and I frequently make the silly mistake of opening my big mouth too soon when an opponent is seeking advice, because more than occasionally he *does* 'get going', and I lose my bet! These mid-round tips which give much pleasure to the player, I find, generally are a slight change of stance, in relation to the ball position, or the adjustment of the tension of the grip. To alter the position of the hands themselves during a round is risky, but a player can be encouraged to loosen-up and let the club swing. Golfers like Sir Dallas Brooks, who find themselves getting flat, do so because they use the flat arc to help them to pivot, and this flat arc causes the swing to be shorter.

Here again is a choice of evils, so to speak: to pivot to the maximum, which is essential for all seniors anyway, hands lower, swing shorter, or to swing longer and more upright, with the risk of less shoulder turn. The answer to this sort of problem is found by experiment, but there is no harm in recalling that the very best golf can be played with the so-called old-fashioned method, which will no doubt become the latest thing one day, judging by the way the pendulum swings in matters

Sir John Musker, finishing a drive, uses his wrists and puts the minimum strain on his body. Deauville, 1958.

of golf technique. By old-fashioned way I mean club-face fully open, toe of the club pointing to the ground at the top of the back-swing and a genuine 'hit past the chin, head down, eye on the ball, wrists crossing at impact' action on the follow through. This is the simplest way, and from my observation and personal experience it makes

golfing a pleasure and diminishes, if not eliminates, all the risk of a 'slipped disc'. The 'stomach' method, shut club-face, is for the young enthusiastic practisers and top-grade pros.

When I watched past-fifty Count John de Bendern (formerly John de Forest) practising at Deauville, he was also working with a flat swing to get his full pivot, but he managed to get his hands quite high and his club-shaft almost horizontal. He told me that he could not pivot adequately unless he did a flat swing. Here was another case of a senior golfer finding it difficult to get his arms up and so using a flatter swing to get the best results. I notice, however, that with the flatter swings there generally goes a sway into the ball because, after all, the hit on to the ball with iron clubs has to be a steep one, and a steep hit is not easily performed without a big lateral shift, if the swing is flat. Here again, this is not wrong and the average handicap golfer, who is erratic anyway, is not going to be much more erratic by 'leaning into it' — certainly he will get the feeling of getting his weight into the shot. Ben Hogan, whose swing to-day is on the flat side, though he is not old nor needing to seek the maximum pivot, performs it so by design, but he has a most pronounced 'slide' into the ball with his body. This is necessary with all flat swings.

FLAT AND SHUT

You can swing at any angle and have a shut-faced club position at the top of the back-swing, but here is a very flat back-swing. This ultimate position comes a little from the placing of the hands on the shaft, but mostly from the angle taken by the arms in the back-swing and the left wrist not being kinked at the top.

This golfer gets results by using a No. 2 wood from the tee, but if he would train his left wrist to get into the position used by Eric Brown (RIGHT), he would get better results and his action would not look so flat. Eric Brown uses various positions of the left wrist in his golf, as do other top golfers.

THE RIGHT WORDS

OCCASIONALLY it is thrown at me that I and others, trying to teach the golf game and write about it, are very casual in our terms. We talk of muscles of the forearm, the back, the legs, and so on, when we should be more explicit.

Even if I were more definite and tried to use the high sounding correct medical names for the muscles I am referring to, it would need the study of a medical chart to identify these muscles, and even then I would not be sure I was using the right word, because there are so many different parts to the arms and hands, for example, and as the reader would not be able to see inside himself, he would be no wiser. Just look at the back view of the human body below. It is a wonder we play at all, moving all those pieces! The sketches explain some common phrases that are used every day by golfers — not always correctly.

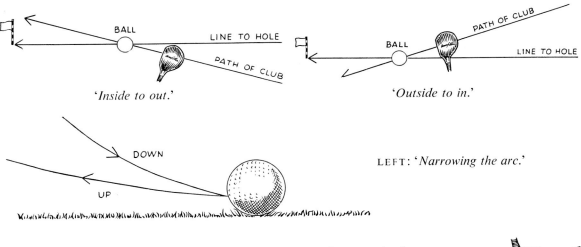

'Inside to out.'

'Outside to in.'

LEFT: 'Narrowing the arc.'

LEFT: 'Hitting on the up swing.'
RIGHT: 'Hitting on the down swing.'

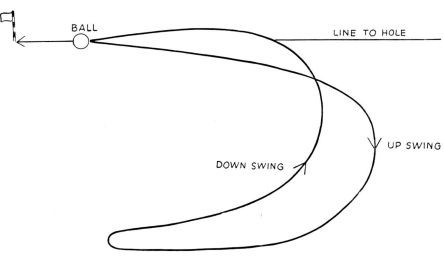
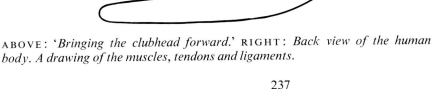

ABOVE: 'Bringing the clubhead forward.' RIGHT: Back view of the human body. A drawing of the muscles, tendons and ligaments.

237

YOUR HEAD CAN DIP

Here is Cary Middlecoff, the very tall American ex-Open Champion, allowing his head to dip considerably as he hits the ball. His very bent right arm at impact has necessitated this bend down of the body. This angling of the trunk, much more at impact than at the address, is clear in these photographs.

HOW THE CLUB-FACE GETS SQUARE

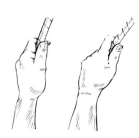

LEFT: *Back of the hand to the hole from this point to impact. This action is always present in every good swing, as it is really the only way to square up the club-face without throwing the clubhead off its true arc.*

RIGHT: *Some golfers talk of this as arching the wrist. I use the expression 'arching the wrist' for the position illustrated in the photograph. It is a swan's neck effect and is an address position. This arching is not maintained at impact, but the back of the hand faces the hole.*

EXTRA UPRIGHT

Jim Ferrier, a tall Australian now living in America, has an upright swing — very upright — and I think his address position (LEFT) and his start back from the ball (CENTRE) are very interesting, but exaggerated, I find. Here he is practising for the Masters at Augusta, Georgia, in 1948.

Ben Hogan.   *My back-swing position.*   *Peter Alliss.*

FLAT VERSUS UPRIGHT

A QUESTION which many golfers ask themselves is this: 'Should I try to cultivate an upright swing, or should I swing around my body?' They usually refer to their golfing heroes when trying to decide this point, going to the trouble of examining the swings of these stalwarts, either from photographs or at first-hand when this is possible.

Every champion who has worked at his game — and few (if any) can claim even in a remote way to being just natural golfers — will have tried out 'the lot'; he will have studied the effect on his play, when using different angles of arcs for his swing, from very upright to very flat.

The present trend among the up-and-coming school is to talk of the upright swing as being best, but I have not yet been able to see that the youngsters making a name in big golf to-day are better shot-makers than the older giants.

Once a player decides to swing in a very upright arc, his hand action needs to be altered and his left shoulder will work less under the head — to point it down towards the ball will give the feeling of dropping the shoulder–and I can only see this action easily performed by the tall athletic types. Yet we have an immediate contradiction in the game of Ben Hogan; thin and athletic, but perhaps not considered anything but medium in height, he has a distinctly flat swing.

I have studied this flat and upright question for many years and feel that the key to the situation lies in where the right elbow wants to go instinctively. The placing of the right hand on the shaft at address, and the shape of the right forearm, also play their parts in this elbow position. See my back-swing position.

When writing of golf, it is very easy to put down one's own impressions and construe them as fundamentals, almost ignoring the physical problems others have to face. So when one reads that the younger school of tournament winners goes for an upright swing, claiming that the extra height leads to more powerful play and that, by keeping the clubhead on the line for a seemingly longer time, more accuracy results, one should not ignore the thought, but try and put it in its right perspective. I think that the tall player tends to go more upright primarily from the need to narrow his hitting arcs when attacking the ball. Peter Alliss comes to mind; he has the opposite problem to the short-of-stature player, who tries all the time to widen his arcs, in order to hit the ball 'in the back' — not too squeezed a blow, that is.

We get Peter Alliss and Cary Middlecoff, both tall men, with the problem of their natural arcs too wide for play through the green, unless they make sure by body, or extra delayed hand-action, that they are able to hit the ball before touching the ground first, which would surely happen if they followed Peter Thomson's or Gene Sarazen's arcs.

In my own case, I come between the two in height, and so have almost a chance, depending on how I feel and how my timing needs adjusting.

LEFT: *Gary Player, the young South African star, swings the club well round his body, but not too flat.*
CENTRE: *This particular upright swing and open club-face presents serious problems, which are aggravated by the open stance and the weight too much on the right heel. There is no doubt that a flatter swing would be better, for it would encourage a full pivot and get the left shoulder under the head; and then, with a shut stance (the right foot pulled well back), there would be less weight on the heel and so a faster hip action in the down swing. The thrust with the big toe of the right foot will be too delayed in this position.*
RIGHT: *Harry Weetman, one of the game's power golfers, gets his hands high and his swing upright. He tends to fade the ball, though; it is perhaps safer at his length. Temple, 1955.*

South African star, Gary Player, a small golfer, uses a 'medium' swing.

The question of the upright swing and the so-called 'dead hand' action, or suppressed wrist action, is, I feel, just another way in which the player can make sure that his wrists are not uncocked too early. The effort to check the natural and instinctive desire to lash the clubhead through is called a 'dead handed' action; but it must be noted that the particularly noticeable exponents of this method, Littler and Winniger, who look to me as if they are pushing the ball, are using fast hip and body action to replace the 'deadness' of the hands. This, of course, is no use to thick-set golfers or older players — or to me.

I do not think that because the club goes more upright in its arc, it will come down faster because of gravity! I think this can be ignored. But if the hands go high in the air it is accepted that this extra length of swing can be of advantage in long driving. Weetman is no exception, yet Hogan, de Vicenzo and Snead, no sluggards in the 'length stakes', all achieve their distance without getting the club-shaft behind their necks (very upright that is). The shaft tends to lie over the right shoulder so that their back-swing, while long, is well round the body, the clubhead travelling in a wide arc. This is more important than the angle of the attack on the ball. Weetman uses an upright swing, as can be seen.

We have always been influenced by the methods of the great players of the day, and this, also, can often make the going tough for the average golfers. Many players, who go on a very upright arc in the back-swing, tend to play with a more shut-faced action and much body unwind, to keep the face square at impact and not too closed. The round-the-body swingers can, to advantage, allow the club-face to open gradually until the left wrist at the top of the swing is well under the shaft. There is no fixed rule on this point, as I show here. Both extremes have produced great players and will continue to do so, I am sure, and it is wrong to select the upright arc as the best, the one and only. An interesting point for students is that tiny Gary Player, one of the greatest short-game players to-day, has a medium-flat swing for all his shots to the pin. There are, fortunately for us all, all sorts of angles of arc in the back-swing to explore. You can check on your back-swing in a mirror, of course.

240

LATE HIT THOUGHTS

THE young golfer from Madrid, Count Fontana (RIGHT), already a fine long hitter of the ball, is caught by the camera in the position so many beginners love to copy, thinking it is obligatory for them to get into this pose if they are to play better.

This delayed hit position is useful only to those with terrific clubhead acceleration. This golfer *is* able to flash in the clubhead, so that at impact the club-shaft and hands are in line with the ball. The body and hands seem to wait for the clubhead because the hands move only to A, while the clubhead moves right round to contact with the ball. Only the speediest and strongest wrists can time a ball with an action like this. The left hand must play a big rôle in helping the right to apply increasing speed to the clubhead.

In the photograph of myself playing a big shot, my hands will also move forward only to position B, while the clubhead reaches the ball, but already the clubhead is going flat out and the hands have not yet played their full rôle in permitting the clubhead to overtake.

Just recall that a clubhead is travelling at impact for a drive at about 140 m.p.h., so to get to this great speed it is not possible to arrive in the positions seen here in the photograph with the clubhead moving slowly; it must already be travelling very fast. The only exception is those with quite 'wicked' acceleration; they can leave the hit late.

One of the most powerful golfers in the world, 'Chick' Harbert (BELOW), is leaving his acceleration really too late to be true, but he will still manage to get his clubhead there on time. His hips have been in position for some appreciable time already, but few golfers have ever lived who dare leave the clubhead so far behind the hands at this point.

LEFT: *The grip: left hand well over to pull club; right hand well under to thrust; club held down the shaft.* CENTRE: *At the address the shoulders are more level than the usual standard hand position. At the start back there is a definite drag back by the hands first. The club is taken back on the inside.* RIGHT: *Full pivot, hands very high and long back-swing. Club-face position is correct and normal and there are no thumbs on the shaft to check the action in any way — a palm grip is used.*

AN UPSIDE-DOWN GRIP

OR THE WRONG WAY ROUND

WHEN little Willie takes hold of father's putter on the lawn and proceeds, with the nose of the club well up in the air, to slog the ball along the ground time after time, he will always hold the club with his left hand below his right in order to play a right-handed shot. Usually he is successful in hitting the ball into the flower-bed every time to the admiring gasps of parents and relatives. Then one day, when little Willie is considered to be old enough, he has to be taught the 'proper grip' — and then his troubles begin.

Just think what might have happened, though, if Willie had not had to switch his hands over. He might have become as good as M. Joseph Charles, of Belgium, who took up golf at the late age of forty-three and, with this upside-down grip, became almost a scratch golfer in two years. After the war, he did become a scratch golfer and won the championship of his country, also winning three rounds in the Amateur Championship at Carnoustie in 1947. Now, at the age of sixty-three, he is still playing to a 3 handicap.

I had seen M. Charles hit an odd shot some years ago, but only when I had the chance to play with him did I realize quite what went on. You really have to be in the game with someone to get the true picture of their ability.

Here was a natural golfer if ever there was one — a golfer who punches at the ball for all he is worth and, curiously enough, still hits the ball with his right hand which is held near to the top of the shaft. 'The left guides', says Joseph, 'but the right punches through.'

A pair of gloves is essential because of the repeated and necessary sliding of the shaft in the hands. The rather ragged gloves he uses seem to be part of his equipment and the rough rubber grips do not readily allow slipping. He had learned to use the friction to control the grip tension in order to get the most out of his attack.

Look at the photograph of his grip. There is quite a space showing between his hands; the club is held in the palm of the right hand but by the fingers of the left hand. At the address, the straight left arm and the distinctly bent right arm keep the right shoulder a bit lower than it might be, for I always feel the shoulders could be level for this grip. But I like the way he executes that principle of

242

LEFT: *This is almost the end of the swing, for the ball is hit on a very definite 'hit and stop' action with a vicious punch. Head beautifully kept down.* CENTRE: *In a position of rest, as it were, after the shot is well on the way.* RIGHT: *Joseph Charles plays a run up shot — which* looks *like a run up from the action. His reverse hand grip is very interesting and effective. A golf shot can be played successfully this way. It sometimes cures a twitch for ordinary grip sufferers.*

keeping the back of the left hand towards the hole.

At the top of the back-swing the hands are incredibly high for a sixty-three-year-old golfer, and there is no doubt that as his club swung back, he had moved his weight well on to the right foot. The actual impact is a sort of hit-and-stop action, and there is little follow-through of the clubhead after the ball has gone.

The same grip is used for putting, but the left index finger is extended down the shaft. This seems to give plenty of control and I think it has possibilities for those who find a normal putting grip to be 'full of twitches'.

I have not experimented with this grip at all except for a few putts and chips. I have never yet hit a real shot with it, but if ever I slip up on the other methods, I like to feel that here is another world to explore. But I do know this: there is a firmness about pitches and putts with this method which will gladden the hearts of many players, and a back spin is put on the ball which I bet many golfers could not produce in any other way.

Joseph Charles has lost length with the passing years, he admits, but at one time he used to drive around the 250-yard mark. Now he settles for less, but some of his iron strokes are real power shots. I saw him hit the green on a 250-yard hole at the Cannes Country Club course with his No. 2 iron, but it was running fast that day and there was a helping breeze — still, it meant a solid blow.

This is the sort of method which reading golf books or taking lessons will not help much; you need to know your own game. Fancy playing golf and not having one of the game's 5,000,000-odd instructors able to say a word to you. There are over 5,000,000 golfers in the game and each one is a potential teacher — at least it looks and sounds that way!

In a letter to me on this subject M. Charles envisages one day a whole group of reverse-handed players with special professionals to teach them — also playing this way. It looked unlikely till, using this method, Sewsunker Sewgolem, an Indian from South Africa, won the Dutch Open Championship in 1959.

The reason M. Charles does not play 'the other way' is that he has no confidence, and as an old 'crosse' player he finds this method easier. 'Crosse', an old national game of Belgium, is gradually dying out, but all the same it is still played in country districts, where egg-shaped wooden balls of various sizes are used, with a long-shafted iron club to drive them over the country-side.

THE BENT LEFT ARM

These two photographs of myself and a high-handicap golfing friend show a great difference in the left arm action. My friend cannot possibly hit his tee shot in 'the back of the ball' — it must be a chopped sort of blow. The arc is far too steep and the hands have already brought the clubhead forward, which will also mean an outside-to-in hit and a slice spin on the ball. In fact the attack on the ball could not be worse. The way to set about rectifying this trouble is to build up the entire left arm, training it to play a proper rôle. Regular swinging of a heavy club and hitting balls one-handed as a start are easy to do and well worth the time and trouble. This golfer plays regularly and has instruction so it is clear that he has not got the right golf muscles.

LEFT: *Here again the muscles are not up to their job — the left arm bends because of weakness and this makes for a 'soft' impact.* RIGHT: *Here the left arm has 'funked' the job — the shot has been pushed with little whip in the clubhead. In this action the left wrist has not 'bent back' to help the clubhead overtake. The two 'V's in the grip are not parallel — they oppose one another.*

DRIVING TESTS — WITH THE GOLF BALL

IN Great Britain driving tests are usually carried out by the makers of golf balls at regular intervals on their own private testing-grounds, where their own products and specimens of their competitor's goods, which are bought through various normal sources, are put on driving machines. The results are tabulated and kept secret.

This has been going on for years and, naturally enough, each maker claims that *his* product goes farther than the rest, which, to the general public, may seem 'poppycock'; but there is often some truth in these statements, because certain balls go farther in the response to certain weights of hit. I mean that a tightly-wound ball of, say, 90 compression (some balls are sold on compression figures in the U.S.A., e.g., 90, 80, 70), needs a very powerful blow to compress it and so get the maximum distance from it; the same ball could not be driven as far by a weaker hitter; he would do better perhaps with an 80, 70 or 60 compression. This is no new disclosure, but so many golfers ignore this point and go for the very ball the champion uses, wound very tightly and tested to the maximum human carry on the driving machine — 260 yards is a *very* long carry indeed. On a still day on flat ground, the average scratch golfer will not do much above 200 yards, and only now and then get to 220 yards (all carry, note).

I have always taken a great interest in the golf

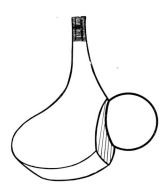

At impact for a full drive, the average player, driving around 225 yards, will flatten the ball at least one inch on the club face. It is the expansion of the ball after this abrupt compression which gives it the length. An American size ball will flatten about $1\frac{1}{4}$ inches for a similar blow and that is why they seek in the U.S.A. always a harder ball, a ball with a higher compression to stand the repeated battering.

This drawing is from a photograph of the exact moment of impact.

The mobile 'driving' unit of the Penfold ball firm at a Southport golf tournament.

ball question and have continued to study this side of the golf game deeply. When the Standard Scratch Score system was established to compete with the American Par some years ago, and to try to get handicaps on a more even basis, various golf authorities made tests to establish the distance the average scratch man drove, and then allowances were made for the type of ground and the way the hole played. Apart from this study and an occasional long-driving competition, public tests are rare in this country, whereas in America they are regular features at golf tournaments. I have not seen much data published in recent years about our golf ball and its performance. Certainly no trouble is taken to collect data and publish it under a suggestive title — maybe, 'The Behaviour of the British Golf Ball'.

In America the golfing public is being educated to be 'compression conscious', and I have even come across pros. with compression-testing machines on hand to show customers exactly what they are buying, in the way of the tension of the winding in a golf ball. As I have already mentioned, a tightly wound golf ball is not necessarily the best for everyone — a 'just middle' must be the soundest investment, and at my tee shot range, which is just good professional average today, I find the very tightest American winding of all is too hard for me, unresponsive and stone-like. I cannot get these 'stones' along as well as my 'made in Britain' ball.

At the Oak Hill Country Club in Rochester, N.Y., the venue of the 1956 U.S. Open, won by Cary Middlecoff, Robert Trent Jones, the well-known golf architect, who toughens up the courses selected by the U.S.G.A. for their major championships, made a study of the behaviour of the golf ball — he does it each year. He selects a flat hole — if possible with no tee elevation — and then records the drives of the top players, taking those playing on the final day in the U.S. Open for his test. From the data collected he regulates the width of the fairways, the placing and size of bunkers, and the length of the rough, as well as the making of new teeing grounds.

The test on the 432-yard 8th hole at Oak Hill was so discreetly carried out that I did not know such a test was happening. A little heap of sand, placed every 10 yards in the centre of the fairway, gave observers a chance to note the length of every one of the fifty-one drives.

The average length of the tee shots for the 1956 test was 253·39 yards, including roll, as against an overall average of previous test of 260 yards. Allowing for a hot sultry morning with the watered fairways being extra moist following a lot of rain during the night, the ball can be said not to have improved much from a length angle over previous years.

Nine drives were caught in a fairway bunker at the left, and one ball went into a bunker on the right. The bunker at the left was 30 yards long, the bunker on the right was 20 yards long, and from the bunkers some seven of the ten players reached the green about 170 yards away. The longest drive was by Roberto de Vicenzo at 280 yards, though an amateur, John Garrett, of Texas, was one yard farther, but just in the rough. The widest drive was by Mike Souchak, some 273 yards long, but 15 yards off the fairway. The fairway width between the two bunkers was 35 yards. This seemed to me to be quite wide as I stood on this tee, and the tee shot never really worried me — my drive of 239 yards, I recall, was not hit very solidly, just a good scoring sort of shot. I felt that

I should have had another 10–15 yards or so on it, which is about all I can expect to do to-day.

Our American colleagues are watching very closely the performance of the modern golf ball, and have tried to establish a control by limiting its velocity at impact, but this sort of check is difficult, it seems to me, to carry out. Provided our ball-makers 'stay put' with their products, I can only think they will be allowed to carry on with the '1·68 × 1·62' ball, but if a definite leap forward in length appears, then I should not be surprised to see a floater tried out seriously.

From a very thorough test carried out in 1957 emerged one interesting point from a mass of statistics (some figures of which have since been proved 30% inaccurate), and that was that the ideal impact loft for a driver, to get the maximum carry, is 11°. My own drivers have 8°–10°, and I hit a lowish ball, so I probably squeeze the ball slightly, so that if I wanted a long carry I should need to catch the ball more 'coming up' and so add to the loft of the club. This is what I do in fact.

This also bears out the fact that most average golfers are better with a No. 2 wood from the tee, for they tend to lean into the ball and so diminish the effective loft. A ball struck off the dead centre of the club-face will go *much further* even if the swing speed is slower than a faster speed swing where the ball is not struck on the centre of the face. This was proved in the tests and shows it pays to hit accurately. I have never seen any figures of tests for mishits with iron clubs, but the variation in distance, apart from direction, must be enormous. My own experience has satisfied me on this point. So each club has a sweet spot — use it.

THE SHAPE OF THINGS TO COME?

Watching the News of the World *P.G.A. semi-finals at Royal Birkdale, 1959. 'Toots' gets a grand-stand view of Weetman and Thomas at the 16th hole from her electric buggy. This is a heavenly way of spectating, but what chaos it would be if there were dozens of these cars in use at the same place. Nevertheless, they are great fun to use.*

THE END

LEFT: *A close-up view of the Open Championship Trophy. It is in the shape of a silver jug. All the names of the early winners from 1872 onwards are on the Cup; later winners have their names engraved on the plinth. When I won 'The Cup' in 1934, my wife got Cartier's to make me a replica, one-quarter size, which has every name on it — legible, too — just as on the real thing. It is a nice souvenir and golfers visiting my home like to see it. Two of the champion's gold medals are made into a bracelet, which 'Toots' wears, and the third into a brooch. Better than leaving them lying in drawers somewhere! The actual Open Championship title dates from 1860 — a Belt being given at first to the winners.*

BELOW: *Firmly grasping the beautifully proportioned Open Championship Trophy — perhaps the most elegant Golf trophy in the world — for the third time and saying 'Thank you' to the many golfers who had cheered me on. At the same time shaking hands with Fred Daly, who was winner in 1947 and runner-up to me on this occasion. Muirfield, 1948.*

I never did receive the Ryder Cup Trophy as Captain. I had one very near squeak, though, in 1953, and have been a member of a winning team, 1929, but I was pleased to receive the huge Joy Cup from the hands of M. Raymond Barbas, who presented it to the European Golf Association for the match British Professionals versus the Continental Professionals. Home professionals have so far won this trophy each time it has been played for.

No golfer ever had to learn to do this — this is just about the only part of the golf game which comes naturally!